Legal Problem Solving

Reasoning, Research & Writing

Fifth Edition

Maureen F. Fitzgerald
Ph.D., B.Comm., LL.B., LL.M.

with
Susan Barker

LexisNexis®

Legal Problem Solving: Reasoning, Research & Writing, Fifth Edition
© LexisNexis Canada Inc. 2010
August 2010

Members of the LexisNexis Group worldwide

Canada	LexisNexis Canada Inc., 123 Commerce Valley Drive East, MARKHAM, Ontario
Australia	Butterworths, a Division of Reed International Books Australia Pty Ltd, CHATSWOOD, New South Wales
Austria	ARD Betriebsdienst and Verlag Orac, VIENNA
Czech Republic	Orac sro, PRAGUE
France	Éditions du Juris-Classeur SA, PARIS
Hong Kong	Butterworths Asia (Hong Kong), HONG KONG
Hungary	Hvg Orac, BUDAPEST
India	Butterworths India, NEW DELHI
Ireland	Butterworths (Ireland) Ltd, DUBLIN
Italy	Giuffré, MILAN
Malaysia	Malayan Law Journal Sdn Bhd, KUALA LUMPUR
New Zealand	Butterworths of New Zealand, WELLINGTON
Poland	Wydawnictwa Prawnicze PWN, WARSAW
Singapore	Butterworths Asia, SINGAPORE
South Africa	Butterworth Publishers (Pty) Ltd, DURBAN
Switzerland	Stämpfli Verlag AG, BERNE
United Kingdom	Butterworths Tolley, a Division of Reed Elsevier (UK), LONDON, WC2A
USA	LexisNexis, DAYTON, Ohio

Library and Archives Canada Cataloguing in Publication

Fitzgerald, Maureen F.
          Legal problem solving : reasoning, research & writing / Maureen
F. Fitzgerald. — 5th ed.

Includes index.
ISBN 978-0-433-46300-9

          1. Legal research—Canada. 2. Legal research. 3. Legal composition.
I. Title.

KE250.F57 2010   340'.072071   C2007-903929-4
KF240.F57 2010

Printed and bound in Canada.

To my life partner Paul Clay Quinn

MFF

To James, Kim and Evan

SB

Preface

Legal problem solving is the backbone to all that lawyers do. Every lawyer is engaged in some form of legal problem solving, every day. Without the skills to be able to solve legal problems, lawyers would be unable to access or understand the law. Every law school in Canada teaches legal problem solving through a first-year legal research and writing course.

This book was designed as a textbook for that course. Unlike other textbooks, this book:

- places legal research in the context of solving legal problems;
- teaches the fundamental steps to all legal research;
- provides enough detail to enable any researcher to solve a legal problem from beginning to end;
- introduces a step-by-step problem-solving process (FILAC) to make research more systematic and memorable; and
- includes learning objectives, examples and exercises to engage students in their learning.

Almost 20 years ago I created the concept of FILAC — a problem-solving technique to teach legal research and writing — after several years of teaching Legal Research and Writing at both the University of Victoria and the University of British Columbia. As a lawyer I understood the importance of making student learning relevant and immediately applicable. I decided that I would teach them the whole process of legal problem solving.

At that time in Canada the course was taught primarily by librarians and the content was essentially about how to find laws in books in a law library. The critical piece that was missing was context. I discovered over the years that to make learning most effective, students needed to understand **why** they were looking for the books and **what** they would do with the books once they located them. I slowly began to understand how to better teach the course and translated that knowledge into this book.

Who This Book Is For

This book can be used by anyone who wishes to solve a legal problem. This includes lawyers, law students, legal assistants and the general public. It is written in a way that should be easily understandable to those who are not familiar with the law.

The Format of This Book

This book teaches the entire process of legal problem solving. All legal problems begin with a set of facts or circumstances. The researcher's task is to analyze facts, determine legal issues, find relevant law, analyze the law, apply the law to the facts and communicate the results.

Each chapter begins with a set of learning objectives and ends with a self test. This enables the reader to quickly see what is covered in each chapter and understand the learning expectations.

Since the skills of factual analysis, issue identification, finding the law, legal analysis and legal writing are learned best through repeated practice, examples and problem-based exercises have been included. In addition to doing these exercises, researchers should practise the skills on their own time or in small groups where the skills can be simulated and feedback can be received.

Enjoy the learning!

Maureen F. Fitzgerald
Vancouver, May 2010

Acknowledgments

When I wrote this book almost 20 years ago I did not imagine that it would go into a fifth edition. I am deeply honoured to be able to help law students learn about this very important skill. Even though my law practice has evolved into one of conflict resolution exclusively, I still believe that legal research is one of the most important skills a lawyer can possess. It's not so much about finding books as it is about *thinking about what you need to solve a problem and how you will use that information once you find it*. It is about being effective and efficient, and not simply about finding relevant cases and statutes. Even today, I go back to the fundamentals contained in this book and have the confidence of knowing that I have all the information I need to solve my legal problem.

I have not wavered from my thinking that legal research is necessarily about legal problem solving and I am proud to say that the success of this book is in the fact that so many law faculty are using it to teach their Legal Research and Writing courses. I have received many complimentary e-mails from students, faculty, law librarians and legal researchers in law firms. Thank you.

I wish to thank those who supported me over the years: Susan Barker, whose brilliance made this edition possible; Melinda Renner, whose endless help is not forgotten; Kathleen McIsaac, who taught me the important things; the students at the University of Victoria and University of British Columbia; Monica Beauregard; John Fairlie; Nancy Hannum; Pat Pitsula; Pat Nelson; Anne Morrison; Joan Honeywell; Joan Fraser; Penny Hazelton; Michael Lee; Emily Quinn; Paige Quinn; Jennifer Leslie and Paul Quinn.

I would also like to thank Michael Silverstein, Ji Hyun (Jenny) Ryu (Thomson Carswell); Mark Bettiol and Tracy Smith (LexisNexis); Mary Mitchell and Anna Holeton (University of British Columbia Law Librarians); and all of the law faculty and legal researchers across Canada who provided me with suggestions for this edition.

Finally, thanks to those publishers who generously granted their permission to reproduce information contained in this book, as well as those organizations that generously provided funding for the first edition in 1996: the Legal Research Foundation (B.C.); the Faculty of Law at the University of Victoria; the Office of the President at the University of Victoria; and the Law Foundation of British Columbia.

I welcome comments and feedback on the book, and can be reached via e-mail at Maureen@CenterPointInc.com.

Maureen F. Fitzgerald
Vancouver, May 2010

I wish to thank, first of all, Maureen for her wise words, humour and support and for giving me the opportunity help out with this cool book. Equal thanks go to Nancy McCormack for her mentorship and encouragement. All my friends and colleagues (who are more family than friends) at the Bora Laskin Law Library, especially Sooin Kim, John Papadopoulos and Gian Medves, deserve thanks, mainly because they make it a pleasure to go to work every day. And finally, thanks to my family for pretty well everything else.

Susan Barker
Toronto, May 2010

About the Author

Maureen F. Fitzgerald, Ph.D, B.Comm., LL.B., LL.M., taught legal research and writing at the University of Victoria and the University of British Columbia for several years. She has practised law for over 20 years in both Ontario and British Columbia and built her own conflict resolution practice: CenterPoint — Conflict & Collaboration Inc. (<http://www.CenterPointInc.com>) that is dedicated to transforming conflict and building trusting teams.

She has a doctorate degree from the University of British Columbia on legal education, and a master's degree in law from the London School of Economics, specializing in alternative dispute resolution. She has written many articles and six books, including *Corporate Circles* (2006); *One Circle* (2006); *Hiring, Managing and Keeping the Best* (2002); and *Mission Possible* (2003).

About the Contributor

Susan Barker is the Electronic Information Coordinator/Reference Librarian for the Bora Laskin Law Library at the University of Toronto, Faculty of Law. She holds a Master of Information Studies from the University of Toronto and a Diploma in Library Techniques from Seneca College.

Table of Contents

Chapter 6: How to Find Secondary Materials

Chapter 10: Introduction to Legal Analysis

Chapter 11: Legal Writing

The Legal Problem Solving Process 1

The ultimate goal of legal research is to find solutions to legal problems. In simple terms, this means finding relevant statutes and cases, interpreting them and applying them to a particular situation. There is no single best way to approach a legal problem; however, all research should be approached systematically.

This book provides a basic introduction, framework and strategy for conducting legal research. It introduces a step-by-step approach to legal research that can be utilized by newcomers to legal research. It teaches all of the skills necessary to complete any research problem from beginning to end by duplicating the entire research process that lawyers use to solve legal problems. It includes instruction on how to analyze legal problems, design a research plan, locate the law, reason legally and present research results in an understandable way.

The skills taught here are designed to supplement other legal education and should assist students at law school, during professional legal training and after call to the Bar. This book should be used as a springboard towards development of expert research skills.

Although the process of legal research has, herein, been broken down into distinct steps for purposes of learning, it must be recognized that legal research is complex and will be shaped by the researcher and the individual problem.

This chapter provides an overview of the entire five-step process of legal problem solving. The remaining chapters discuss these steps in more detail.

LEARNING OBJECTIVES

At the end of this chapter you will be able to:

- Describe the five-step process of legal research
- Explain what is meant by factual analysis
- Explain what is meant by issue determination
- Explain what is meant by legal analysis

THE LEGAL PROBLEM SOLVING PROCESS (FILAC)

All legal research begins with a legal problem and ends with a solution or conclusion about how the law applies to that problem. The complete process of legal research involves tasks that can be translated into the FILAC five-step approach to legal research:

Step 1:   Facts — Analyze the facts
Step 2:   Issues — Determine the legal issues
Step 3:   Law — Find the relevant law
Step 4:   Analysis — Analyze the law and apply it to the facts
Step 5:   Communication — Communicate the results of the research

These five steps overlap and are repeated over and over as a researcher begins to solve a legal problem. For example, a researcher will analyze the facts initially but will continue to hone the facts as the research continues. Each of the steps is revisited periodically as the research evolves.

The following is a brief description of each step.

Step 1: Analyze the facts — Each new legal problem will have aspects to it that are totally foreign to the legal researcher. The first task, therefore, is to make some sense of the problem by gathering the necessary facts and separating the legally relevant facts from the irrelevant ones. This is called factual analysis.

Step 2: Determine the legal issues — After the facts have been analyzed, the next step is to identify the legal issues raised by the facts. This involves determining the legal questions that need to be examined. This is called issue determination and requires reading about the law generally.

Step 3: Find the relevant law — After the legal issues have been identified, the researcher should visit the library, use online resources or the Internet to locate the relevant cases, statutes and other legal sources. In order to do this, the researcher must have a basic understanding of what the law is and where it is located. The majority of research time is spent at this stage.

Step 4: Analyze the Law and Apply It to the Facts — Analyzing the law involves reading the relevant law, synthesizing it and applying it to the facts. Some refer to this step as thinking like a lawyer, legal reasoning or legal analysis.

Step 5: Communicate the Results of the Research — The last step involves communicating the results of the research to the person in need of the research — such as clients, judges or other lawyers. The results must be communicated either orally or in writing and must be understandable, accurate, clear and concise. This communication usually takes the form of a memorandum of law or an opinion letter.

The researcher should continually review each of the above steps and confirm the results of each as the law and the problem become clearer. Although the research process has been divided into five steps, it must be emphasized that the process is an art as opposed to a science. Researchers should feel free to develop their own techniques in addition to the basics learned here.

In the FILAC model, as with any research model, the researcher must be systematic. Research should never be approached in an *ad hoc* way. Each step should be planned and the results of the search should be recorded, as the research process sometimes extends over weeks or months.

AN EXAMPLE OF THE PROBLEM SOLVING PROCESS

The following is a simplified example of the five steps of the legal problem solving process.

Fact Pattern

Ms. Safety

Your client, Ms. Safety, is a security guard for a toy store. One night, after carefully checking the store, she inadvertently locked in Sam, a small boy, who was hiding in the building. The boy was found the next day unharmed. The boy's parents, however, are threatening a false imprisonment suit. Ms. Safety claims she had no intention to confine the boy and would like to know if the boy's parents have a basis for their threatened suit.

Facts: The relevant facts are that Ms. Safety inadvertently locked Sam inside a store. His parents suggest that this is false imprisonment.

Issues: After reading about the law you decide that the legal question to be answered is: Was the inadvertent locking of Sam in the store false imprisonment?

Law: You search the law library and electronic materials and find that there are no statutes that describe the law of false imprisonment, but there are a number of cases. You read these cases and synthesize them. See the example below.

Analysis: After reading the relevant cases, a researcher might synthesize this part of the law into a statement something like this:[1]

> To be found guilty of false imprisonment the person imprisoning the other must have been aware of the imprisonment. If there is no intent to imprison there cannot be false imprisonment.

---

[1]   This is only an example and should not be considered an accurate statement of the law.

Applying this law to the facts, it is likely that because Ms. Safety was not aware of the boy hiding in the store, she had no intent to imprison and therefore likely cannot be said to have falsely imprisoned Sam.

Communication: You can tell your client that it is unlikely that her inadvertent locking of Sam in the store would be considered to be false imprisonment.

SELF TEST

The following is a self test based on the information provided in this chapter. The answers to these questions, and the answers to all the other self test questions at the end of chapters, are found at the end of the book in the "Answers to Self Tests" section.

1. What is the five-step process of legal research?
2. What is factual analysis?
3. What is issue determination?
4. What is legal analysis?

Factual Analysis

2

The first step in the legal research process is factual analysis. Every research problem begins with a set of facts or circumstances which must be analyzed in order to determine which legal issues need to be researched. The researcher must read the facts and elicit the legally relevant facts prior to entering the library.

Every new legal problem presents new challenges to students and lawyers alike. No two situations are identical and the variety of situations that clients present to lawyers is infinite. As well, many problems involve multiple legal issues that may not be immediately obvious. It is therefore necessary to develop a method by which to break down the facts. This method may then be used on each new legal problem.

This chapter explains what factual analysis is, describes a method of analyzing facts and provides an example of factual analysis.

LEARNING OBJECTIVES

At the end of this chapter you will be able to:

- Name the three steps of factual analysis
- Describe what PEC stands for
- Identify legally relevant facts
- Formulate or restate facts

WHAT IS FACTUAL ANALYSIS?

Factual analysis is the task of extricating legally relevant facts from the mass of facts in a legal problem. Legally relevant facts are those with the most legal significance or that raise issues of law. These facts dictate the issues of law to be researched.

The relevant facts are those facts that the courts will take into consideration if the case proceeds to trial. Determining which facts are relevant is a judge's first task when deciding a case. Indeed, every written judgment begins with a recitation of relevant facts.

Although it is difficult to determine the legally relevant facts without some knowledge about the law, an initial attempt at sorting relevant facts from irrelevant ones can provide focus and considerably narrow your research.

HOW TO ANALYZE FACTS

Factual analysis involves figuring out the who, what, where and why of the problem presented, separating the relevant facts from the irrelevant ones and restating the facts in a concise fashion. There are a number of ways to analyze facts. The method described here is a recommended systematic approach.

Although there is some skill involved in analyzing the facts of a problem, a researcher who is systematic about the process will find that it soon becomes second nature. Usually a first attempt at factual analysis will not be complete. Factual analysis should continue throughout the research process as the legal issues are defined and narrowed. The process necessitates that researchers return to the facts after looking at the law and revise their statement of the facts accordingly.

There are essentially three steps in factual analysis. They are as follows:

Step 1:   Gather and organize the facts
Step 2:   Identify the legally relevant facts
Step 3:   Formulate the facts

The following fact pattern will be used to explain each of these steps.

Fact Pattern

Paul Quint and Melody Jones

Paul Quint and Melody Jones are residents of British Columbia who, after ten years of marriage, are getting divorced. They have two children, Lindsay and Wayne, and have agreed that the children will stay with Melody. However, they cannot reach an agreement as to the division of property. They own a house and a boat on Salty Island. In addition, two years ago, Melody was given a $20,000 gift from her grandmother, which she put into a separate bank account in her own name. She wants to know whether the judge will consider the gift to be a family asset when making a decision about the division of property.

Step 1: Gather and Organize the Facts

The first step in factual analysis is simply to determine what happened. This involves gathering facts and putting them in some kind of order. Researchers should select a method of gathering facts that is easy to use but comprehensive.

In law school, fact patterns are often provided to students in exercises or exams. Therefore, students are often not required to gather facts. Gathering facts, however, is an important step in legal research since the particular facts drive the research and determine the outcome.

Gathering facts usually involves speaking to people such as clients, witnesses and experts. It also includes gathering information from books or reports and collecting physical evidence such as contracts or weapons.

Typically, fact gathering involves answering who, what, where, when, why and how. Who is involved or affected? What happened — directly or indirectly? Where and when did it happen? Why did the situation arise? How did it occur? At this initial stage there should be little attempt to control the facts, except to enable the researcher to detect gaps or inconsistencies.

One technique that is frequently used to start thinking about facts is brainstorming. This approach simply requires that the reader think of all possible parties, events and claims regardless of their significance, relevance or order.

Although there are a number of ways to gather and organize facts,[1] a recommended method is called the PEC method (Parties, Events and Claims). In every legal problem there are parties, events and claims. In each problem presented there is a person or persons with a legal problem, events happen which lead up to the problem and a claim is made by one or several parties. In analyzing facts, researchers should think about every potential party, every possible event and any claim that comes to mind.

Some of the questions that should be asked under each of these headings are as follows:

Parties

- Who are the people involved in the problem?
- What are the parties' roles or occupations?
- What are the relationships between the parties?
- What are the parties' special characteristics?

Events

- What occurred?
- When did it occur?
- Where did it occur?
- What is the nature of the location where it occurred?
- How did it occur?

Claims

- What are the parties complaining of?
- What are the parties claiming?
- What are the injuries or harm?
- What will the defence to the claim likely be?

A researcher should be able to state in non-legal terms the answers to the above questions. At this stage it is important to stay open to as many ideas as possible. There is a danger of defining a problem too narrowly, too early, and rushing into the library.

---

[1] Two popular methods used for legal problems are called TAPP (Things, Acts, Persons, and Places) and PAPO (Persons, Actions, Places, and Objects). Both TAPP and PAPO provide four-step tools with which researchers can determine what legally significant events happened.

The following are the facts which were gathered and organized in the Paul Quint and Melody Jones situation:

Parties

Paul Quint: husband of Melody and father of Lindsay and Wayne
Melody Jones: wife of Paul and mother of Lindsay and Wayne
Lindsay Jones: daughter of Paul and Melody
Wayne Quint: son of Paul and Melody
Grandmother: grandmother of Melody

Events

Paul and Melody were married ten years ago and are now divorcing and splitting their property. Two years ago, Melody's grandmother gave her $20,000. Melody held the money in a separate bank account.

Claims

Melody: claims that the $20,000 is hers and should not be part of the family assets, which will be divided upon marriage breakdown.

Paul: claims that the $20,000 is part of the family assets and should be included in the assets to be divided upon marriage breakdown.

Step 2: Identify the Legally Relevant Facts

Once you have gathered and organized the facts, it is necessary to identify which of those facts are legally relevant and which of those facts are irrelevant. The law determines which facts are legally relevant so that is what must be looked at. The following is an example of how to identify the relevant facts in Paul and Melody's situation.

We will assume that initial research of the law pertaining to marital property disclosed that there is a provincial statute called the *Family Property Act* (fictitious). This statute applies to all residents of British Columbia and all marriages that are entered into in British Columbia. It describes particular rules for the division of property upon marriage breakdown. Sections 8–10 provide as follows:

s. 8   Upon marriage breakdown each spouse is entitled to a half interest in the family assets.

s. 9   (1) Property owned by one or both spouses and ordinarily used by a spouse or a minor child of either spouse for a family purpose is a family asset.

         (2) Without restricting the generality of subsection (1), the definition of family asset includes:

             (a) money, including inheritances or gifts, obtained while in the marriage;

(*b*)   a right of a spouse under an annuity or a pension, home ownership or retirement savings plan; or

(*c*)   a right, share or an interest of a spouse in a venture to which money or money's worth was, directly or indirectly, contributed by or on behalf of the other spouse.

s. 10   Where the provisions for division of property between spouses under section 8 would be unfair having regard to:

(*a*)   the duration of the marriage;

(*b*)   the duration of the period during which the spouses have lived separate and apart;

(*c*)   the date when property was acquired or disposed of;

(*d*)   the extent to which the property was acquired by one spouse through inheritance or gift;

(*e*)   the needs of each spouse to become or remain economically independent and self-sufficient; or

(*f*)   any other circumstances relating to the acquisition, preservation, maintenance, improvement or use of property or the capacity or liabilities of a spouse,

a court may order that the property covered by section 8 may be divided into shares fixed by the court.

There is only one case which discussed this statute: *Bogman v. Bregman* (B.C.C.A.) (fictitious). In that case Jill Bogman petitioned for a divorce from her husband, Kevin Bregman, and asked the court to make a determination about the division of assets. The court declared that pursuant to s. 8 of the *Family Property Act* a summer cabin, a camper van and the contents of the matrimonial home were family assets and were divided equally between Jill and Kevin. A question arose as to whether Jill's registered retirement plan was a family asset. Jill acquired the plan through a monetary gift from her mother and kept it in a separate bank account under her name.

The court held that the retirement savings plan was not to be divided equally between Jill and Kevin. Although the savings plan was automatically included within the definition of family assets under s. 9(2)(*b*) of the *Family Property Act*, the fund was a gift from her mother, not used for family purposes, and was kept in a separate bank account. Therefore, the court exercised its jurisdiction under s. 10 of the *Family Property Act*. Although the court considered the fact that the gift had been received ten years prior and was fairly entrenched in the family assets, this factor was not deemed to be as relevant as the other factors in this particular situation.

The following is a brief summary of the statute and case law:[2]

The law provides that upon marriage breakdown "family assets" must be shared equally between the marriage partners. Family assets include gifts, inheritances and registered retirement savings plans obtained while in the marriage. However, a court may alter this division if the division would be unfair having regard to a number of factors including "the extent to which property was acquired by one spouse through inheritance or gift" pursuant to s. 10(*d*) of the *Family Property Act*.

A case that interpreted this section (*Bogman v. Bregman*) found that in determining whether the inclusion of a gift is unfair and the extent to which the property was acquired by gift the court would look at the following three factors:

- whether the gift was kept in a separate bank account;
- whether it was used for family purposes; and
- how long it had been in the hands of the recipient.

For each component of the law there is a matching legally relevant fact in Paul and Melody's situation. For example, the above law states that family assets include gifts. Thus, one legally relevant fact is that Melody received the money as a gift. Also relevant is the amount of time the gift was held. The following schedule helps to differentiate the legally relevant facts from the law.

The Legal Questions	The Legally Relevant Facts
1. Is the money a "family asset"?	
(a) Was the gift obtained while in the marriage?	(a) Melody received the gift while she and Paul were married.
2. Would the distribution be unfair?	
(a) What was the extent to which the property was acquired by gift?	(a) Melody received the $20,000 from her grandmother.
(*i*) Was it kept in a separate bank account?	(*i*) Melody kept the money in a separate bank account.

---

[2] See Chapter 4 (Introduction to Law and Legal Materials) for an explanation of case law.

The Legal Questions	The Legally Relevant Facts
(*ii*) Was it used for family purposes?	(*ii*) The money was not used for family purposes.
(*iii*) How long ago was it received?	(*iii*) Melody received the money two years ago.

Since the only legal issue is whether the $20,000 gift will be considered a family asset, only those facts related to the gift are legally relevant. It is likely, therefore, that the house and the boat are not relevant. It is also likely that the children are not legally relevant. Remember that the relevance of these facts may be revised as the law and the legal issues become clearer.

Step 3: Formulate the Facts

Once you have gathered and organized the facts and determined which ones are legally relevant, it is a good idea to restate or reformulate the facts. This restatement must, of course, include all the relevant facts but will also usually include some facts that help to put the situation into context and enable a reader to understand more clearly what happened.

There are no strict rules for formulating the facts. Some prefer to list the facts chronologically, while others prefer to state a critical fact first. The following are examples of two different approaches to restating the facts in the Paul and Melody situation.

Formulated Facts A

Melody and Paul are divorcing. Melody does not want a gift of $20,000 to be included in the division of family assets. She received the gift two years ago from her grandmother and has kept it in a separate bank account in her name since.

Formulated Facts B

Melody received a gift of $20,000 two years ago from her grandmother. She placed it in a bank account separate from her husband's, under her name. Melody is now divorcing her husband, Paul, and is concerned that the $20,000 will be split equally between her and Paul as part of the division of their family property.

Tips on Reformulating Facts

When restating or reformulating the facts, the following tips should be kept in mind:

- *Often "emotional" facts are irrelevant.* For example, the fact that Melody and Paul may have had a traumatic separation is not legally relevant.

- *Try to use objective language.* Avoid using adjectives or descriptive words. These words tend to make the reading more exciting, but, at the same time, indicate subjectivity or bias. For example, it is preferable not to refer to the home as "beautifully decorated". Later, during advocacy, these words may come in handy, but not at this particular stage.

- *Put the facts in an order that is best suited for the reader.* Writers often gravitate to a chronological description, but be conscious of the fact that a reader may prefer a catchy introductory line which talks about the crux of the issue.

- *Draw attention to any missing facts and their relevance.* Clearly state any necessary assumptions in the facts. If, for example, a critical factor in determining the division of family assets was whether the children had sufficient funds, you would need to either find out about the children's finances or make an assumption about their financial status.

- *Do not be afraid to include facts that may not be entirely relevant, but that make the facts readable.* Often a first attempt at restating the facts will be too abbreviated. Facts that are too bald are difficult to understand. Although tabulation of the facts is acceptable, it sometimes comes across as being sterile or too cut-and-dried.

SELF TEST

The following is a self test based on the information provided in this chapter. The answers to these questions are found in the back of the book in the "Answers to Self Tests" section.

1. What are the three steps of factual analysis?
2. What does PEC stand for?

SAMPLE EXERCISE

The following is an example of the three steps of factual analysis.

Fact Pattern

Ravi, May, and Jan

Ravi and May are being sued jointly by the Regal Bank for $30,000, which was misappropriated from the bank by Jan, their law partner. Unsure of their liability, Ravi and May have asked for your opinion as to the likelihood of successfully defending the action in court. The circumstances leading up to the action are as follows:

Jan, Ravi, and May met and became good friends while they were attending law school in the mid-1980s. They talked often about opening a small firm together some day. All three were interested in blending traditional legal practice with other forms of dispute resolution services. Jan in particular developed a keen interest in mediation while she was at law school.

After being called to the Bar, the three friends decided to form a partnership under the name "JMR Legal Services", to practise law in Toronto. Their partnership agreement included the following terms:

...

14. All profits from the law practice will be shared equally among the partners.

15. Any income or profit received by a partner from business activities, investments, or other sources not forming part of the law practice shall belong to that partner separately, and shall not be subject to sharing under paragraph 14.

16. No partner may use the firm name, letterhead, equipment, or facilities for any purpose not connected with the law practice.

...

In the beginning, the partners worked cooperatively to build their fledgling practice. While all three provided legal representation to clients on a variety of matters, Jan also took some cases as a mediator. She had to keep these roles separate, of course, or she could be in breach of the Law Society's conflict of interest rules. That is, Jan could act *either* as the lawyer for one party to a dispute *or* as a mediator between the parties, but not both.

May and Ravi soon got into the habit of referring some of their clients to Jan when they thought a dispute could be handled more fairly or efficiently through mediation, rather than through adversarial legal action. The troubles began when Jan decided that since her mediation services were separate from her traditional law practice, any profits from mediation should be hers alone to keep. In order to make this clear, Jan began to meet with her mediation clients at home, rather than at JMR's offices, and she arranged for separate bookkeeping, banking and advertising for "Jan's Mediation Services". Jan continued to take legal clients as well, doing this work at the office and sharing any billings with her partners. Although she bent over backwards to keep the two aspects of her practice separate, Jan occasionally asked the secretary who worked at JMR to type correspondence relating to her mediation files as a personal favour.

Ravi and May were surprised and displeased by Jan's move. In their view, the mediation services were integral to the kind of law practice the three of them had envisioned. Indeed, this was one of the main attractions of going into partnership with Jan. Ravi and May wrote a letter of protest to Jan, in which they argued that mediation

> profits were subject to sharing under the partnership agreement.
>
> All of this suddenly became irrelevant, however, when Jan was charged with several counts of theft, and admitted that she had misappropriated $30,000 from the Regal Bank. The bank had retained her to provide mediation services in a major dispute with one of its corporate depositors, and she was holding the money in the trust account she had opened for Jan's Mediation Services. Upon discovering that Jan had no assets, the bank sued May and Ravi as partners in the JMR firm.

ANSWERS TO SAMPLE EXERCISE

Step 1: Gather and Organize the Facts

Parties

Ravi:	lawyer and partner of May and Jan
May:	lawyer and partner of Ravi and Jan
Jan:	lawyer and partner of May and Ravi
Bank:	client of Jan for mediation services

Events

- Ravi, May and Jan formed the law partnership of "JMR Legal Services".
- Their partnership agreement stated that all profits from the law practice were to be shared, and the firm's name and facilities were only to be used for activities related to the law practice.
- Ravi and May regularly referred clients requiring mediation work to Jan.
- Jan started "Jan's Mediation Services", set up her own book-keeping, banking and advertising, met her mediation clients at home, and kept all the profits generated from this work. She occasionally asked the secretary at JMR Legal Services to type correspondence relating to her mediation work.
- Ravi and May wrote a protest letter to Jan stating that the mediation profits should be shared.
- Jan misappropriated $30,000 from the Regal Bank and held the money in a trust account under the name "Jan's Mediation Services".
- The bank sued Ravi and May as partners in JMR Legal Services.

Claims

- Ravi and May: claim that they do not owe the Regal Bank $30,000 since Jan was working outside the partnership.
- The Regal Bank: claims that Ravi and May owe the Regal Bank $30,000 for the fraud of their partner Jan.

Step 2: Identify the Legally Relevant Facts

The Law

Initial research of the law pertaining to legal partnership and liability of partners disclosed that there is a provincial statute called the *Partnership Act* (fictitious). This statute applies to all partnerships entered into in Ontario. It describes particular rules for the liability of partners. Section 12 of the *Partnership Act* states:

> s. 12 Where by any wrongful act or omission of any partner acting in the ordinary course of the business of the firm, or with the authority of his or her co-partners, loss or injury is caused to any person not being a partner in the firm, or any penalty is incurred, the firm is liable for that loss, injury or penalty to the same extent as the partner so acting or omitting to act.

The following two cases interpreted this section of the *Partnership Act*:

Public Trustee v. Morton (Ont. C.A.) (fictitious)

The defendant, Ms. Morton, a solicitor and partner in a law firm, acted as an executor and trustee of an estate. Morton stole money from the estate. In the course of administering the estate, Morton used the staff and facilities of her law firm. Specifically, Morton used a junior solicitor and the firm's staff for the typing and bookkeeping work on the estate. The executor's fees were included in the firm's revenues. The court found the defendant's partners liable for Morton's wrongful acts because she was acting within the ordinary course of the firm's business. The court outlined several *indicia* as possible ways to separate a partner's activities as an executor of an estate from the ordinary course of the firm's business:

> There would probably be an agreement between the partners to that effect, and one might expect to find that the partner would not charge the estate on an account issued in the firm's name, would personally keep any fees and compensation paid, rather than treat them as revenues of the firm, would keep the funds of the estate in an account separate from her firm's trust account, and would keep a set of accounting records from the estate separate from those of his firm. If she wanted to be careful to make it clear that his work as an executor was not part of the firm's business, she would not use the firm letterhead when writing as an executor.

Kozy v. Pierre (S.C.C.) (fictitious)

Mr. Kozy, a solicitor in a law firm, entered into a business agreement with two clients to form a company and serve as one of its directors. When the company went bankrupt he did not contribute his share of the financing, nor did he help his two clients settle the debts. The court, applying the *Partnership Act*, found Kozy's partners liable for Kozy's wrongful acts because he was acting in the ordinary course of the business of the firm. Kozy acted as the solicitor to the company and, by extension, the directors. He also spent several years working for both clients prior to the company's formation. In addition, all meetings of the company's directors were held in Kozy's law offices. Although there were no profits *per se*, the firm benefited by having Mr. Kozy act as a director of such a prestigious company.

Summary of Statute and Case Law

From the statute and these two cases, the factors that indicate when a partner is acting in the ordinary course of business of a law firm are whether:

- there is an agreement excluding the activity from the firm's business;
- the firm's staff (including lawyers, secretaries, and bookkeepers), facilities (including accounts and offices), and name (including letterhead) are used; and
- the profits from the activity are shared.

The law and the corresponding legally relevant facts could be set out in a diagram as below:

The Law	The Legally Relevant Facts
Words in Statute	
Was the partner acting in the ordinary course of business of the firm?	Ravi, Jan, and May carried on business in a partnership called JMR Legal Services to provide legal and mediation services.
Factors from Cases	
1. Is there an agreement excluding the activity from the firm's business?	There is a partnership agreement. It does not exclude mediation from JMR's business, but it states that "all profits from the law practice will be shared equally" and "no partners may use the firm name, letterhead, equipment, or facilities for any purpose not connected with the law practice".

The Law	The Legally Relevant Facts
2. Did the partner use the firm's staff (including lawyers, secretaries, and bookkeepers), facilities (including accounts and offices), and name (including letterhead)?	Jan "occasionally" asked the secretary who worked at JMR to type correspondence relating to her mediation files "as a personal favour". Jan kept banking and bookkeeping separate and met mediation clients at her home.
3. Were the profits from the activity shared between the partners?	Jan kept her mediation profits to herself but Ravi and May disputed this.

Step 3: Formulate the Facts

The following is a restatement of the facts:

Ravi, May and Jan formed the law partnership of "JMR Legal Services" (JMR) to provide traditional legal and mediation services. Their partnership agreement stated that all profits from the law practice were to be shared, and that the firm's name and facilities were only to be used for activities related to the law practice.

In building their practice, Ravi and May regularly referred clients requiring mediation work to Jan. However, Jan eventually decided that since her mediation work was separate from the traditional law practice, she would keep the profits generated from this work. Consequently, she started "Jan's Mediation Services" (JMS), set up her own bookkeeping, banking and advertising, and met her mediation clients at home. Although Jan tried to keep the two areas of her practice separate, she occasionally asked the secretary at JMR to type correspondence relating to her mediation work "as a favour". It is assumed that the secretary did not use JMR letterhead.

Viewing the mediation services as integral to the firm's practice, Ravi and May wrote a protest letter to Jan stating that the mediation profits should be shared. However, before this dispute was resolved, Jan was charged with theft for misappropriating $30,000 from the Regal Bank, which had retained Jan to provide mediation services. During the mediation process, Jan had held the money in a trust account under the JMS name. Since Jan had no assets, the bank sued Ravi and May as partners in JMR. It is assumed that there was no previous relationship between Regal Bank and JMR, and that the bank did not know that Jan was a lawyer.

Note that a few assumptions were made, such as the assumption that the secretary did not use JMR letterhead. Note as well that certain important facts were placed in quotations, indicating their importance.

Issue Determination

3

After you have analyzed the facts, you are in a position to determine the legal issues.

Issue determination involves eliciting relevant legal issues from a set of facts. This takes some skill and an understanding of the law. Defining the legal issues is central to the research process. If you are clear about the issues and ask the correct questions, your research will be direct and efficient. Time spent at this stage saves significant time later in the research process.

This chapter explains how to identify legal issues, describes how to formulate legal issues and provides an example of issue determination.

LEARNING OBJECTIVES

At the end of this chapter you will be able to:

- Name the three steps in determining legal issues
- Name a few techniques to help you think about applicable areas of law
- Name two library sources that might help in defining legal issues
- Distinguish between a legal issue and factual issues

HOW TO DETERMINE LEGAL ISSUES

Issue determination involves translating facts into legal issues. The goal of issue determination is to ask yourself: What are the legal questions that must be answered in order to solve this legal problem?

Since researchers are rarely familiar with all areas of law, they must devise an efficient and effective way to determine the legal issues. A recommended way to do this is to think generally about the areas of law that are likely to apply to the facts, read the law generally in relevant areas and formulate the legal issues.

Step 1: Determine Applicable Areas of Law

There are some techniques that can help get researchers started in thinking about which areas of law might apply to a set of facts. The methods suggested below are: using the subjects of law courses, brainstorming and word association and using library sources.

Using Subjects of Law Courses

When determining what the legal issues are, researchers are most likely to attempt to fit the facts into a framework with which they are familiar. Some with past experiences may recognize a few areas of law that might be applicable (*e.g.*, criminal or family law). Most first-year law students, however, have limited experience and typically try to fit issues into the framework of one of their first-year law courses (*e.g.*, torts, contracts, property, *etc.*).

Using the subjects of law courses to define legal issues may be helpful in situations where the problem fits clearly within the subject area. However, there are two problems with this approach. First, law school courses do not cover the ambit of the law. Second, legal problems rarely fit neatly into these particular divisions. It is important to recognize that law courses are divided into particular subjects for teaching purposes. These divisions are not always helpful when analyzing problems with several dimensions. For example, a situation involving divorce may involve issues of property, contract, tax law and custody, among others. Therefore, if a researcher categorizes the divorce as involving only an issue of property, other areas of the law may be overlooked.

Brainstorming and Word Association

Brainstorming is another way to start thinking about areas of law that might apply. Brainstorming is a process whereby a few people sit in a group and freely share random ideas about the facts and potential legal issues. Brainstorming results in a list of words or phrases that helps describe possible legal issues. This method is particularly helpful if the people involved have a reasonably good understanding of the law.

Word association is a process similar to brainstorming. Word association involves listing words from the facts presented and creatively thinking of synonyms, antonyms, related words and categories. This method assists in breaking down pre-established frameworks and assumptions, which can be barriers to creative thinking. Word association enables researchers to think of the issues from different perspectives and avoid narrowing the issues too early in the research process.

As a general rule, when determining issues, researchers should work from the general to the specific like an inverted pyramid: think about broader categories of law first, while working towards narrower subcategories of law. The following is the result of an actual brainstorming session:

Brainstorming Scenario

Facts

Mr. Red and Ms. Green had a birthday party for a close friend and served drinks to most of their guests. Later that night, one of the guests who had been drinking drove into a telephone pole and injured a passenger in the vehicle. Are the hosts liable for the injury?

↓

Results of Brainstorming and Word Association

Hosts, guests, liable, property, alcohol, invitations, driving, drinking, consumption, risk, harm, responsibility, torts, duty of care, joint liability, driver's responsibility, negligence, parties, friends, drunk, inebriated, passenger's responsibility, contributory negligence.

Using Library Sources

A final way to think about potentially applicable areas of law is by using sources in the law library. Every book that describes the law has organized it into various compartments. The following are some library sources that have highly developed categorizations of law and are most helpful in determining applicable areas of law. Each of these are called "secondary materials" and are discussed in more detail later in Chapter 6 (How To Find Secondary Materials).

The Canadian Encyclopedic Digest

The *Canadian Encyclopedic Digest* (CED) is a comprehensive encyclopedia of Canadian law. It is published by Carswell in two formats: in a paper loose-leaf multi-volume set (available in most law libraries), and online from Westlaw Canada. The CED divides Canadian law into approximately 225 different subject titles. Each title is written by an expert in that area of law and is divided into detailed headings and subheadings.

In the online version, these titles are presented as a table of contents. If you decide to use the electronic version, it is best to simply look at the main headings in the table of contents first, and then the drop down subheadings. Full text searching is also available but, if you begin your research with a full text search, unless you are fairly sure about what you are looking for, you may spend a lot of time looking at topics that are not directly on point. It should be pointed out that some of the CED's categories are not very current, so always check the date the title you are looking at was last updated. See Chapter 6 (How to Find Secondary Materials) for illustrations of the CED.

The print set provides a table of contents for each title as well as a Key and Research Guide which lists all of the subject titles.

Halsbury's Laws of Canada

This new comprehensive Canadian encyclopedia was introduced in 2006 by LexisNexis Canada. It is modelled on the widely used English legal encyclopedia *Halsbury's Laws of England* and presents current commentary on the full range of Canadian law in approximately 50 legal topics. Each subject is authored by a Canadian expert on the topic and is divided into logical divisions and detailed subheadings.

Halsbury's Laws of Canada is available online through LexisNexis Quicklaw. Each topic area is both browsable and searchable. As with the CED, it is more productive to start your search by browsing the tables of contents for the appropriate titles rather than searching the full text as you may end up filtering out information that is not relevant to the issue you are researching.

The print version of *Halsbury's Laws of Canada* comprises 70 hardbound volumes. At the end of each volume is a detailed subject index, a recommended list of additional secondary sources for further research and a glossary of relevant terms.

Textbooks

Every law library has a collection of legal textbooks. A few of these textbooks are now available in electronic form. These books include summaries of the law in a number of areas. You can find these books by simply searching a library computer catalogue for your particular subject.

Almost all legal textbooks have tables of contents and subject indices. Both provide examples of the ways in which the law is categorized. For example, a textbook on employment law might have one chapter on unionized employees and one chapter on non-unionized employees. By perusing a table of contents or subject index, researchers can gain ideas about the divisions and categories of the law, which will help determine applicable areas of law.

Periodical Indexes

Legal periodical indexes are published to assist researchers in finding journal articles and other legal sources such as book reviews and reports. These indexes list legal journal articles and other legal sources by subject and author. They therefore have extensive subject categories. These subject categories are extremely well-developed divisions of legal concepts. A researcher can go to the library equipped only with a factual analysis and a list of key words and after perusing these indexes have a good idea about the area of law that might apply and how it is categorized. See Chapter 6 (How to Find Secondary Materials) for more information about periodical indexes.

Each of these secondary sources categorizes the law in very different ways, so it is best to use them in combination. For example, in the Melody and Paul situation in Chapter 2 (Factual Analysis), the issue of division of family assets was labelled in the following ways in the three sources:

- CED Table of Contents: Family Law - Divorce
- Textbook on Family Law Index: Proprietary Rights in Matrimonial Property
- Periodical Index: subject headings of Marriage Law or Marital Property

All of these sources are fairly easy to find and, as you will see, are the first sources that you should look at when you begin to look for the law.

Researchers should be careful to keep open minds about potentially applicable areas of law. It is wise to look at as many areas of law as possible to avoid overlooking relevant areas. Do not delve too deeply into the text of the library sources until you have perused a few. Just look at the indexes of each source until you have a better idea about the specific areas of law that may be relevant. Beware of going off on tangents into areas of law that may be irrelevant.

Step 2: Identify the General Legal Issues

Once you have an idea about the general areas of law that might apply, you can read about these areas generally, and identify the legal issues. This means reading a few secondary materials such as textbooks, the CED or journal articles. You cannot identify the legal issues without knowing some law.

Although the process of issue determination is ongoing, you should attempt to identify the broader legal issues early in the research process. This will help you focus your research.

Reading about the subject generally will enable you to formulate the general issues and arrange them in a logical pattern, which will form an outline for your research. For example, if you read about family law, you will learn that there are statutes in most provinces that determine how property is divided upon marriage breakdown. These statutes may then form the starting point for your research.

As you read about the law in more depth you will be able to formulate the legal issues.

Try This Example

Jill's Will

Jill died last night and her daughter, Madeline, found a handwritten will under Jill's bed. Madeline has come to you to find out if the will is valid.

Assume that you read about the law generally and found that there is a provincial statute that regulates the making of wills. You find out as well that in order for a will to be effective it must be in writing and must be witnessed. This is described in case law.

The first question you will likely want to answer is: Is Jill's will valid? This is a broad legal issue. The next question you might ask is: Did Jill's will have all the necessary requirements of a will? More specifically: Is Jill's handwritten, unwitnessed will valid? These last two questions are more focused legal issues which emerge as you read about the law. This focusing of issues is ongoing throughout the research process.

The more you learn about your particular area, the better you become at drafting legal issues.

Step 3: Formulate the Specific Legal Issues

Only after you have a fairly clear idea about the law will you be able to formulate the specific legal issues. A legal issue is a question arising from the facts that demands an answer in law. The following is an example of a well-drafted legal issue based on the Paul and Melody situation (from Chapter 2):

> Will the $20,000 gift that Melody received from her grandmother two years ago, which she kept in a separate bank account in her name, form part of the family assets to be divided upon marriage breakdown?

Because each and every situation is different, each situation has a legal question specific to its particular circumstances. Legal issues should, ideally, include enough information to enable a researcher to go into the library and find the answer to the problem.

Factual Issues vs. Legal Issues

Legal issues combine facts and law into questions. The legal issue must be put into the context of the facts. Without some facts, the issue is incomplete.

The object in drafting issues is to include just enough facts to make the question answerable in that particular situation and no other. Sometimes beginners at research confuse factual issues and legal issues. Factual issues demand a factual answer and can be answered without referring to the law. They do not contain questions about the law. The following are examples of factual issues:

- Why did Melody's grandmother give her the money?
- In whose bank account was the money placed?
- Did Paul know about the money?
- When did Jill write the will?
- Was the will signed?
- Did anyone witness the will?

Sub-issues

There may be more than one issue or one large issue and several sub-issues. Sub-issues emerge through the identification of the larger issues. They usually take the form of necessary components of the larger issues. For example, there are two sub-components of every crime: *mens rea* (intent) and *actus reus* (act). These sub-components will often be the sub-issues of the larger issue of whether the accused is guilty of a crime.

Try This Example

Nancy and Steve

Nancy slipped and fell on Steve's icy driveway today and broke her wrist. Steve had been away on a business trip for a week and there had been a major snowfall over the last three days. Steve was too tired last night to shovel the driveway when he got in from the airport and he was hoping it would warm up overnight and the snow would melt.

Summary of the Law

Negligence law provides that every person has a duty to take reasonable care to prevent foreseeable harm. The duty owed by homeowners to the public is that of the reasonable homeowner in a similar situation (*i.e.*, standard of care).

Possible Main Issue

Is Steve liable for Nancy's fall and broken wrist for failing to clear his driveway of snow for three days?

Possible Sub-issues

1. Did Steve owe a duty of care to Nancy to clear the driveway? Was it reasonably foreseeable that Steve's failure to shovel the driveway would result in Nancy's slip and fall?
2. Did Steve meet the standard of care required of a reasonable homeowner when he failed to shovel the driveway?
3. Did Steve's failure to shovel the driveway cause Nancy's broken wrist?

Often the sub-issues are elements of a cause of action. For example, the three sub-issues above are the three elements you must prove in a negligence action: duty of care, standard of care and causation. Each sub-issue should be able to stand on its own as a distinct question of law.

Defining the issues sets the stage for the eventual organization required to write the results of research. Often the logic arising from the formulation of the issues is good logic to follow when explaining the law later.

Although defining the legal issues is important, researchers should not become too concerned about the specific wording of the legal issues too early in the research. It is best to err on the side of defining legal issues too broadly. As the research evolves, these issues will become clearer and more defined. It is wise to review the issues periodically to ensure they are complete and accurate. Often this may not be accomplished until the research is near completion.

SELF TEST

The following is a self test based on the information provided in this chapter. The answers to these questions are found at the end of the book in the "Answers to Self Tests" section.

1. List three steps in determining legal issues.
2. Name a few methods that might assist you in thinking about possible areas of law that might apply to legal problems.
3. What library sources might assist you in determining legal issues?
4. Do correctly formulated legal issues include just facts, just law, or a combination of facts and law?
5. Should legal issues be drafted as questions?

SAMPLE EXERCISE

Instructions

Assume you are given the following fact pattern and you know nothing about this area of law. Do a factual analysis; then go through the three steps for determining legal issues and attempt to formulate the legal issues.

Fact Pattern

Homes and Watson

Sherly Homes asked Mr. Watson, a trusted friend, to assist her in purchasing an automobile. She specified the type and price of automobile Mr. Watson was to search for and stipulated that he was to consult her prior to concluding a deal.

A few weeks later, Mr. Watson found a car suitable for Homes. Unfortunately, he forgot to obtain her prior approval of the vehicle and concluded a deal to purchase the automobile by signing the sale papers in her name.

Before Mr. Watson was able to inform Homes of the purchase, the vendor telephoned him and stated that "the deal is off". Mr. Watson then advised Homes of the automobile purchase and the vendor's telephone call. Homes approved Watson's purchase of the automobile.

Ms. Homes wants to know if she gets to keep the car.

ANSWERS TO SAMPLE EXERCISE

Factual Analysis

The following is a restatement of the facts:

> Sherly Homes asked Mr. Watson to help her buy a car. She specified the type and price of automobile and stipulated that he was to consult her before concluding a deal.
>
> A few weeks later Mr. Watson found a car and, before obtaining Ms. Homes' approval, signed the papers of sale in her name. Before Mr. Watson told Ms. Homes of the purchase, the vendor telephoned him and stated that "the deal is off". Mr. Watson then advised Ms. Homes of the automobile purchase and the vendor's telephone call. Ms. Homes approved Mr. Watson's purchase of the automobile.

Issue Determination

Step 1: Determine applicable area of the law by using any of the following:

- *Law Courses* — Two law courses that could potentially be relevant are Contract Law and Property Law. A review of a typical Contract Law set of course materials indicates that these facts may fall into the categories of offer, acceptance, and ratification.

- *Brainstorming and Word Association* — Some words that might come to mind during a brainstorm are: contract, car, automobile, ratification, offer, acceptance, agent, principal, on behalf of, authority, apparent authority and ostensible authority.

- *Library Sources* — There are several textbooks on contracts. Some of the indexes of these texts have chapters devoted to offer and acceptance. Both *Canadian Encyclopedic Digest* and *Halsbury's Laws of Canada* have a section devoted to contract law.

Step 2: Identify the legal issues by reading the law in more depth; read generally at first. The following three cases describe the relevant law in this area.

Monty's Insurance Co. v. McGill (Alta. C.A.) (fictitious)

An employee of the plaintiff insurance company accepted a promissory note as payment for a policy of insurance. He then entered a notation of the policy on the company's record book. The promissory note was subsequently dishonoured, although no attempt to return the note or to change the notation in the book regarding the policy was made. Several months later, the policy-holder's premises were destroyed by fire. The insurance company refused to honour the insurance policy because the employee did not have authority to accept a promissory note as payment for the policy. The court stated:

> For it cannot be doubted that an agent may bind his principal by acts done within the scope of his general and ostensible authority, although those acts may exceed his actual authority as between himself and his principal; the private instructions which limit that authority, and the circumstances that his acts are in excess of it, being unknown to the person with whom he is dealing.

The court held that by accepting the promissory note, the employee acted outside his scope of authority, as promissory notes were not a recognized method of payment for a policy of insurance. Therefore, the employee did not bind the company to a contract of insurance.

Tillman v. Leader (Sask. C.A.) (fictitious)

Mr. Jones, purporting to act as agent for Mr. Tillman (the plaintiff), contracted with Mr. Leader (the defendant) in the name of Mr. Tillman. Mr. Jones was actually contracting on his own behalf and with fraudulent intent. When the defendant discovered the identity of the agent, he refused to complete the contract. Mr. Tillman, however, then ratified the act of Mr. Jones. The court held that the ratification was valid and stated:

> ... we think that the contracts could be validly ratified by the person in whose name they purported to be made, even although they were in fact made without his actual authority, and although the agent had in his mind some fraudulent intent. ... They were, therefore, contracts which not only purported to be made by him, but which he had the means to carry out. ... It is not found that Tillman the principal was guilty of any fraud. If there was such a finding, the question would be altogether different. ...

Bilder v. Lampton (B.C.C.A.) (fictitious)

The defendant, Lampton, made an offer to the agent of the plaintiff, Bilder, which was accepted by the agent, although the agent had no authority to bind his principal to a contract. The defendant subsequently withdrew the offer. The plaintiff then ratified the acceptance made by his agent. The court held that the contract was binding, and that the ratification went to the date of the acceptance. The court stated:

> The rule as to ratification by a principal of acts done by an assumed agent is that the ratification is thrown back to the date of the act done, and that the agent is put in the same position as if he had authority to do the act at the time the act was done by him.

Step 3: Attempt to formulate the specific legal issues.

The legal issues appear to be:

Issue 1: Did Mr. Watson have authority to bind Ms. Homes to the purchase of the automobile?

Issue 2: Did Ms. Homes' retroactive ratification of the purchase make the contract binding?

Appendix 3A: Summary of Steps of Issue Determination

The following is a summary of the steps of issue determination:

Step 1: Determine applicable areas of law by using any of the following techniques:

    a.   use law school course subjects (*e.g.*, Tort or Contracts);
    b.   brainstorm or word associate; and
    c.   use library resources such as indices, the *Canadian Encyclopedic Digest*, *Halsbury's Laws of Canada* or textbooks.

Step 2: Identify the general legal issues by reading the law generally in the relevant areas. The *Canadian Encyclopedic Digest*, *Halsbury's* or textbooks are a good place to start. Also, check relevant subject headings in periodical indexes to locate articles on point.

Step 3: Formulate the specific legal issues. Read the law in more detail and attempt to articulate the legal issues into questions of law and facts. Remember to continually hone the legal issues as you progress in your research.

Introduction to Law and Legal Materials

4

In order to conduct legal research, you must have a basic understanding of what the law is and how it is made. You must also know about other legal resources, sometimes called secondary materials, and their importance to finding and learning about the law.

This chapter provides a basic introduction to legal systems, the law and the law-making process. It describes both primary sources such as statutes and cases and secondary materials such as journals and textbooks. This chapter also describes what regulations and municipal bylaws are and how they are made.

Chapter 5 (How to Find the Law and Legal Information) explains how these legal materials are typically organized in law libraries, on CD-ROMs, online and on the Internet.

LEARNING OBJECTIVES

At the end of the chapter you will be able to:

- Explain the difference between civil and common law systems of law
- Understand the relationship between statutes and cases
- Define what is meant by "the Constitution"
- Describe the law-making process
- Describe some secondary materials

SYSTEMS OF LAW

An understanding of legal systems and the way that laws are made is critical to legal research. It assists you in recognizing the relationship between legislation and cases, and in understanding why and how law is put in written form, published and categorized.

There are two types of legal systems that prevail in Canada: the civil law system that applies in Quebec and the common law system that applies in all other provinces and territories. In addition, there is an international system of law that governs the relationship between Canada and other countries in the world.

The Civil Law System

The civil law system is based on a complete set of written laws or a civil code. Unlike the common law system, judge-made cases simply interpret that code and need not be treated as precedents. In practice, however, judges informally recognize precedent and, when cases are appealed, higher courts will not forget what they have said in prior cases. Another feature of the civil law system is that the actual cases are inquisitorial as opposed to adversarial. This means that civil law judges play an active role in eliciting information. They are even permitted to call witnesses and order investigations.

The Common Law System

Canada (with the exception of Quebec) inherited a system of "common law" that originated with travelling courts in England. Because there were few written laws in England, English judges developed a system whereby prior decisions from one area of the country were applied to other areas of the country. These decisions were based on the "common custom" as the judges saw it. These decisions slowly became uniform across the country and were referred to as the "common law".

The common law is, therefore, law made by judges and found in decided cases. Each decided case modifies the law slightly as it is applied to a particular set of circumstances; this system of precedents is called case law. By applying prior case law and interpreting statutes, the courts build upon and revise the law. They clarify ambiguities and elaborate upon the intentions of Parliament as they see them.

Another type of case law is found in the decisions of administrative tribunals. In order to better administer the law, governments create administrative bodies. Governments delegate to these bodies the authority to make decisions but not to pass laws. Although these decisions also form part of the law, they have not been fully integrated into the common law. This is partially because administrative law is not made by judges and, therefore, judges are not compelled to follow it as precedent.

International System of Law

Various international laws also affect Canadians and cannot be overlooked in legal research. These laws include international treaties and covenants, which are agreements signed by the Government of Canada and other countries. The government is ultimately bound by these agreements and Canadians are required to act in accordance with them. These treaties and covenants are sometimes interpreted by Canadian courts and administrative bodies.

WHAT IS THE LAW?

There are essentially two types of written law in Canada: case law and legislation. Case law is judge-made law and legislation is government-made law. Cases and legislation form the law in Canada and are called "primary sources".

Case Law

As described above, case law or court decisions are the written decisions of judges and tribunals. Therefore case law consists of cases from all levels of courts from all jurisdictions, from various provincial courts to international tribunals. The next chapter explains how these cases are published and filed in libraries and databases. Chapter 10 (Introduction to Legal Analysis) explains the hierarchy of these cases and how they are interpreted.

Legislation

Legislation is that part of the law that is made by elected members of Parliament. Legislation is made by each level of government: federal, provincial and municipal. Federal and provincial legislation is usually in the form of statutes and regulations, whereas municipal legislation is manifested as bylaws.

The main products of legislatures are statutes and regulations. The government is constantly introducing or repealing statutes and thereby creating new law. Although statutes are new law, they are often codifications of case law and are created to clarify case law.

Legislation is introduced primarily to create new laws or to clarify or amend case law. There is rarely a legal problem that is not touched in some way by legislation. Although Canada has a common law legal system based on the rule of precedent or decided cases, it seems that, with the increased creation of statutes, Canada is moving towards a more legislative legal system.

Statutes are published by the federal government and each provincial government. These governments also publish research aids such as indexes of statutes, although many of the tools researchers use to locate statutes are published by commercial publishers.

Statute-making Authority

In Canada, the federal government and provincial governments share governing and, therefore, have separate spheres of law-making powers. This division between federal and provincial powers is described in ss. 91 and 92 of the *Constitution Act, 1867*.[1] Essentially, the provincial governments regulate provincial matters (*e.g.*, education and property) and the federal government

---

[1]   R.S.C. 1985, Appendix II, No. 5.

regulates matters that extend across Canada (*e.g.*, banking, national defence and postal services).

There is often overlap between these two spheres and, therefore, legislation affecting certain matters sometimes appears in both federal and provincial laws. For example, there are both federal statutes and provincial statutes dealing with employment and labour law. As a general rule, the federal laws apply to employees in businesses that cross provincial boundaries and provincial laws apply to employees of businesses of a local or provincial nature; however, this distinction is not always clear. A good researcher will look at both federal and provincial statutes to determine what they cover.

It is a good idea to review ss. 91 and 92 periodically to recall the fundamental divisions and the differing law-making powers.

Regulations and Municipal Bylaws

Because the day-to-day administration of statutes can be time-consuming, Parliament and the legislative and territorial assemblies often delegate some of their law-making authority to other government bodies. These more detailed laws, which deal with the implementation of statutes, are called regulations or rules and have as much force in law as statutes.

Regulations and municipal bylaws and ordinances are laws created by a delegated authority and are called subordinate or delegated legislation. Elected representatives delegate their law-making power to other authorities who, in turn, make laws on their behalf.

Regulations describe the day-to-day administration of a statute. They "put meat on the bones" of statutes. For example, while the British Columbia *Name Act*[2] sets out the basic law permitting British Columbians to change their names, the regulations under the *Name Act* describe the process involved in changing names and the cost of doing so. Federal regulations are called statutory instruments (SI) or statutory orders and regulations (SOR).

At the present time, there is no one single online source for Canadian municipal bylaws and ordinances. However, many municipalities post bylaws on their websites.

The Constitution

The most important piece of legislation in Canada is the Constitution. The Constitution will almost always have some effect on a legal problem and thus usually plays a role in research.

The Constitution is the highest law in Canada. All other laws must be consistent with the Constitution or they can be struck down and declared invalid by the courts. Section 52 of the *Constitution Act, 1982*[3] states:

> The Constitution of Canada is the supreme law of Canada, and any law that is inconsistent with the provisions of the Constitution is, to the extent of the inconsistency, of no force or effect.

---

[2]   R.S.B.C. 1996, c. 328.
[3]   R.S.C. 1985, Appendix II, No. 44, Sched. B.

In simple terms the Constitution describes the rules about how a country governs itself. It specifically describes:

- who can make laws (legislative power);
- who will enforce the laws (executive powers); and
- who interprets the laws (judicial powers).

The Constitution also defines the rights and freedoms of Canadians in the *Canadian Charter of Rights and Freedoms* (the *Charter*).[4] Specifically, it restricts governments from interfering with certain basic rights of individuals. Indeed, there are few areas of law that are not affected in some way by the *Charter*. It protects fundamental freedoms (*e.g.*, speech and religion), democratic rights (*e.g.*, voting), mobility rights (*e.g.*, travel), language rights, equality rights, and legal rights (*e.g.*, consulting a lawyer).

The Constitution of Canada originated as a statute of the United Kingdom entitled the *British North America Act, 1867* (*B.N.A. Act*) (see the *Constitution Act, 1867*). This statute includes ss. 91 and 92, which describe the powers of Parliament and the courts. It established Ontario, Quebec, Nova Scotia and New Brunswick as the first provinces of Canada. The remaining provinces joined Canada afterwards. Because the *B.N.A. Act* was a statute of the United Kingdom, only the United Kingdom could amend it.

In 1982, that statute was patriated. The United Kingdom introduced the *Canada Act 1982* (U.K.) and its schedule, the new *Constitution Act, 1982*. The *Canada Act 1982* renamed the *B.N.A. Act* to the *Constitution Act, 1867* and contains the amending formula. It gives Canadians sole power over their own constitution and includes the *Charter*. The Act also states that the United Kingdom will not pass any laws affecting Canada.

Therefore, the Constitution consists of a number of documents: the *Canada Act 1982* (U.K.), the *Constitution Act, 1982*[5] and the Acts listed in the schedules to the *Constitution Act*. Part I of the *Constitution Act, 1982* is the *Canadian Charter of Rights and Freedoms* and one of the schedules is the *Constitution Act, 1867*. The constitutional documents can be found in the Appendices volume of Revised Statutes of Canada, 1985.

The Constitution is important to legal research for two fundamental reasons: it defines the limits of legislative authority and defines the rights and freedoms of Canadian citizens.

Treaties

In Canada, a treaty is formed with one or more other sovereign states by the federal Executive (the Prime Minister).

Treaties are considered primary legal authority. However, unless a treaty's commitments coincide with existing Canadian law, they are not enforceable in Canada until implemented by statute passed by the appropriate legislative body (federal or provincial) in accordance with the division of powers set out in

---

[4]   R.S.C. 1985, Appendix II, No. 44, Sched. B, Part I.
[5]   R.S.C. 1985, Appendix II, No. 44, Sched. B.

Canada's Constitution. Hence, when a treaty deals with a provincial power, the Executive will seldom ratify it before obtaining the consent of all the provinces.

Treaties are negotiated by delegates of the Prime Minister and reviewed by the Treaty Section of the Department of Foreign Affairs and International Trade (DFAIT) to ensure that they conform both to the principles of international law and to Canadian practices. Since it stems from the royal prerogative, the power of treaty ratification resides with the Executive. It is carried out by an Order in Council issued by the Governor General in Council.

After being signed, treaties are published by the Treaty Section of DFAIT in the *Canada Treaty Series* which has been published since 1928. DFAIT maintains a free, publicly available searchable resource at <http://www.treaty-accord.gc.ca/> that lists titles, signing dates, other details, and the full text of every bilateral and multilateral treaty to which Canada is a signatory. This website advises that it "also maintains a Registry of many non-treaty arrangements or understandings (MOUs) entered into by the Government of Canada, government departments and agencies, and Canadian provinces". Print copies of individual treaties may be purchased from DFAIT, and an annual print volume for each year is also for sale. DFAIT is responsible for maintaining the original copies of treaties.

Like all other states, Canada adheres to Article 102 of the *United Nations Charter*, which requires that Member states register "every treaty and every international agreement" with the UN Secretariat. As a result, all treaties since the coming into force of the *Canadian Charter of Rights and Freedoms* appear in the *United Nations Treaty Series* (U.N.T.S.).

Aboriginal Law

Aboriginal law consists of the *Indian Act*[6] as well as agreements made between First Nations and governments. The *Indian Act* authorizes band councils to make bylaws governing issues on reserves in relation to local matters such as health, traffic control, zoning, building construction and the residence of band members, as well as to levy property taxes, impose business licences and regulate the use of intoxicants on reserves. General regulations made by the Governor in Council under the *Indian Act* are published in the *Canada Gazette, Part II*. Until 1987, the index to the *Gazette* also listed individual band bylaws, but the texts themselves were not published in the *Gazette*. Band bylaws are generally available from the bands themselves, sometimes on their websites, or copies may be requested from Indian and Northern Affairs Canada.

First Nations that have entered into land claims and self-government agreements are not subject to the *Indian Act* limitations on the authority of band councils. Such agreements, ratified by each First Nation and then enacted as federal and provincial statutes, define the governmental authority of the First Nation and the relationship of its laws to federal and provincial laws. Examples

---

[6] R.S.C. 1985, c. I-5.

include the *Nisga'a Final Agreement Act*,[7] and the *Nisga'a Final Agreement Act*.[8]

The *First Nations Gazette*, co-produced since 1997 by the Native Law Centre, University of Saskatchewan, and the Indian Taxation Advisory Board, publishes the full texts of reserve property tax bylaws made under the *Indian Act*, s. 83. This gazette also contains texts of some other finance-related bylaws.

The *Canadian Native Law Reporter* (known as *Canadian Native Law Cases* until 1978), also published by the Native Law Centre, is an excellent and fairly comprehensive resource for full texts of judicial decisions involving Canadian native persons and bands. It also contains occasional secondary legal material such as case comments, articles, and other commentary.

In the area of criminal law, courts have used the sentencing provisions of the *Criminal Code*[9] to authorize alternative forms of sentencing for Aboriginal persons, under certain conditions. Forms of restorative justice and community service are being implemented by use of band-based sentencing circles.

The Law-making Process

As described above, statutes and cases combine to form the law of Canada. The law-making process looks something like this:

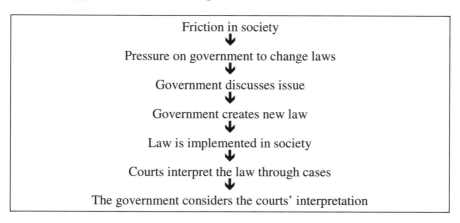

Friction in society
↓
Pressure on government to change laws
↓
Government discusses issue
↓
Government creates new law
↓
Law is implemented in society
↓
Courts interpret the law through cases
↓
The government considers the courts' interpretation

If friction exists in society, groups or individuals will often pressure the government for change (*e.g.*, through lobbying). The government will often investigate the issue by setting up commissions or committees. If, after an investigation, the government believes that the conflict can be resolved by creating a new law, it will introduce legislation (*e.g.*, a statute). Eventually, that legislation will be implemented in society. If there is a dispute about the law, it can be challenged in court. If the court finds that the new law is inconsistent

---

[7] S.C. 2000, c. 7.
[8] S.B.C. 1999, c. 2.
[9] R.S.C. 1985, c. C-46.

with existing law, it will make a decision stating this. Courts interpret the legislation. Each case that is decided affects prior cases and legislation. The following fictional example assists in describing the law-making process.

Example of Law-Making Process

In 2005, research was conducted indicating that the taking of vitamin BX7 prolongs life and general happiness. Activists for preventive medicine pressured the Canadian government to introduce legislation making the use of BX7 mandatory. In 2006, the federal government created a Vitamin Commission, which travelled across Canada gathering data and opinions about the use and effect of BX7. The results were astounding. All those people who had taken BX7 were much happier and appeared to live longer. As a result of this investigation, the government passed legislation, the *Vitamin Act*, requiring that all Canadians take BX7 three times a day. The penalty for non-compliance was ten years in prison. An administrative body was set up to enforce the statute.

Mr. Beauregard, a resident of Vancouver, refused to take BX7 and was imprisoned. He hired a lawyer who brought an action in the courts arguing that Mr. Beauregard's rights and freedoms were violated. The court hearing the case agreed with Mr. Beauregard and stated in its decision that the *Vitamin Act* was inconsistent with Mr. Beauregard's constitutional rights and, therefore, was of no effect. When the government of the day heard about the court decision it decided to repeal the law and remove it from the statute books.

It is important to recognize the interplay between legislation and case law. In Canadian law, neither stands alone and research will always involve a search of both types of law.

It is also important to keep in mind the entire legislative process when researching legislation. Since statutes are only the final product of a long process of consultation and debate, researchers should be aware of documents such as reports of government commissions, which can assist in interpreting statutes or understanding the policy reasons for their introduction.

Secondary Materials

Other types of legal materials are sometimes considered to be part of the law. These are called "secondary materials". They are, however, only aids in interpreting and finding the law; they are not the law. Secondary materials include such things as textbooks, encyclopedias and journal articles. They assist legal researchers in two ways: in understanding the law and in locating the law. For example, encyclopedias and textbooks summarize the law and, in doing so, provide references (*i.e.*, citations) to cases and statutes. They are most frequently used at the beginning of the research process, primarily to gain an understanding of a particular area of law. Chapter 6 (How to Find Secondary Materials) describes these in more detail.

SELF TEST

The following is a self test based on the information provided in this chapter. The answers to these questions are found at the end of the book in the "Answers to Self Tests" section.

1. What are the two types of law in Canada?
2. Where does the term "common law" originate?
3. What is legislation?
4. Describe the law-making process.
5. What is the difference between primary sources and secondary materials?

How to Find the Law and Legal Information

5

Once you have completed your factual analysis and determined your legal issues, you will be ready to look for the law and relevant legal resources.

This chapter explains the steps you need to take when looking for the law before you delve into the law library and the vast world of electronic legal resources. It describes how legal information is sorted, explains differences between commercial service providers and public collections, and outlines how to find law and legal information using several different sources.

LEARNING OBJECTIVES

At the end of the chapter you will be able to:

- List the six steps to doing effective research
- Explain why Google is not the best place to start your research
- Name the two main commercial providers of Canadian legal information
- Describe a few public (no-fee) providers of legal information
- Describe the four doors to any law library

PLANNING IS CRITICAL

Whether you are searching online or in a law library you must always plan ahead. This means thinking about what you need, where it is likely located and how you can access it efficiently before you start.

For example, you can find legal cases in at least three specific locations: in books in a law library, online through a commercial provider and via the Internet on a courthouse website. You need to decide which is the most cost- and time-effective for your particular search.

Although planning is important for in-library research, it is even more important for online research since computers do only as instructed. If a search is conducted in the wrong database or if it is constructed improperly, the results will be wrong. If the problem is defined too narrowly, the information retrieved will be incomplete. If it is defined too broadly, too much information will be provided.

Even if you have some idea about the information you need, in order to avoid duplicating or missing any relevant information, you will want to be systematic about your search. There is nothing worse than going in circles because you forgot that you had taken a step before.

Don't Start With Google

Although you may be inclined to begin your research by simply launching into Google, you will quickly discover that the information you find is vast, inconsistent and unfortunately not the "real law". Although Google is useful (explained below), most lawyers start with one of the established legal publishers to save themselves time and money.

The Big Three

The first thing law students learn is that there are two big commercial providers of legal information: LexisNexis (which provides Quicklaw) (LN/QL), and Westlaw Canada (WC). These two companies compete to collect as much law and legal resources as possible and provide tools to lawyers and law students to make research as easy as possible. All Canadian law students have free access to these two services.

CanLII, on the other hand, is a free public service, paid for by all of the provincial law societies. It is giving these two big companies a run for their money. Other publishers of law include the various governments (who publish legislation) and the various provincial and federal courts (who publish cases), as well as the many companies who publish legal news, journals, textbooks, *etc.*, as you will see below.

In order to decide where to start, you need to know a bit about these providers of legal information. Specifically, you need to know:

- what they have in their collections;
- how they sort, tag and index the information;
- how their search engines work; and
- how to use their templates and tools to conduct an efficient search.

And in order to answer these questions in a systematic fashion, you will want to follow the following steps.

EFFICIENT RESEARCH IN SIX STEPS

Effectiveness and efficiency are driven by a host of factors, such as your particular problem, your access to the information, and your skill at searching.

Never assume that one method is better than others for all purposes. At this stage you must look not just at the financial and time costs. You must also look at the likelihood that your research will be accurate and complete. If, for example, you are not skilled at constructing word searches then you might be better off starting in the library with secondary sources or printed reporters, or perhaps confirming your computer research in print in a library afterwards. At the end of the day you may decide to contact your library and speak to a librarian. Sometimes this approach is most efficient.

In order to produce effective results from your research, you need to ask the following six questions:

- What information are you looking for?
- Where is that information likely located?
- Which resources are available for your use? At what cost?
- What resource likely contains your content?
- How easy is it to use the service?
- How will you formulate your search?

Each of the above questions is discussed here, followed by detailed descriptions of each of the main providers of legal information.

By working through these steps you will ultimately decide which legal resource is most effective and most efficient for your situation.

1. What Information Are You Looking For?

If you have completed your factual analysis you will likely have some idea about what you are looking for. All legal research involves looking for cases and some involves looking for statutes and regulations. A researcher should have some idea about the particular legal issues raised in a problem and the general area of law before looking for specific resources. So if you know you are looking for cases, you would not look in a statute database.

Keep in mind that although it is easy to conduct a word search on a computer, the search is only as good as the researcher's knowledge and skill at using that particular provider's system. Choices must continually be made about where and how to search. Here are some general questions to prime your mental pump:

- Are you looking for cases, legislation or secondary materials?
- Is the information needed from a specific jurisdiction (*e.g.*, Canada, a province, the United States)?
- If you are looking for a case, is the case from a specific court (*e.g.*, Supreme Court of Canada or British Columbia Court of Appeal)?
- Is the information from a specific period of time?

As mentioned previously, when beginning your research it is best to read generally about the law, particularly in secondary sources (textbooks and encyclopedias) to determine what specific legal materials are needed.

The reason law librarians recommend that law students use print-based sources first is simply because most of the secondary sources are most easily accessed in a few shelves in the library. The textbooks and encyclopedias tend to be located in a small area and can be located and reviewed fairly easily. However, as more textbooks and encyclopedias are being converted to electronic format, these searches may soon become easier.

2. Where Is That Information Likely Located?

Once you know what you are looking for, you must decide where you are likely going to find the information. In the library? From commercial providers? From free public websites? Then you must find out which sources are available for your use and which are most effective and efficient. For example, if searching for a federal statute, you could look in a library, on a government website or through a commercial provider. Each has its benefits and drawbacks.

The law and legal resources are available in book form in all law libraries and in electronic form in various public and private collections. Most research involves making appropriate use of both paper and electronic resources.

It is important to know that although there is a lot of free information out there on the World Wide Web, you usually get what you pay for in legal research. This is because most of the law and legal resources are still in the private domain,which means you must purchase access to it.

Libraries and lawyers buy books, CDs and online services from a variety of publishers and legal information providers. Although this is slowly changing, the legal profession is slow to accept information that is not from an original or well-recognized source.

The following table gives you an idea of the possible sources (providers) of law and legal resources:

Law	Sample Sources
Cases	LN/QL, WC, CanLII, Fed. or Prov. Court websites
Legislation	LN/QL, WC, CanLII, Fed. or Prov. Gov. websites
Citators	LN/QL, WC, to some extent CanLII
Case Digests	LN/QL, WC
Journals	LN/QL, WC, HeinOnline, other collections of online journals available to you, often through a law society, courthouse or law school library

Don't Disregard the Law Library

Keep in mind that most research begins in a law library. This is because unless you have a very clear idea about the exact item you are looking for, you need to begin your search by reading broadly. This means you will most likely start by looking at secondary sources such as textbooks, lawyers' manuals or encyclopedias that are most easily located, and easy to peruse, in a law library.

3. Which Resources Are Available for Your Use? At What Cost?

Because access to computer information can be expensive, law libraries and law firms do not necessarily subscribe to all of the information available. A decision is often made to only maintain access through one or two commercial online providers. Some of the questions you must ask when deciding where to look for information are:

- Which sources do you have access to (*e.g.*, commercial online providers, a library or Internet access to public websites)?
- Do you have to pay for the information or is it available for free?
- If there is a fee, what is it?
- How can you keep your costs low?
- What format will the information be in (*e.g.*, a PDF file that is identical to the original, html only or in a Word document)?

4. What Resource Likely Contains Your Content?

Each provider is unique, and has a unique collection of law and legal resources. Therefore, when looking at the content of any provider you will want to look at each of the following:

- Does it have statutes, cases, secondary sources, journals, *etc.*?
- Does it have abstracts, summaries, headnotes?
- How far back does the information go?
- How current is the information?

A discussion about what each of the providers offers can be found below under "How easy is it to use the service?", and comprehensive lists of what the main providers offer is found further below. Although all of the service providers post this information online, it is not always easy to locate in a summary fashion.

Will the Courts Accept the Information?

A final question you must always ask is whether the courts will accept the information that you find. Many courts, recognizing that electronic documents can be altered, are hesitant to use them. Also, when referring to particular excerpts from cases or statutes, it is easier for all parties to be working from one document when referring to particular pages or passages. PDF files are replicas of the original documents with original pagination and often are the preferred format for electronic documents. Legal publishers have created standards to get past this problem, but it is still necessary for you to check to ensure that the document you retrieve is considered legitimate for all purposes.

5. How Easy Is It to Use the Service?

As you become familiar with each of the electronic resources, you will find that some are easier to use than others, depending on what you need. And as you can imagine, each service provider works very hard at designing websites, research engines, templates, tools and hyperlinks to make your searches faster and better.

Separate Databases

Although each provider is unique, you will quickly discover that each has its own particular collection of databases.

Like the shelves in a library, each database contains different information and since not all information can be in one place, the legal information is typically sorted just as it is in a law library: by legislation, by cases and by secondary sources. For example, statutes and regulations are usually contained in one database, cases in another and secondary sources in several others. These databases are also often subdivided by jurisdiction, topic and time span.

Contents of Databases

When doing a search, you want to make sure that you are searching all the relevant databases, and this requires an understanding of exactly what each contains. Each service provider provides a list of its databases and their contents (see summaries below). These lists are available online and sometimes in print, and must be completely up-to-date to be useful. Often you can click on a description of the contents of a database before you enter it.

Some commercial providers allow researchers to combine databases to make research easier. You can customize your combinations to get what you want with fewer searches. If you do combine it, try to click on the description of the contents to ensure you have picked the right file(s) for your research.

Full Text or Digest

Databases of cases are in either full text or digest form. They are sometimes organized in a similar way to the print case reports: by court, jurisdiction and subject. For example, there is a database on LN/QL for the Supreme Court of Canada Judgments that includes only Supreme Court of Canada decisions. The corresponding print case report is called the *Supreme Court Reports* (S.C.R.), which includes only Supreme Court of Canada decisions. Statutes and regulations are also available online, in jurisdiction-specific databases.

Search Tools

The most significant advancements provided by electronic searches are not just the speed at which you can locate a case or statute, but also the search tools and hyperlinks that allow a researcher to move between various resources, including books, cases, statutes and commentaries. For example, some online textbooks and encyclopedias include hyperlinks that can lead you directly to the case or statute that they are referring to in the text.

If you begin your research, as many beginners do, with an encyclopedia, you will need to locate that encyclopedia in the database. If you go to Westlaw Canada and do a general search you will not be forwarded to the CED. If you go to LexisNexis/Quicklaw and to a general search you will not be searching *Halsbury's*. You still need to know where the various secondary sources are and access them directly.

Keeping Track of What You Do

If you use electronic sources when just beginning to learn about a topic, always keep track of where you looked and how you conducted a search. For example, did you search the CEDs and if so, what words did you use to search the sources? If you find yourself sinking into the huge number of cases, back up and remember how you got there. The commercial online providers enable you to keep track of your searches. Westlaw Canada has a Research Trail feature that remembers all your searches for 14 days. LexisNexis/Quicklaw has a History and Alerts feature that remembers your searches for seven days. You can return to these searches and edit or rerun them at any time.

Library or Electronic Collections?

Your decision about whether to use the library will usually be based on the amount of time and money you have and how close you are to a well-stocked law library. However, there are several reasons why you might still want to use a law library.

I wish I could tell you that electronic sources have finally replaced paper-based law libraries, but in reality, physical libraries are still necessary for most research. This is primarily because none of the electronic collections contain *all* of the law and legal resources, but also because looking in a library may actually be faster. As well, some courts are hesitant to accept electronic versions of cases or statutes because there is still a lack of confidence that the electronic version is completely accurate. This reluctance likely will diminish over time.

As a rule of thumb, the better you understand your problem and specifically what you are looking for, the more efficient electronic research will be. For example, if you are looking for one case and you have the complete citation, it is fairly easy to find the case in an electronic collection by searching by citation.

Print Is Similar to Electronic

There is another reason why library search skills are so important: electronic searches are very similar to print-based research. This is because most of the companies who publish laws and legal materials in electronic form are the very same publishers who provide the information in print form. These publishers have been collecting and organizing print versions for years and now organize electronic versions in a similar way. For example, they collect and publish cases in specific collections and design search tools that are useful at finding cases.

They each develop specially designed tools for use in both the law library and the electronic version. You may also prefer to turn to a library because of cost and time constraints.

Another advantage of library sources is that they can be easier to read and scan than electronic sources. Researchers can quickly view a whole case or statute instead of just one page or section at a time.

6. How Will You Formulate Your Search?

To retrieve electronic information, a researcher must instruct the computer to find that information. This is done by conducting a word search. A researcher asks the computer to search for a word or words or a phrase, often through a template. The search engine simply scans all of the information in a database for the words requested and any documents containing those words. This is called a literal search.

    The first thing that law students should notice when using Westlaw or QL is that the first page of the website is designed for a busy lawyer looking for information fast.

The First Screen

The first screen you will see, after you enter your password, describes the general contents and provides you with a number of choices such as links or templates. You will find "quick search templates" for locating cases and statutes. You will also find links to news and current changes to the law, which are of interest to lawyers who wish to stay up-to-date on the law. Commands can be completed by easy point-and-click options or selecting the appropriate template.

No Quick Searches for Beginners

But for law students, who are trying to solve a complex legal problem, there are no "quick search" templates. You will need to look in several places within the website to begin to sort through your research problem, exactly as you would in a law library — systematically from general (secondary sources) to specific (cases, statutes and regulations).

Constantly Changing Interfaces

Since new interfaces are created regularly to meet the ever-expanding needs of lawyers, always take your time on the first page. It is always a good idea to familiarize yourself with the tools and look at a map of the site to get a sense of what the site includes. The first step usually involves selecting a database; therefore you must know what information is included in each and that most systems search words on the basis of Boolean logic rather than literal searching. This means that the computer simply searches for words in different permutations and combinations (this is explained further in the section below on constructing searches).

Selecting a Database

If you are using a commercial provider or free website that sorts the information into distinct types of databases, then it is fastest to select — from a drop-down list or template — the particular database that is likely to contain what you are looking for. For example, if you are looking for Alberta Court of

Appeal decisions, select the database or template that covers only cases from that jurisdiction and court level. A search through a database containing Ontario case reports would not prove fruitful. Here are some questions to ask before delving in:

- Which database likely has the information you are looking for?
- Does the databases provide full text, digests or indexes?
- Does the databases include headnotes, summaries or annotations?
- Does the database have hyperlinks or special searching tools?

Formulating a Search

In order to conduct an effective search you must understand not only what databases you are searching in, but also how the search tool you are using works and how it retrieves information. You therefore need to be able to construct a word or phrase search. Here are some questions you need to ask before going online:

- What words or phrases do you want the computer to locate?
- How should the words be grouped?
- Do you want to limit the search by dates?
- Do you want to limit the search by other factors such as judge's name, jurisdiction or level of court?

The following are some basics about searching online databases and free public websites. The success of your search depends not only on your ability to select the correct database but on your ability to construct a proper search. You must articulate your search in a way that a computer will understand. You will have already analyzed the facts and determined the legal issues before beginning your search, so you have a good idea of the terms to use in your search.

The skill in formulating a search is in arranging the words or phrases in a particular way so that the search will be broad enough to include all relevant information and narrow enough to exclude irrelevant information.

Although most service providers have templates, these are only as effective as what you place in the correct template.

Tips on Database Searching

In order not to retrieve too much information, researchers can control or limit searches by combining several words together or doing multiple word searches.

For example, a search for cases with the word "doctor" in them would result in a phenomenal number of cases, whereas a search for cases with the words "doctor" and "cancer" would result in fewer cases being selected. Multiple-word searches involve the use of "connectors" or "proximity indicators".

Using Connectors and Proximity Search Tools

In multiple-word searches, connectors are used between each word. The connectors used are "or", "and", and occasionally "but not". They are linked to the software's system of logic, which is called Boolean logic. Each database has its own system of logic; LexisNexis/Quicklaw, for example, interprets a space between words to be a phrase search while Westlaw Canada interprets a space between words to mean OR, so a search in LN/QL for *customs duties* would yield vastly different results than a search for the same expression in WC. Each database has a button or link that leads to a page which defines all the Boolean operators and how they are used, so it is not necessary for you to learn or memorize the differences in each database. The most commonly used Boolean expressions are:

- "Or", which searches for "wife" *or* "assault". It locates cases containing either the word "wife" or the word "assault".
- "And" searches for "wife" *and* "assault". It locates cases containing both the word "wife" and the word "assault".
- "But not" (often represented by a per cent sign) searches for "wife" but not "assault". It locates cases containing the word "wife" but not the word "assault". Caution should be used with "but not" since it is nearly impossible to think of all the situations that you do not want. In this case, perhaps a better search would be just the word "wife".

By placing "proximity indicators" between words, researchers can request those cases where a word is found within a certain distance of another word. These searches involve searching for one word in a defined proximity to another word. Numerical connectors find words within a certain number of words of each other. Grammatical connectors locate words within the same paragraph or sentence. Once again, you do not need to learn or memorize these connectors.

Within each search, single words can be given special treatment. Most databases have a "wild card" or universal character command that instructs the computer to search for *any* letters where a wild card is placed in a query. In many systems the wild card is an asterisk (*) or an exclamation point (!). So, since practice can be spelled two ways — with a "c" or an "s" — a single word search might look like this: practi*e.

Most search engines also allow for the truncation of a word. Truncation is a technique used to search for words with the same root. For example, employment, employee, employed all have the same root: employ. In many systems an exclamation mark (!) placed at the end of the word directs a computer to search all words with that root. Therefore, a search for employ! will retrieve sources that include words such as employee, employees, employment and employer. Some systems also handle plurals by retrieving both the singular and plural forms of any searched word.

Using Field Search Tools

Searches can also be narrowed down to a specific location with a document. To save time, researchers can direct a computer to restrict a search to a particular part of a case such as the names of one or more parties or the name of the court. Generally these fields are available through a drop down menu on the search screen.

Cases are stored in databases in much the same format as they appear in the published hard copy in the case reports. Each segment of the reported case is searchable in Boolean logic or in a dedicated search box, and each field is coded for purposes of searching. One field may contain the "style of cause". So if a researcher is searching for a case by the names of the parties in the action, it would be most efficient to search only that particular field or template search box for this information, rather than to search the entire text of all decisions.

Tips on Internet Searching

Because of the huge amount of information available through the Internet and the increasing capacity of search engines, it would be impossible to describe a generic way to conduct an Internet search. For legal research, the best method is to go to a legal site you know, such as those mentioned in this book. The best law sites are those maintained by legal experts or librarians who have selected and sorted legal information in meaningful ways.

In most cases, you can begin with a legal website and use their hyperlinks and list of resources to access other sources of information. The only step you may ever need to think about is which site to go to first. This site will lead to a chain of other sites. Some useful Websites for legal research are:

Access to Justice Network (ACJNet Canada)
<http://www.acjnet.org/splash/default.aspx>

Best Guide to Canadian Legal Research
<http://legalresearch.org/>

Doing Legal Research in Canada (Ted Tjaden)
<http://www.llrx.com/features/ca.htm>

Canadian Law Blogs
<http://www.lawblogs.ca>

Legal Tree
<http://www.legaltree.ca/>

If you decide to conduct a general Internet search, keep in mind the limitations of search engines and directories. Although search engines, spiders or crawlers search through massive amounts of data to locate specific information, they may either be searching the tags on a site or the contents of a specific website. As well, although they are a very fast way to find information, your search may only be searching through their index — not all that is available on the Internet.

Even the biggest search engines only index part of the Internet's public domain. However, they scan sites periodically to update their indexes. Also, all of the search engines use Boolean logic. It uses operators such as AND, OR and NOT to refine your search. If you do not include Boolean operators the engine will still use Boolean operators automatically. For example, most search engines will interpret the words "mutual funds" as a search for the words mutual AND funds. In other words, they default to AND. Therefore it is best to use operators when conducting a search.

The main drawback of search engines is that they locate *too much* unsorted information. Another drawback is that they usually do not search inside files or documents such as PDF (Adobe) or proprietary information.

THE MAIN PROVIDERS OF LEGAL INFORMATION

Many organizations collect law and other legal information so that other people can use it. Historically all resources could be found in a law library collection; now, although most still remains there, much of the information is collected and sold online by large commercial publishers. At the same time, smaller publishers and not-for-profit organizations publish both print and electronic resources. More and more access is by way of the Internet.

In this section I describe:

- the law library collections;
- the collections of the two largest commercial legal publishers;
- some of the smaller legal publishers; and
- the public (no-fee) providers of legal information.

Law Library Collections

Each law library sorts its books on the shelves in a particular manner and many create its own search tools. At the same time, publishers publish materials in a certain manner and create their own search tools to be used with their own publications.

A law library is simply a storehouse of the law and other sources relating to the law. Like other libraries, law libraries contain books and journals about a variety of subjects written by various authors. Unlike other libraries, law libraries contain the written laws and specialized tools to assist researchers in both finding and interpreting the law. For example, most governments publish lists of statutes to enable researchers to find the citation (location) of the statute and any revisions to statutes by looking at just one resource.

Books and journals are filed in law libraries in much the same way as they are filed in all other libraries. To locate a book, you use a computer catalogue, and to locate articles in periodicals, you use periodical indexes that are compiled to assist researchers in locating articles by subject, author or title. Textbooks and other treatises are filed by subject and call number, and journals are filed by the journal title.

However, legal researchers also need to locate the law itself: cases and legislation. The specific research tools for locating legislation and cases are described in later chapters. Cases, statutes and regulations are kept in distinct places in a law library and are not sorted by subject. Tools have been developed to help researchers locate this law.

In a law library there are four access points: one for general materials such as textbooks; one for journals and periodicals; one for cases; and one for legislation. I refer to access points as the "four doors" to the law library. All four doors should be used for comprehensive legal research.

The Four Doors to the Law Library

Door	What You Are Looking For	Where It Is Shelved	How To Find It	Example
1.	Textbooks	By subject and classification number	Computer catalogue	Search the law library catalogue by subject, author, title or keywords.
2.	Journal and periodical articles	By the title of the periodical or journal	Periodical indexes	Search for a topic in a periodical index in print or online.
3.	Legislation	By jurisdiction (federal and each province and territory)	The relevant federal, provincial or territorial table of statutes	Look in the Federal *Table of Public Statutes* under the letter "L" for the Labour Code.
4.	Cases	By the title of the case reporter (*e.g.*, Dominion Law Reports)	Indexes of cases or case digests	Look in *Case Digests (Cdn. Abridg.)* under your subject to locate digested cases on that topic.

Novice legal researchers will almost always enter the library first through the first door: the library catalogue, which provides access to most general sources.

The door to journal articles is an important one. Articles are usually ahead of books in terms of currency and new areas of the law because of the relative speed with which articles can be published compared to books. Only after gaining a general understanding of the law will a researcher use the two doors leading to the cases and legislation. Since each law library has its own particular filing scheme, it is best to always look at the floor plan of a library before beginning research.

Large Commercial Legal Information Providers

Commercial providers collect and purchase cases, statutes and other legal resources and put them in electronic form in databases, which grow every single day. In the last few years the key providers have merged so that there are only two main online service providers, in competition with each other: Westlaw Canada (WC) and Quicklaw through LexisNexis (LN/QL). Initially these providers had very different content but now, as you will see, the content of these commercial providers' databases is very similar. The key differences between the two databases lie in the value-added content that each provider supplies. This content includes privately held information like textbooks, as well as the research tools, citators, search engines and user supports that make searching easier.

LexisNexis/Quicklaw Collection

LexisNexis/Quicklaw is a comprehensive database of full-text Canadian case law, legislation, journals and commentary. Created in Canada in the 1970s, Quicklaw was purchased by LexisNexis in 2002 and is now known as LexisNexis/Quicklaw. Depending on their needs and the subscription they purchase, users can access foreign and international secondary and analytical information specifically intended for their type of firm or organization, in addition to the extensive Canadian primary law collection that LN/QL contains. Quicklaw can be accessed on the Internet at <http://www.lexisnexis.com/ca/legal/>.

In addition to providing full-text material, Quicklaw also provides a number of useful research tools including the *Canada Digest*, which provides summaries of Canadian reported and unreported cases, fully searchable and organized by subject with links to the full text, *Halsbury's Laws of Canada*, a comprehensive legal encyclopedia, and *Canadian Legal Words and Phrases*. It also contains an online case and statute citator (*Quick*CITE Canada) which enables researchers to update and note up cases and statutes. For cases, *Quick*CITE provides parallel citations, case histories, citing cases and judicial treatments. The *Canada Digest* and *QuickCITE Canada* are two highly useful sources for case law research as you will see in Chapter 9 (How to Find and Update Cases).

LexisNexis Canada has been expanding Quicklaw by gathering and compiling cases, legislation and other information for legal practitioners since 1973 and, more recently, by building a comprehensive collection of practice-specific secondary and analytical content, which provides access to commentary, legal texts, encyclopedias and current awareness sources, as well as case law and legislation. These practice areas include:

- Criminal*Practice*
- IP&IT*Practice*
- Employment *Practice*
- Labour*Practice*
- Family*Practice*
- Litigation*Practice*
- Immigration*Practice*

One additional important tool for first-time users is the Quicklaw source directory, available as part of the Quicklaw service. By scanning or searching the directory, you can find a particular source that is likely to contain the information you are looking for. Each source contains different content from one point in time to another. Supreme Court of Canada and Ontario court decisions date back to the 1800s, and full-text cases for most other jurisdictions go back more than 30 years.

Illustration 5.1
LexisNexis/Quicklaw Collection

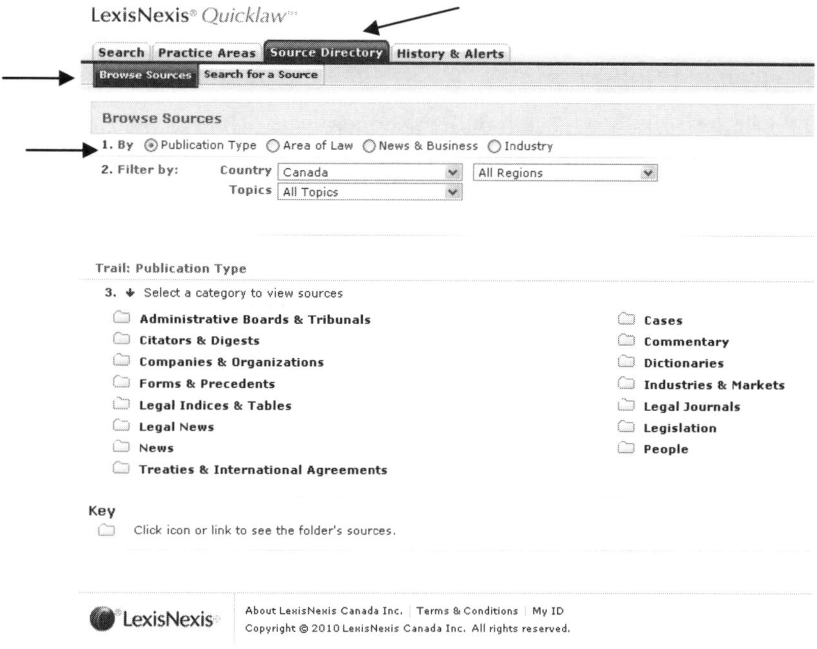

Summary of Content on Quicklaw

- **Case law:** All Canadian common law decisions reported in print since 1970 and decisions rendered prior to 1970 and cited by a court after 1970, plus full-text cases from more than 100 federal and provincial administrative tribunals.

- **Case digests:** More than 900,000 case digests available in the *Canada Digest*, organized by area of law.

- **Statutes:** Statutes, regulations and court rules updated regularly for federal, provincial and territorial jurisdictions. Enhanced collections for Canada (English and French), Alberta, British Columbia and Ontario, offering daily updates, point-in-time searching and historical archives.

- **Citators:** *Quick*CITE Case Citator with over 1 million records and over 2.8 million treatment relationships, with links to full-text cases and case law summaries, as well as the *Quick*CITE Statute Citator.

- **Secondary sources:** Current awareness services including over 100 *NetLetters* on 40 legal topics. Over 45 legal treatises, over 800 international journals and law reviews, plus legal newsletters. The *Index to Canadian Legal Literature*, with links to law journal articles, plus other legal indexes.

- **Premium collections:** Canada Quantums, Forms & Precedents, News & Companies, and international legal content.

Westlaw Canada Collection

In 2002 Carswell integrated its online service with United States-based Westlaw to produce Westlaw Canada, an online, web-based service. It is an integrated database that provides online access to most Canadian cases, statutes and rules (plus regulations in specialty areas) and provides access to all the United States and other collections on the Westlaw platform. It can be accessed at <http://www.westlawecarswell.com/home>.

Westlaw Canada contains Canadian case law, statutes and secondary materials, and includes two of the main Canadian legal research tools: the *Canadian Encyclopedic Digest* (CED) and the *Canadian Abridgment*, including the case digests and citator services, that is, the original *Canadian Abridgment*, *Case Law Digests* and *Canadian Case Citations*. You will see in Chapter 9 (How to Find and Update Cases) that these two sources are the main tools for case law research in a library. This also enables researchers to search for cases by using the *Canadian Abridgment* subject classification scheme.

Westlaw Canada is organized into eight services:

- LawSource
- CriminalSource
- Estates&TrustsSource
- FamilySource
- InsolvencySource
- IPSource
- SecuritiesSource
- Litigator

As you can see, seven of these services are designed specifically for practitioners in the areas of criminal law, estates law, family law, insolvency law, intellectual property law and securities law. They include all of the information a busy practitioner might need, including books, loose-leaf services, cases and legislation on a particular subject, all hypertext linked. These services also provide weekly newsletters, published only electronically.

LawSource is an extremely comprehensive collection of Canadian statutes and case law. It includes a case citator (KeyCite*Canada*) to help researchers update and note up cases, statutes and rules. It contains judicial treatments, parallel citations and case histories. The LawSource service also includes the

Canadian Encyclopedic Digest (CED), journals, law reviews and the *Index to Canadian Legal Literature* (ICLL).

Litigator provides users with online access to a large collection of litigation resources, including: precedent galleries, quantums, expert directory, lawyer directory, profile awards by judge or counsel, practice guides, commentary and current awareness.

Illustration 5.2
Westlaw Canada Collection

Reprinted by permission of Carswell, a division of Thomson Reuters Canada Limited.

Summary of Content on Westlaw Canada

- **Case law:** Over 550,000 full-text Canadian cases with headnotes. The collection, which may be searched globally, or as broken down by jurisdiction, topic or Carswell law report series, provides decisions from all Canadian courts comprehensively since 1986, with coverage of reported cases generally back to 1977 or earlier for key courts or report series.

- **Litigator:** includes several thousand court filings (pleadings, motions and facta) from important cases in selected areas of law.

- **Case digests:** Over 750,000 case law digests in the *Canadian Abridgment Case Law Digests* collection, covering Canadian reported cases since 1803, and unreported cases since 1986, with links to the full text of all decisions on Westlaw Canada.

- **Statutes:** All federal and common law provincial statutes, plus key Quebec legislation; comprehensive rules of practice; comprehensive regulations for specialties; selected regulations for LawSource.

- **Citators:** KeyCite*Canada* based on the print version of the *Canadian Abridgment*, *Canadian Case Citations*, *Canadian Statute Citations*, and *Rules Judicially Considered*, linked to cases and legislation.

- **Secondary sources:** The *Canadian Encyclopedic Digest* (CED), *Index to Canadian Legal Literature* (ICLL), law reviews and journals for LawSource; treatises, newsletters and other secondary material for specialty areas; rules annotations and practice guides for Litigator.

Other Commercial Providers

Although Westlaw Canada and LexisNexis/Quicklaw are generally considered to be the main commercial online providers of Canadian legal resources, there are others that have specialized scope and content.

Maritime Law Book Online

For many years, Maritime Law Book (MLB) has published printed collections of cases (or case reporters) such as Nova Scotia Reports and Alberta Reports, along with their National Reporter (covering Supreme Court of Canada and Federal Court of Appeal cases) and Federal Trial Reports. MLB now provides "mirror images" of their printed reporters in online databases available at <http://www.mlb.nb.ca>. These files of cases are searchable by keyword, judge's name, names of parties, year, *etc.*, but the most helpful feature is the MLB "Key Number System" that assigns a specific, unique classification number to all cases pertaining to the same legal issue, regardless of jurisdiction. Through a "key number" search, you can avoid excessive lists of cases that often result from broad keyword searches and quickly retrieve very similar cases exactly on point.

MLB also provides free access to all its cases in a database called Raw Law <http://www.rawlaw.ca>. These cases do not include headnotes and cannot be searched by MLB key numbers.

CCH Online

CCH publishes specialized books, textbooks and loose-leaf practice manuals. Most of the content of these printed resources is now available online by subscription at <http://www.cch.ca/>.

The CCH Canadian search portal has four categories: tax accounting, legal, business and financial. Your access to these resources will depend on the print subscriptions that your library has purchased. Of most interest to lawyers is the legal online product group which contains a growing number of subject-based sets of materials, including alternative dispute resolution, environment, family, health, real estate, insurance, technology and securities. A new tracking service, *Legislative Pulse*, continuously monitors the progress of all federal and provincial bills and is keyword searchable; users can also set up a profile to track only selected bills of interest. The full text of bills at various stages is also provided.

Canadian Human Rights Reporter Online

All decisions published in the printed reporter *Canadian Human Rights Reporter* (C.H.R.R.) from 1980 to the present are available by subscription through <http://www.cdn-hr-reporter.ca>. These full-text decisions originate from Canadian courts, and federal and provincial human rights tribunals and boards of inquiry. Associated with the decisions are summaries and keywords, prepared by human rights specialists, that facilitate speedy research. Researchers can search the full text by year, jurisdiction, adjudicator, legislation cited or keyword. This service includes a citator to note up decisions, as well as lists of pending and in-process cases that help researchers stay current.

Canada Law Book and BestCase

Canada Law Book, a publisher of law texts, loose-leaf services and reports since 1855 (<http://www.canadalawbook.ca>), now provides subscription-based online comprehensive "libraries" in such specialty areas as criminal, patents, labour and employment law.

Two online services provided by CLB are *Criminal Spectrum* and *Labour Spectrum*, which integrate and make searchable all available CLB loose-leafs, journals, case reporters and commentary, including such leading texts as *Martin's Annual Criminal Code* in *Criminal Spectrum* and *Labour Arbitration by Brown and Beatty* in *Labour Spectrum*.

CLB's new flagship service is *BestCase*, a searchable database of case law from all CLB's print reporters from their inception to the present, including the *Dominion Law Reports*, the *Canadian Criminal Cases* and other regional and topical reports, as well as case digests from the *All-Canada Weekly Summaries* and the *Weekly Criminal Bulletin*. These cases are available in both html and PDF format. The PDF version is an image of the printed reporter and includes headnotes and its original pagination. The database also provides unreported decisions from 1977 onwards. Reported cases are edited for accuracy. Until recently, this information was available via LN/QL, but now the only access to electronic versions of CLB resources is through *BestCase*.

SOQUIJ Online

The Société québécoise d'information juridique, headquartered in Montreal, publishes databases containing over 900,000 documents, including summaries and the full text of decisions, plus other legal publications. It offers the most comprehensive body of Quebec case law available online. Its search engine, AZIMUT, allows searching of summaries and full-text decisions in one unified file or via 13 separate subject databases. SOQUIJ also offers an annotated *Civil Code of Québec*, searchable Quebec court records and seven current online newsletters, the most well-known of which is the weekly *Jurisprudence Express*.

World Law Reform Collection

The World Law Reform Collection published by Manas Media (<http://www.manasmedia.com>) provides a searchable online index to over 7,500 law reform commission reports and other publications from common law countries, including those published by Canadian commissions. These secondary sources are very helpful for determining the state of the law at a point in time, or how experts felt it should have been changed. Such reports may be "prescriptive" in recommending needed reforms. For most reports published after 1999, a link to the full text is also provided.

Public (No-Fee) Providers of Legal Information

The main providers of free legal material on the Internet are governments and law libraries who continually place materials on their websites. However, over the last few years CanLII has established itself as a substantive key website for free access to Canadian law. Here are some tips on using free sources and a description of the more popular non-fee websites.

Tips When Using Free Sources

As electronic access has evolved, more and more information has become available to the public through various providers and various websites. Therefore it is important to be able to determine the relevance and authenticity of the site and the information you are retrieving from the site. As a general rule, you should always evaluate your Internet source by looking at the following:

- the organization or individual who maintains the site;
- the author of the specific information;
- the scope, accuracy and links; and
- the date of the information.

Government Websites

The federal government and each of the provinces and territories maintain websites with information on both legislation and case law. Statutes and regulations are usually maintained by the provincial Queen's Printers in each province and territory, and bills are maintained by the legislature. Cases, on the other hand, may be made available by the particular federal court or the various provincial courts. Courts vary greatly in the scope and depth of cases they make publicly available.

A list of the government websites that contain legislation is appended to Chapter 7 (How to Find and Update Statutes) and a list of the court websites that contain cases is appended to Chapter 9 (How to Find and Update Cases).

Here are some selected Canadian government websites that are very good for general legal research, including legislation, government reports, and identifying various agencies and departments:

Seneca Guide to Canadian Federal Bills, Statutes and Regulations
<http://dsp-psd.communication.gc.ca/Reference/seneca-e.html>

Guides to Government Information
<http://dsp-psd.pwgsc.gc.ca/Reference/guides-e.html>

Canada: Departments and Agencies
<http://canada.gc.ca/depts/major/depind-eng.html>

Canadian Depository Services Program E-Collection
<http://dsp-psd.pwgsc.gc.ca/Epubs/epubs-e.html>

Law Library Websites

Another source of law is law library websites. This includes every university
law school and most provincial courthouse libraries. Many of these law library
websites are open to the public and their catalogues are searchable through the
Internet. As well, more and more information is being placed online to help
researchers locate law and other law-related resources. Many public sites have
simple instructions about how to find information on their sites. Here are some
of the better law library websites:

Bora Laskin Law Library Legal Resources (University of Toronto)
<http://www.law-lib.utoronto.ca/index.htm>

Cornell Legal Information Institute
<http://www.law.cornell.edu>

York University Law Library
<http://library.osgoode.yorku.ca/>

Gerard V. La Forest Law Library (University of New Brunswick)
<http://lawlibrary.unbf.ca/>

University of British Columbia Law Library
<http://www.library.ubc.ca/law/>

CanLII

CanLII is a bilingual, web-based, public legal information resource, accessible
at <http://www.canlii.org>, that provides very convenient free access to a
growing body of Canadian law. CanLII's aim is to support the legal profession
in the performance of its duties and to provide the public with permanent open
access to the legal heritage of Canada.

Originally designed as a prototype project by University of Montreal Law
Professor Daniel Poulin, the public version of CanLII was created in 2001.

CanLII is a non-profit independent corporation managed and funded by the Federation of Law Societies of Canada.

Presently, CanLII provides searchable full-text access to virtually all current consolidated Canadian legislation (federal, provincial and territorial statutes and regulations) and to a very significant and growing number of recent cases from all levels of federal, provincial and territorial courts. The service also contains a number of Canadian board and tribunal decisions, and it provides links to the business of Parliament and the provincial and territorial legislative assemblies, such as progress of bills, debates and other activities, where available.

CanLII is not a "value-added site" in the sense that it only provides links to the law from the originating sources, without editorial additions and enhancements such as headnotes, summaries, key numbers or indexes. However, there are key terms, automatically generated, that are associated with every decision retrieved. CanLII provides helpful hypertext linking between case law and legislation and the capability to note up case law with links to other cases available in CanLII only.

As noted above, the quality and timeliness of the information to which CanLII links depends completely on the originating source of that data, such as the relevant government legislative assembly, Queen's Printer or court. CanLII's depth and coverage of case law and decisions of tribunals continues to grow but is understandably somewhat behind that of Canadian for-fee legal resources, due to CanLII's youth relative to longer-established systems. At present, CanLII does not contain secondary sources of commentary on the law such as full-text journals, newsletters or texts.

CanLII is one of a number of web-based free "legal information institutes" from around the world. (See Appendix 5B for a complete list.)

Social Science Research Network

Another source of useful legal information is the Legal Scholarship Network which is part of the Social Sciences Research Network <http://www.ssrn.org>. This site provides an excellent searchable database of very current legal research from legal academics and researchers. The vast majority of these papers can be downloaded at no charge.

Other Sources of Free Legal Information

There are a number of other sources of free legal information on the Internet. Law firms often publish substantive newsletters on a variety of legal topics. Many law schools, law libraries and practising lawyers publish law blogs which comment on current issues, and which, although they often will reveal a particular bias or viewpoint, may also include valuable information on the latest legal developments. Listservs or electronic discussion lists distribute e-mail messages to subscribers who want to communicate with others who share a particular interest or specialty. The Canadian Bar Association, for example, provides a number of listservs on various topics to their members.

SELF TEST

The following is a self test based on the information provided in this chapter. The answers to these questions are found at the end of the book in the "Answers to Self Tests" section.

1. Describe the six steps of efficient legal research.
2. What are some of the questions you might ask when formulating an online search?
3. Describe the "four doors" to the law library.
4. Name two or more online providers of Canadian legal information.
5. Name three other sources of free legal information.

Appendix 5A: Helpful Sources for Foreign Law

Although this book does not address foreign law, it is sometimes helpful for researchers to have online links to basic foreign resources, in the event that Canadian law does not address a legal subject adequately. This is especially true in certain emerging areas of the law that foreign jurisdictions may already have begun to examine.

Here are some respected free websites that will give you starting points. These will lead you to other useful sites — mostly official but some from commercial providers — in the countries and regions listed.

Website Name and Jurisdiction	URL
AsianLII – Asia excluding Australia and New Zealand	<http://www.asianlii.org/>
AustLII – Australia and New Zealand	<http://www.austlii.edu.au/>
BaiLII – Great Britain and Ireland	<http://www.bailii.org/>
CommonLII – a combination of a number of Commonwealth countries including African nations	<http://www.commonlii.org/>
CyLaw – Cyprus	<http://www.cylaw.org/index-en.html>
Droit francophone – a combination of French-speaking countries	<http://droit.francophonie.org/>
HKLII – Hong Kong	<http://www.hklii.org/>
ITTIG – Italy	<http://www.ittig.cnr.it/IndexEng.htm>
JuriBurkina – Burkina Faso	<http://www.juriburkina.org/juriburkina/>
LII – United States	<http://www.law.cornell.edu/>

Website Name and Jurisdiction	URL
NZLII – New Zealand	<http://www.nzlii.org/>
PacLII – Pacific Islands	<http://www.paclii.org/>
SafLII – Southern Africa	<http://www.saflii.org/>
WorldLII – leads to many sites worldwide that do not fit into the above categories. Links to the laws of many individual countries not covered above are also provided.	<http://www.worldlii.org/>

Appendix 5B: Checklist: How to Find Legal Information

Before searching for legal information, you need to ask yourself the following six questions:

1. What information are you looking for?

- Are you looking for cases, legislation or secondary materials?
- Is the information needed from a specific jurisdiction (*e.g.*, Canada, a province, the United States)?
- If you are looking for a case, is the case from a specific court (*e.g.*, Supreme Court of Canada or British Columbia Court of Appeal)?
- Is the information from a specific period of time?

2. Where is that information likely located?

Once you know what you are looking for, you must decide where you are likely going to find the information, for example:

- In the library?
- Through commercial providers?
- On public websites (no-fee)?

3. Which resources are available for your use? At what cost?

- Which sources do you have access to (*e.g.*, commercial online providers, a library or Internet access to public websites)?
- Do you have to pay for the information or is it available for free?
- If there is a fee, what is it?
- How can you keep your costs low?
- What format will the information be in (*e.g.*, a PDF file that is identical to the original, html only or in a Word document)?

4. What resource likely contains your content?

Each provider is unique, and has a unique collection of law and legal resources. Therefore, when looking at the content of any provider you will want to look at each of the following:

- Does it have statutes, cases, secondary sources, journals, *etc.*?
- Does it have abstracts, summaries, headnotes?
- How far back does the information go?
- How current is the information?
- Will the courts accept the information?

5. How easy is it to use the service?

As you become familiar with each of the electronic resources, you will find that some are easier to use than others, depending on what you need. And as you can imagine, each service provider works very hard at designing websites, search engines, templates, tools and hyperlinks to make your searches faster and better.

Some questions you might ask are:

- Can you do global searches or just search in individual databases?
- Can you use natural language or do you need to know Boolean logic?
- Are there hyperlinks between databases (*e.g.*, digests and full cases)?
- Are there citators (statute and case) that link legislation and cases?
- Will search engines search the full text of cases and statutes or just the headnotes?
- Are there tools you can use to keep track of what you do?
- Is the search mechanism robust?
- Can you build your own specialized search?

6. How will you formulate your search?

When selecting a database:

- Which database likely has the information you are looking for?
- Does the database provide full text, digests or indexes?
- Does the database include headnotes, summaries or annotations?
- Does the database have hyperlinks or special searching tools?

When constructing your word search:

- What words or phrases do you want the search engine to locate?
- How should the words be grouped?
- Do you want to limit the search by dates?
- Do you want to limit the search by other factors such as judge's name, jurisdiction, or level of court?

How to Find Secondary Materials 6

Secondary materials are books and other sources that assist legal researchers in doing two things: understanding the law and locating the law. They are essential to most research problems and are usually the first sources referred to upon entering a law library. Wise researchers "let the experts begin the work" by finding sound scholarly and practice-oriented materials that explain legal concepts and lead to cases and legislation.

This chapter describes how to locate and use the most popular secondary sources.

LEARNING OBJECTIVES

At the end of this chapter you will be able to:

- Locate and use textbooks and legal dictionaries
- Use periodical indexes to locate journal articles
- Find and use the two Canadian legal encyclopedias: *Halsbury's Laws of Canada* and the *Canadian Encyclopedic Digest*
- Locate case digests and case indices
- Explain what a citator is
- Cite secondary sources

WHY USE SECONDARY MATERIALS?

Almost all research involves looking at secondary materials. These author-written commentaries are invaluable not only to explain the law, but also to locate the law. Even lawyers who know the name of a particular statute or case will refer to secondary sources since they put the law into context and explain how the cases and statutes work together to form the law. Because they are created by editors and experts who know the law well, it is usually a good idea to read what they say and refer to the cases that they mention.

The following are the main sources used to **explain** the law:

- Textbooks, treatises, casebooks and loose-leaf services
- Journals and periodicals
- Encyclopedias (such as the *Canadian Encyclopedic Digest* and *Halsbury's Laws of Canada*)
- News sources

- Legal dictionaries
- Books of words and phrases
- Abbreviations lists
- Government documents
- Legal directories
- Legal education materials and seminar papers
- Forms and precedents
- Legal Wikis
- Law blogs
- Legal research network papers
- Law firm newsletters

The following are the main sources used to **locate** the law:

- Case Digests
- Case and Statute Citators

Each of these will be covered in the chapter.

TEXTBOOKS, TREATISES, CASEBOOKS AND LOOSE-LEAF SERVICES

Textbooks are books designed to teach a single subject and usually summarize the law on a specific legal topic. Treatises include textbooks and usually cover broader subject areas than textbooks. Textbooks and treatises are extremely useful to those new to a particular area of law. They provide summaries of the law and often include helpful tables of contents, tables of cases and subject indexes.

Every law library has a collection of law textbooks in print or in electronic format that can be located and retrieved by using a computer catalogue. Researchers can search the catalogue by subject, keywords, title, author or call number.

Although textbooks and treatises are not primary sources of law, they have come to be regarded as having a considerable degree of "persuasive" authority because they are often written by academics and scholars. They are sometimes cited as "secondary authority" in Canadian judicial decisions.

Casebooks, unlike textbooks, do not summarize the law. They are collections of excerpts of cases and brief discussions about these cases. They are almost exclusively used in first-year law classes and are designed to help students learn by the case method. These books are used almost exclusively for educational purposes and are rarely referred to after the first year of law school, nor are they cited in decisions.

Loose-leaf services, usually purchased by ongoing subscription, consist of one or more volumes (usually in a binder) of very current material about a fairly narrow area of the law, such as family law or environmental law. Replacement or update pages are sent out periodically for insertion into the binder so that the contents will be up-to-date with changes to the law.

Loose-leaf services usually contain commentary by experts, including citations to leading cases and relevant statutes pertaining to the topic at hand. Some may provide the full text of relevant statutes and regulations, along with legislative histories of Acts. Some also include practitioner aids such as research checklists, sample forms, tables of costs and damages, *etc.* Check the holdings of your local academic or law society library to determine what loose-leaf services are available, or check the websites of prominent Canadian publishers such as Thomson Carswell, LexisNexis Canada/Butterworths, Canada Law Book, CCH Canadian, *etc.*

A growing number of electronic versions of texts, treatises and loose-leaf services are being included in the subject-specific services provided by the commercial database providers. Westlaw Canada's *Family*Source, for example, includes the full text of a number of key loose-leaf family law services including the second edition of MacDonald and Ferrier's *Canadian Divorce Law and Practice.* LexisNexis/Quicklaw's Criminal*Practice* includes such texts as the seventh edition of Ruby *et al*'s *Sentencing* and the third edition of Sopinka, Lederman & Bryant, *The Law of Evidence in Canada.* These versions are all browsable and full-text searchable.

JOURNALS AND PERIODICALS

Legal journals and periodicals are particularly helpful when researching new or changing areas of the law. If you happen to locate a very recent article on your topic you will save hours of research.

Journals are periodic publications consisting of collections of articles. They can also include other useful information such as advertisements, job postings, legal literature, book reviews and current news. They tend to include very current information because the time required to produce an article about a new topic is considerably less than that required to produce a book. Many lawyers subscribe to periodicals relevant to their area of practice in order to stay up-to-date on the law.

The following are a few types of legal journals:

* General interest (*e.g., Canadian Lawyer Magazine*)
* Special interest (*e.g., Canadian Journal of Family Law*)
* Bar association (*e.g., Canadian Bar Review*)
* Scholarly (*e.g., Journal of Law & Equality*)

Some common features of print journals include helpful research tools such as detailed tables of contents, subject indexes, author and title indexes, tables of cases commented on and book review indexes. The contents of journals are rendered accessible through these research tools as well as through periodical indexes. Recently, journal research has been made much more straightforward with the advent of full text journal databases and electronic journal indexes.

Over the last few years a huge number of published law journals have been made available in electronic form through a number of commercial providers. In addition, libraries will often subscribe to collections of other social science electronic journals in law-related areas.

Law Journal Library (HeinOnline)

The most well-known legal journal collection is HeinOnline's *Law Journal Library* (<http://www.heinonline.org>), which provides access to close to 1,400 legal periodicals in pdf format. Most university law libraries and many law firms subscribe to the *Law Journal Library*. One valuable feature of HeinOnline is that, for virtually all the journals included, coverage goes back to the first volume ever published. HeinOnline also contains volumes of old and rare journals, mostly U.S. and Canadian, that have ceased publication. Both of these features are useful for historical research. HeinOnline provides its own search engine for the *Law Journal Library* which enables the researcher to search the full text of each article. Another useful feature of HeinOnline is its **ScholarCheck**, which lists and links to articles that have cited a particular article, thus making it possible to easily locate additional articles on the subject in question.

Journals on Westlaw and LexisNexis

A growing number of journals are now available through commercial online providers. For example, LexisNexis/Quicklaw (LN/QL) provides searchable full-text access to about 30 Canadian academic journals and to a huge number of non-Canadian journals. Some Canadian firms and government agencies purchase this part of LN/QL as an "add-on" to their basic Canadian service. LN/QL also contains many "netletters", which are digital newsletters of great help to practitioners and researchers who are seeking the very newest information on emerging topics. Likewise, Westlaw Canada (WC) contains many searchable full-text Canadian journals, including those published by Thomson Carswell, as well as articles and case comments printed within Carswell's many topical reporters, such as *Reports of Family Law*. There is an "add-on" service to WC, offering many non-Canadian journals, that some researchers choose to purchase in addition to the basic Canadian coverage.

Tips for Searching Online Journals

When searching for articles in electronic journals, it is best to narrow your search as much as possible before beginning. You can do this in three ways:

(1) Select a specific database that only contains certain journals (*e.g.*, only Canadian journals).
(2) Select a specific field search so that your search will be limited to such fields as author or subject (*e.g.*, environmental law journals).
(3) Construct a keyword search in a general journals database that uses connectors such as and/or, not or adjacent words.

Sometimes this last way is best, because you might miss a useful, subject-specific article that happens to have been selected for publication in a general-interest journal.

Periodical Indexes

Periodical indexes are research aids designed to assist researchers in locating periodicals. In times past, the printed versions of these indexes were critical to locating print journal articles. Almost all of the printed indexes have now been replaced by online versions that make searching by keywords or legal topics much easier. It is very important to check indexes as well as full-text journal databases in order to ensure you have done a thorough search, since only 50 per cent of law journals are available in full-text electronic format. Indexes enable the researcher to locate even those articles that are not available electronically.

The few remaining indexes that are only available in print are usually published a few times throughout the year (*e.g.*, quarterly), and a cumulative volume is usually published annually. Print versions of periodical indexes list periodicals by subject, author and title so that researchers can approach the periodical indexes in any of the following ways:

(1) **By title of journal**. If you know the title of a journal that is likely to be helpful to your area of research, such as the *Canadian Journal of Family Law*, but do not know the title or author of any articles, it is often easier to go directly to that periodical on a library shelf and leaf through its index rather than using the periodical indexes.

(2) **By author or title**. If you do not know the title of the journal but know the author or the title of the article, look in the author or title index in a printed index or do an electronic word search of either a periodical index or a full-text journal database.

(3) **By subject**. If you know only the subject, it is best to start by looking in the subject indexes in one of the many periodical indexes, either in print or online. The subject categories are different for each journal.

The print versions of indexes are particularly helpful when trying to find out how a legal subject is categorized or to narrow down a subject area. This is because you can scan back and forth quickly, searching for keywords that can ultimately be used for your electronic search. Each legal publisher describes subjects differently and there are usually a number of topics that are relevant to any research problem.

Printed periodical indexes are hardbound and thus are updated by supplements, so you must look in both. Occasionally, the supplements are consolidated into cumulative volumes, so it is always important to read the spine of the volume to determine whether the index is a consolidation or a supplement. It is usually necessary to search through several hardbound volumes and several softcover supplements to do a thorough search. Often the indexes provide instructions at the front of the volumes to assist researchers in using them. Most indexes include a list of all of the periodicals referred to in that index.

Many periodical indexes are published by geographical region. For example, the *Index to Canadian Legal Periodical Literature* includes only Canadian periodicals.

There are a few main legal periodical indexes with Canadian coverage. They are as follows:

Index to Canadian Legal Literature (**ICLL**): Since its inception in 1981, it has indexed Canadian journal articles, books, book reviews and other legal literature such as continuing legal education (CLE) papers and speeches. It attempts to include all Canadian journal articles and as many of the other types of materials as possible. Hence, it is the closest thing to a complete bibliography of Canadian legal writing. It is available in print by subscription from Thomson Carswell and online through WC and LN/QL. The Westlaw Canada version has a more detailed search template than the LN/QL version.

Illustration 6.1
Excerpt from the *Index to Canadian Legal Literature*

INDEX ANALYTIQUE

MARINE RESOURCES CONSERVATION

– Australia
Oceans law and policy in the post-UNCED era: Australian and Canadian perspectives. ed. by Lorne K. Kriwoken ... [et al.]. (International environmental law and policy series). London; Boston; Cambridge, MA. USA: Kluwer Law International. 1996. xvii. 453 p.: maps.
– International cooperation
Towards regional ocean management in the Arctic: from co-existence to cooperation. by David Vanderzwaag, John Donihee and Mads Faegteborg. (1988) 37 U.N.B. L.J. 1-33.
– Law and legislation
Bill C-98: Oceans Act. by Daniel Dupras. (Legislative summary ; LS-225E). Ottawa: Library of Parliament, Research Branch, 1995. 19 p. Issued also in French.
Canadian ocean law and policy. by David L. VanderZwaag. Markham, Ont.: Butterworths. 1991.
Canadian ocean law and policy. ed. by David L. Vanderzwaag. Toronto: Butterworths. 1992. xxxiv. 546 p.
Implementation of the new law of the sea in West Africa: prospects for the development and management of marine resources. by Peter C. Underwood and Phillip M. Saunders. Halifax: Dalhousie Ocean Studies Programme, 1985.
Implementing international environmental agreements: advocating a functional analysis of hard law and soft law documents. by Sari Graben. (Spring 2000) 15 Inter. Insights 29-52.
Marine structures *see*
Offshore structures

MARINE TERMINALS
Liability equals responsibility: Canadian marine transport terminal operators in the 1990s. by Roger Harris. (Jan. 1993) 21 Can. Bus. L.J. 229-253.
– Safety measures
Performance audits: British Columbia Ferry Corporation. (Report ; 1995/96 : 2). Victoria: Office of the Auditor General, 1996. 107 p.: ill. Also issued in electronic format on the Internet at http://www.aud.gov.bc.ca.
Marine transportation *see*
Shipping
Mariners *see*
Sailors
Marines de guerre
= Navies
Marins
= Sailors
Marins (Marine merchande)
= Merchant seamen
MARIS
= Husbands
Les Groupes thérapeutiques à l'intention des maris violents: étude d'un programme mis au point à Vancouver. par Andy Wachtel et Bruce Levens. [Rapport pour spécialistes / Direction des programmes ; no 1984-75). Ottawa: Solliciteur général Canada, Secrétariat, 1984. 243 p.
Maris violents *voir*
Hommes violents
MARITAIN, JACQUES, 1882-1973
Le Droit naturel et le droit des gens d'après J. Maritain. par Léon Charette. (1988) 19 R.G.D. 947-960.
Marital condition *see*
Marital status
Marital contracts *see*
Antenuptial contracts

Marital infidelity *see*
Adultery
MARITAL PROPERTY
= Biens communs
"Running hard to stand still": the paradox of family law reform. par Mary Jane Mossman. (Spring 1994) 17 Dalhousie L.J. 5-34.
A Critique of the Manitoba matrimonial property regime. by Jim Stoffman and Sharon Kravetsky. (1988) 3 C.F.L.Q. 269-286.
A Matter of difference: domestic contracts and gender equality. by Brenda Cossman. (Summer 1990) 28 Osgoode Hall L.J. 303-380.
A Note on British Columbia's Personal Property Security Act and the Family Relations Act. by Greg Lanning. (Spring 1990) 8 Can. J. Fam. L. 395-399.
Aboriginal women and matrimonial property: feminist responses. by Mary Ellen Turpel. (Feminism and law workshop series ; WS 94-95 (11)). Toronto: Faculty of Law, University of Toronto. 1994. 40 p. Not for commercial sale.
Advising the family business: impact of the Family Law Act. by Robert Halpern. (April 1995) 10 Money & Fam. L. 25-32.
Advising the family business: impact of the Family Law Act. by Robert Halpern. (May 1995) 10 Money & Fam. L. 39-44.
Alberta introduces changes to pension legislation. by J.M. Norton. (June 1999) 14 Money & Fam. L. 46.
All things come to he (she) who waits: Da Costa v. Da Costa in the Court of Appeal. by Stephen M. Grant. (June 1992) 7 Money & Fam. L. 41-43.
An Overview of pension sharing under the Family Law Act. by Julie A. Colden. Ottawa: [s.n.]. 1993. 26. xxxviii p.
Are gifts and constructive trusts inconsistent? (Mar. 1991) 6 Money & Fam. L. 18-22.
Are gifts and constructive trusts inconsistent? by Lorne H. Wolfson. (1992) 9 C.F.L.Q. 119-131.
Asset hide & seek. by James D. McAuley and Valerie Steele. (June 1993) 8 Money & Fam. L. 45-47.
Bankruptcy and family law problems and solutions. by Robert A. Klotz. (1993) Spec. Lect. L.S.U.C. 253-280.
Bankruptcy and family law. by Anne-France Goldwater. (Jan. 1998) 15 C.F.L.Q. 139-186.
Bankruptcy and family law. by Anne-France Goldwater. dans: Développements récents en droit familial (1997) (Cowansville, Qué.: Éditions Y. Blais. 1997). p. 1-52.
Bankruptcy issues in family law. by Robert A. Klotz. (July 1992) 14 Advocates' Q. 18-69.
Belman v. Belman: a corporate divorce. by A. Scott Davidson. (July 1996) 11 Money & Fam. L. 49-50.
Business agreements and the Family Law Act. by Wolfe D. Goodman. (1986/87) 8 Est. & Tr. Q. 193-203.
Business assets and family law: valuation and income determination workshops. Toronto: Osgoode Hall Law School of York University, Professional Development Programme. Continuing Legal Education. 1998. 1 v. "January 8, 1998".
Business interests and family law. by Stephen M. Grant. (June 1999) 17 C.F.L.Q. 67-85.
CPP [Canada Pension Plan] credit system can work against divorced couples. by Bruce Cohen. (June 1999) 14 Money & Fam. L. 43-44.
Can a trustee in bankruptcy elect under the FLA [Ontario Family Law Act]? (Nov. 1991) 6 Money & Fam. L. 86-88.
Canada Pension Plan credit splitting. (Dec. 1991) 6 Money & Fam. L. 91-93.

The above example is an excerpt from the *Index to Canadian Legal Literature*. As you can see, the section that relates to the Paul and Melody situation is the heading "Marital Property".

LegalTrac: The most comprehensive, widely purchased online index to legal journals indexes approximately 1,500 journals from most of the common law countries, including French-language journals from Canada. Indexing begins in the mid-1980s for most of the included titles. For over 200 of its journals, there is a direct link to the full text of some or all articles. University libraries very often purchase a subscription to LegalTrac, making access to it available through their online catalogues. The print equivalent, **Current Law Index**, is almost never consulted due to its huge size and difficulty of use. Both the online and print versions are available from Gale Cengage (<http://www.gale.cengage.com/pdf/facts/legal.pdf>).

Index to Legal Periodicals and Books **(ILPB)** **in print or Index to Legal Periodicals online:** Indexes about 1,100 journals from the U.S., Canada, the U.K., Ireland, Australia and New Zealand. Indexing begins in approximately 1982 for most of the included titles, but a separately priced database (*Index to Legal Periodicals Retrospective: 1908-1981*) offers online indexing back to the inception of most of the journals. For approximately 270 of the current journals, a link to full-text articles is provided. In addition, ILPB indexes approximately 1,400 legal books per year and displays the contents online. A printed version of ILPB, beginning in 1926, is also available, and both online and print versions may be purchased from H.W. Wilson Co. (<http://www.hwwilson.com/default.cfm>).

***Index to Canadian Legal Periodical Literature*:** This index was published from 1961 through 2002 in print format only. It is available in most Canadian academic and larger bar society law libraries. For the period 1961 to 1981, it was the only tool that covered Canadian journals exclusively, and it is still critical to research for that period of time. With the advent of online indexes in the 1980s, most with Canadian content, it became less useful, although it remained the only source for the majority of Canadian legal newsletter indexing until its cessation in 2002.

This index, now identified as the Scott *Index to Canadian Legal Periodical Literature*, <http://biblio.caij.qc.ca/web2/tramp2.exe/log_in?setting_key=BIBLIO> has recently been made available online from the Centre d'accès à l'information juridique. Covering from 1998 to present and updated weekly, this free resource indexes Canadian legal and related journals, case comments and law conferences. In some cases there are links to full-text journal articles. At the moment the search interface is in French only but there are plans to build an English language interface. To use this index, select the *Articles de périodiques et commentaires d'arrêts (Index Scott)* radio button and begin your search.

Illustration 6.2
Scott Index to Canadian Legal Periodical Literature

Abstract of the website of the Centre d'accès à l'information juridique at <www.caij.qc.ca>. ©2010 Centre d'accès à l'information juridique — All rights reserved.

Additional journal indexes that may be useful to researchers are:

> **Legal Journals Index:** An index of 400 journals from the U.K. and Europe from 1986 to present. Available in print and online through CLI (Current Legal Information) from Sweet and Maxwell <http://cli.sweetand maxwell.co.uk/> or via Westlaw Canada (database code LJI).

> **Index to Foreign Legal Periodicals:** An index of more than 450 legal journals focusing on international law (public and private), comparative law, and the law of non-common law countries. Coverage of American, British or British Commonwealth laws is not included in this database.

ENCYCLOPEDIAS

There are two Canadian legal encyclopedias, the *Canadian Encyclopedic Digest* and *Halsbury's Laws of Canada*.

Legal encyclopedias are similar to other encyclopedias in that they summarize large amounts of information. They are heavily footnoted with references to both statutes and cases. They are a good place to start research if you know very little about the legal topic you are researching.

These summaries are not the law. They are only an editor's opinion about what the law is, what the cases stand for, or what the statutes mean. All cases and statutes referred to should be checked to ensure that the editors of the encyclopedia have interpreted their meaning correctly.

Encyclopedias consist of volumes covering legal subjects organized alphabetically by topic. Because the law is categorized into specific legal topics, researchers must have some understanding of the way in which the subjects are categorized before beginning research. This is usually accomplished by reviewing the indexes and tables of contents in the encyclopedias.

Canadian Encyclopedic Digest

The *Canadian Encyclopedic Digest* (CED) is published by Carswell, in two editions, a Western version (CED, Western 4th ed.), which contains the law of the Western provinces, and an Ontario version (CED, Ontario 4th ed.), which contains the law of Ontario. Researchers use one or the other, depending on where they practise in Canada.

They are available in print in almost all law libraries as well as online through Westlaw Canada. A word of caution is in order: despite the fact that the CED has recently issued a fourth edition, not all the subject titles have been updated. Thus, the timeliness of cited cases and the coverage of emerging directions within certain legal topics of law are beginning to be somewhat questionable. With the publication of the fourth edition, the publisher has, however, committed to updating the key titles annually and every title every three years. (See Appendix 6A for instructions on using the CED.)

Halsbury's Laws of Canada

The other comprehensive Canadian legal encyclopedia is *Halsbury's Laws of Canada*. It is based on the widely used legal encyclopedia, *Halsbury's Laws of England*, and was introduced in 2006 by LexisNexis Canada. The set contains a series of alphabetically arranged subject titles. Some subject titles are still in production and, upon completion, the encyclopedia will provide current commentary on the full range of Canadian law. (See Appendix 6A for instructions on using *Halsbury's*.)

ADDITIONAL USEFUL SECONDARY RESOURCES

A description of secondary legal materials would not be complete without mentioning the following sources.

News Sources

Often lawyers research news and other media. Criminal and civil issues are covered extensively by news media long before such matters enter the courts, if indeed they ever do. Also, since jury trials do not result in written decisions (because a jury is not required to give reasons for finding guilt or innocence), researchers and lawyers often turn to news sources to provide information before, during and after trials.

Many newspapers provide current and some archival news files. Current issues are often free but the use of the archival files generally requires that the researcher subscribe to the print version of the paper or purchase access on a "pay-per-view" basis. As an alternative to such newspaper websites, researchers may subscribe to collections of Canadian and world news sold by commercial online providers. *OnlineNewspapers.com* <http://www.onlinenewspapers.com/> is a huge directory of links to newspapers that are available on the Internet from countries throughout the world.

Libraries often subscribe to online news databases which provide comprehensive access to a wide range of newspapers and news magazines.

One news service is **FPInfomart**, available through the CanWest Global group of companies (<http://www.fpinfomart.ca>), which provides same-day and archival access to over 4,600 full-text newspapers, magazines, newswires, broadcast transcripts and web newsblogs. Both subscription and pay-per-view options are sold.

Another news source is **LexisNexis Canada** which, on the "Nexis" side, sells full-text retrieval of articles and news stories from thousands of different sources worldwide, via subscription (<http://www.lexisnexis.com>). Most of this news is from English-language sources including newspapers, magazines, wire services, company news and profiles, and trade and industry journals.

Newscan (<http://www.newscan.com/>) is a Canadian-based virtual news library, specially designed for public libraries and the education sector, which offers access to an impressive database of current and archival Canadian and European news sources, including French-language sources. Users can subscribe to selected media sources or to the entire service.

ProQuest Canadian Newsstand <http://www.proquest.com/en-US/catalogs/databases/detail/canadian_newsstand.shtml> provides searchable access to over 300 Canadian newspapers from the late 1970s onward. These newspapers include not only the national and leading newspapers but also many smaller local publications.

Factiva <http://www.dowjones.com/product-factivacom.asp> from Dow Jones is one of the largest news databases and contains information from over 28,000 sources from 157 countries in 23 languages. It also includes web and blog content.

Legal Dictionaries

Legal dictionaries define legal terms and common words with special legal meanings. Like standard dictionaries, they list words alphabetically. The most frequently used dictionary is *Black's Law Dictionary*, an American publication (Thomson West) which is available on Westlaw Canada (database code BLACKS). The two main Canadian dictionaries are the popular *Dictionary of*

Canadian Law, 3d ed., by Dukelow (Thomson Carswell) and the *Canadian Law Dictionary*, 4th ed., by Yogis (Barron's Educational Services), now out of date. Dictionaries are typically located in the reference sections of libraries.

Books of Words and Phrases

In some situations legal research is conducted on the basis of particular words or phrases. To assist researchers in this search there are secondary materials called "books of words and phrases". These sources list and define words and phrases that have been interpreted by courts and administrative tribunals. They also provide citations to cases and statutes that **define** certain words or phrases. The main Canadian sources for words and phrases are:

Words and Phrases Judicially defined in Canadian Courts (part of the *Canadian Abridgment* and also available on Westlaw Canada). This source consists of eight bound volumes that are updated by supplements. It includes over 50,000 considerations of words and phrases from Canadian judicial and tribunal decisions, and provides citations for the cases referenced.

Canadian Legal Words and Phrases (on LexisNexis/Quicklaw) includes words and phrases defined in Canadian courts since 2000. It also contains over 13,000 words and phrases defined in statutes, rules and regulations from every jurisdiction in Canada.

Sanagan's Encyclopedia of Words and Phrases, Legal Maxims, Canada (Thomson Carswell). This is a four-volume loose-leaf source. For each word or phrase listed, the authors provide summaries of the judicial comments and/or relevant quotations relating to each word or phrase and also provide ratios of the cases that have spoken most recently and most distinctly to the meanings of the words or phrases in question. This resource largely continues the product below. *Sanagan's* is also available online as part of the Carswell eReference library.

Words and Phrases, Legal Maxims. This source consists of three loose-leaf volumes and defines words and phrases interpreted by Canadian courts. It was originally published by DeBoo and is now largely being continued by *Sanagan's Encyclopedia* (see above).

Abbreviations Lists

Researchers may encounter hundreds of legal abbreviations every day. Interpreting these quickly and correctly is crucial to finding the cited sources, whether they be secondary materials, cases or legislation. One excellent, free online source for interpreting abbreviations is the *Cardiff Index to Legal Abbreviations* (<http://www.legalabbrevs.cardiff.ac.uk/>) produced by Cardiff University's Law Library. This index is updated twice a year. Another free website for this purpose is Monash University Law Library's Abbreviations of Legal Publications List (<http://www.lib.monash.edu.au/legal-abbreviations/>).

The best printed resource is *Index to Legal Citations and Abbreviations*, 2d ed., compiled by Donald Raistrick (London: Bowker-Saur, 1993); the contents of this index are also included in the *Cardiff Index to Legal Abbreviations.* All three of these sources cover abbreviations for case reporters, statutes, journals and other secondary sources from the common law countries.

Government Documents

Numerous government bodies produce studies or publications on different areas of the law. For example, federal and provincial law reform commissions investigate problems in the law and recommend changes. These commission reports are very useful summaries and critiques of the law. Often parliamentary committees or royal commissions produce reports on investigations or controversial areas of law. In law libraries these are often treated like textbooks and categorized by subject and call number. Often they are listed in periodical indexes and, more recently, they can be located on government websites.

In addition, ministries, departments and agencies of the federal, provincial and territorial governments produce annual reports as well as unique, documents that have both legal and policy implications. Again, law libraries treat these either as serial publications, arranging them by jurisdiction and year, or as books with call numbers. They can be highly persuasive and may be cited as secondary authority in judicial decisions. Frequently they appear on government websites, but there are no guarantees that they will remain permanently archived for public access, so many libraries download and process the most important ones for permanency.

Other government documents consulted by researchers include the debates of the House of Commons and Senate of Canada and those of the provincial and territorial legislatures, often referred to as the "Hansard". Most large law libraries will have these in print format, and some recent years are on legislative websites. Debates can inform about the reasons for passing or amending legislation, but they are almost never cited as authority in judicial decisions.

Legal Directories

There are literally hundreds of legal directories. Some list lawyers and firms, or legal services such as title searching, or addresses, phone numbers and e-mail information for government officials, corporations or non-governmental organizations. Two particularly helpful directories for locating Canadian practitioners and firms by practice area are the Canadian Law List (Canada Law Book) in print and online (<http://www.canadianlawlist.com/>) and the Martindale-Hubbell Canadian Law Directory (LexisNexis Martindale-Hubbell) in print and online (<http://www.martindale.com/>).

Legal Education Materials and Seminar Papers

Other useful sources are materials published by continuing legal educators, law societies and bar associations. Often materials are published as part of a course or workshop for practising lawyers or articling students seeking bar admission and are written by experts. Similar materials include proceedings of bar society conferences and symposia. To help you locate these papers, the *Canadian Law Symposia Index* on LexisNexis/Quicklaw provides an index to papers presented at legal seminars, continuing education workshops and symposia going back to January 1986. These materials can be found at law libraries or through the originating organization. Sometimes they can be purchased online through the organization's website.

Forms and Precedents

There are a few publications of forms and precedents. These are used primarily by lawyers in practice as examples or templates of commonly used forms. Examples include: *O'Brien's Encyclopedia of Forms* (Canada Law Book), in print and online for those who have purchased the print version (<http://www.clbonline.ca>) and *Canadian Forms and Precedents* (LexisNexis Butterworths), currently in print only. They include reusable forms related to commercial law, corporate law, banking, real estate and wills. Some courts provide access to their court forms through their websites. A quick Google search for the name of the province and "court forms" should take the searcher directly to the appropriate website. The court forms for Ontario can be found on the Ontario Court Services website for court forms at <http://www.ontariocourtforms.on.ca/english/>.

Legal Wikis

Legal Wikis are web-based online collaborative collections of legal information. When relying on information provided by any collaborative source, it is important to be aware of the provenance of the information and to confirm all information with an authoritative source.

Some of the best known legal wikis are:

Wikipedia <http://www.wikipedia.org> is one of the first and the classic example of a free collaborative online encyclopedia, and has many entries relating to various legal topics.

Legal Tree <http://www.legaltree.ca/> is the most prominent Canadian legal wiki. Canadian lawyers are invited to contribute "well drafted, professional" articles on substantive points of law in a variety of subject areas.

Wex <http://topics.law.cornell.edu/wex> is a legal dictionary and encyclopedia from the Legal Information Institute at Cornell. Although it is a collaborative project, content is only added by qualified legal experts who are selected to contribute. This selectivity gives the information provided some authority.

Jurispedia <http://en.jurispedia.org/index.php/Main_Page> has over 1,000 subject pages and identifies itself as an "academic initiative devoted to worldwide law, legal and political sciences". Sponsored by a number of law faculties from around the world, this site can be edited by registered users only.

Law Blogs

There are a number of blogs online which contain self-published commentary on general or specific legal issues. Blogs can be produced by individuals alone, individuals within organizations or as the official voice of an organization or institution. Blogs from lawyers, law firms, law professors or law libraries in a particular area of law are very useful in terms of locating the most recent information on current or controversial issues. Researchers, however, must be aware that not all blogs are equal. Some are highly authoritative, while others may contain errors or omissions that render their contents useless, so make sure you find out about the source of the information. You can likely trust the information if it comes from an academic institution, government department or law firm. Usually blogs will have an "About" section which will enable you to check the authority of the author. Always double check the information that blogs provide to ensure that it is accurate. The *Canadian Law Blogs List* <http://www.lawblogs.ca> is a great resource for locating Canadian blogs.

Legal Research Network Papers

The Legal Research Network, which is part of the Social Sciences Research Network <http://www.ssrn.org>, provides an excellent searchable database of very current legal research. SSRN is unique; it enables researchers to post their current research online, thereby facilitating its speedy dissemination to researchers worldwide. Researchers should be aware that these papers are not peer-reviewed but often they are part of a working paper series of an academic institution, and many are eventually published in scholarly journals. Many of the papers are free to the public, but academic institutions may also pay for additional access. Each paper is available as a downloadable PDF file.

Law Firm Newsletters

Many law firms publish newsletters highlighting their current cases and legal issues, and which often include substantive legal information. To help you locate law firm information you can search Fee Fie Foe Firm Canada <http://www.feefiefoefirm.com/ca/>, which is a search engine of Canadian Law firm websites, newsletters, bulletins and press releases.

Case Digests

Case digests are summaries of reported and unreported cases. They are written by editors and compiled in periodic publications and newsletters. They are prepared primarily for use by lawyers so that they can quickly read about current cases in their area of practice. A lawyer who wants the full text in print can retrieve it from the print reporters in the library, order it from the publisher or the courts or go online to one of several commercial online providers. The digests are arranged according to subject matter. Unlike the encyclopedias, digests are simply abstracts and are rarely used by beginning researchers.

The main Canadian case digest collection is the *Canadian Abridgment: Case Digests*. It is organized in a fashion similar to the CED; cases are filed according to a similar classification scheme. Each topic is assigned a multi-level number. These same digests and numbering scheme can also be found online in Westlaw Canada.

The *Canada Digest* on LexisNexis/QuickLaw also contains case summaries written by legal editors from all jurisdictions. Digests are organized by broad and then more specific subject headings for browsing. The database is also searchable. There is no print equivalent of the *Canada Digest*.

The case digests are explained in more detail in Chapter 9 (How to Find and Update Cases).

Case and Statute Citators

Citators are very useful annotations of the law. They typically identify the law and list all of its updates and judicial considerations. There are both statute and case citators. Statute citators consist of lists of statutes, including revisions, and cases that refer to statutes. Case citators consist of alphabetical lists of decided cases, each followed by a list of cases that have judicially considered the original case. The two most comprehensive paper-based citators are published as part of the *Canadian Abridgment: Canadian Case Citations* and *Canadian Statute Citations* and are also included in KeyCite*Canada* on Westlaw Canada. On LexisNexis/Quicklaw, legislation and cases can be noted up using the *QuickCite Statute Citator* and the *Quickcite Case Citator*.

Citators are explained in more detail in Chapter 7 (How to Find and Update Statutes) and Chapter 9 (How to Find and Update Cases).

CITATION OF SECONDARY MATERIALS

The authoritative book on Canadian legal citation is the *Canadian Guide to Uniform Legal Citation* (the "McGill Guide" published by Thomson Carswell). Be sure to use the current edition, since this guide often changes when it is reissued. The main rule of citation of any source is to remain consistent. Each part of a citation has a purpose with the ultimate goal of enabling the reader of the citation to locate the source. The following is an example of a proper citation:

Author   Title   Edition   Publication Info.   Page
↓   ↘   ↘   ↓   ↓

Peter W. Hogg, *Constitutional Law of Canada*, 2d ed. (Toronto: Carswell, 1985) at 73.

The following are some tips about textbook citation:

Author:	List the author's name exactly as he/she used it in the work being cited, followed by a comma
Title of textbook:	Italicized or underlined, followed by a comma
Volume:	If there is one
Edition:	Use abbreviations, *e.g.*, 3d
Place of publication:	Name of city followed by a colon
Publisher:	Full name of publisher
Year of publication:	Of that particular edition
Page reference:	Only if referring to a specific passage (this is known as a "pinpoint" citation)

The following are the parts of a journal article citation and some tips:

L. Eisenstat Weinrib, "Learning to Live with the Override" (1990) 35 McGill L.J. 541 at 562.

Author:	List the author's name exactly as he/she used it in the work being cited, followed by a comma
Title of article:	Put in quotation marks
Year of publication:	Place in round brackets
Volume number:	If there is one
Name of journal:	Use proper abbreviations
First page of article:	Always included in citation
Page reference:	Only if referring to a specific passage (this is known as a "pinpoint" citation)

Electronic Citation

If your secondary material is taken from an electronic source, it is helpful to your readers if you add that information to the citation so that the material can be found easily. If a commercial online system was used, add the abbreviation for the provider (*e.g.*, WC, LN/QL). If a website was used, after the citation (above) add a comma and then the word "online" followed by a colon. Add the name of the website followed by the name of the specific part of the site, then the URL (Uniform Resource Locater) in angled brackets. This information is necessary so that your reader can locate the information, but also to prove the prior existence of the information should the website be taken offline in the future.

SELF TEST

The answers to these questions are found at the end of the book in the "Answers to Self Tests" section.

1. How do you locate a textbook?
2. How do you locate journal articles by subject?
3. What is the *Canadian Encyclopedic Digest*?
4. What is a book of words and phrases?
5. What is a case digest?
6. What is a citator?

SAMPLE EXERCISES — FINDING SECONDARY MATERIALS

Objectives

At the end of this exercise you should be able to:

- Locate and use relevant books and treatises
- Through periodical indexes, locate and use relevant journal articles
- Locate and use the *Canadian Encyclopedic Digest* (CED)
- Properly cite a journal article and a book

Instructions

- Do background reading on secondary materials.

- Keep a record of all the steps and the time taken to complete the exercise.

Fact Pattern

Mr. Green
Your client Mr. Green has recently been charged with hunting for deer without a licence. He can't understand why he is now being charged with an offence as he is a "Treaty Indian". He believes that because of his status as a Treaty Indian he has a constitutional right to hunt and fish anywhere and anytime he chooses. Is your client correct? Can you fight the charges on the basis of your client's Indian status?

1. Brainstorm and list five words or terms that you might look for in the library. Before looking at the law, list the facts you think are relevant.

Words:

Relevant facts:

2. Go to the *Canadian Encyclopedic Digest* and look in the first few volumes for the *Contents Key* and *Index*. List those subject titles and volumes that appear to be relevant to the fact pattern. Or look in the Westlaw Canada online version in the Table of Contents.

    Subject titles:

3. Go to the volume that contains the most relevant subject title (from Question 2). Look in the *Index* to that volume and find the most relevant sections. List the most relevant heading, subheading(s), and paragraph(s) that appear to be relevant to the fact pattern.

    Number:

    Heading:

    Subheading(s):

    Paragraph Numbers:

4. Check the cumulative index to *Halsbury's Laws of Canada*. List the subject title(s) that appear to be relevant to the fact pattern. Or browse the Table of Contents in the online version on LexisNexis/Quicklaw.

    Subject titles:

5. Go to the volume that contains the most relevant subject title (from Question 4). Look in the *Index* to that volume and find the most relevant sections. List the most relevant heading, subheading(s), and paragraph(s) that appear to be relevant to the fact pattern.

    Heading:

    Subheading(s):

    Paragraph Numbers:

Books and Treatises

Use the library computer catalogue to locate a treatise/book on the subject of criminal law by D. Stuart. Provide the proper citation and record the call number.

1. Citation:

2. Call number:

Periodicals

Go to the legal periodical indexes (paper or electronic). Give the proper citation for one periodical that addresses the following:

1. By subject. Use the *Index to Canadian Legal Literature (Canadian Abridgment)*:

   Naskapi Indians (Innu) of Labrador and an environmental impact assessment.

   Citation:

2. By author (use the *Index to Canadian Legal Periodical Literature*):

   A 2000 article by Randall Echlin on labour law.

   Citation:

3. By a keyword search in LegalTrac online:

   A 1999 article by Penny about municipal solid waste.

   Citation:

Dictionaries

Give a complete clear and succinct legal explanation in your own words for the following term. Name the source you used.

> *Res judicata*:

> Source:

ANSWERS TO SAMPLE EXERCISES

Canadian Encyclopedic Digest

1. Words: Constitution, Native or Indian or Aboriginal Rights, Hunting and Fishing Rights, Treaty Rights.

   Relevant Facts: A man was charged with hunting without a licence. He is a "Treaty" Indian.

2.

Title Numbers	Subject Titles	Volumes
1	Aboriginal Law	1
73	Fish and Wildlife	29

3. Volume 1, title 1, section V: Constitutional Aspects, part 2: Legislation at par. 107, and section III: Treaties part 5: Provisions: (c) Fishing and Hunting at pars. 76 to 85. Also Volume 19, title 73, section 1: Provincial Legislation: (a) General interpretation at par. 26 and 65

4. Hunting and fishing.

5.   Hunting and Fishing, Section I: Jurisdiction, Subsection 1. Right to Hunt
     and Fish, (2) Aboriginal Rights at par. HHF-2: Constitutional Basis.

Books and Treatises

1.   Citation: Don Stuart, *Canadian Criminal Law: A Treatise*, 5th ed.
     (Toronto: Carswell, 2007).

2.   Call number: KE8809 .S78 2007 (The call number may be different in
     different libraries.)

Periodicals

1.   Patricia Fry, "A Social Biosphere: Environmental Impact Assessment,
     the Innu, and their Environment" (1998) 56 U.T. Fac. L. Rev. 177.

2.   Randall Scott Echlin, "Developments in Labour and Employment Law:
     The 1999-2000 Term" (2000) 13 S.C.L.R. (2d) 247-267.

3.   William L. Penny, "The Municipal Solid Waste Landfill Presumptive
     Remedy" (1999) 13 Natural Resources & Env't 471.

Dictionaries

Res judicata: An issue that has been definitively settled by judicial decision.

Source: *Black's Law Dictionary*, 8th ed. (St. Paul, Minn.: West Publishing Co.,
2004).

Appendix 6A: How to Use Legal Encyclopedias

This appendix provides a "walk-through" of the *Canadian Encyclopedic Digest* and *Halsbury's Laws of Canada* — the two Canadian legal encyclopedias.

THE CANADIAN ENCYCLOPEDIC DIGEST (CED)

The Main Set

The complete *Canadian Encyclopedic Digest* (CED) consists of two sets (the Western set and the Ontario set) consisting of approximately 50 loose-leaf volumes each (called the Main Sets). They are in alphabetical order, so the first volume includes a summary of the law on *Aboriginal Law* and the last volume contains a summary of the law on *Youth Criminal Justice*. The volumes are loose-leaf so supplements can be inserted.

The Titles

Like any encyclopedia, each volume contains a number of legal subjects (called Titles). Each title is essentially a summary of the law on that subject and includes references to specific statutes and cases. Each subject is written by a practitioner or academic who is considered to be an expert in that particular subject area.

Supplements and Updates

These topics are often updated and appear as yellow-coloured supplements that are inserted in the front of section they update. These supplements are cumulative. Every page in the CED, including supplements, has a date on it. This is the cut-off date of the information and shows its currency. If the main information has been recently updated there will not likely be any supplements.

The Research Tools

In addition to these "main sets", the print version of the CED has several research tools located in the *Research Guide, Index and Keys*, which is the first binder in the collection. This binder contains all of the following tools:

Research Guide:	Explains how to use the CED.
Index:	Lists all titles alphabetically with subheadings.
Contents Key:	Lists all subject areas or titles.
Statutes Key:	Lists statutes alphabetically.
Rules Key:	Lists rules alphabetically.
Regulations Key:	Lists regulations alphabetically by enabling statute.

The CED uses a particular indexing system that categorizes *all* of Canadian law into over 150 different subjects so researchers often start by looking for their topic in these subject areas.

The best way to approach the CED is by taking the following steps: go to the *Index*, then to the *Main Set*, and finally to the *Supplements*. Here are the steps in detail:

Step 1: Locate either the *Index* or the *Contents Keys* and look for areas of law that are relevant to your problem. These sources will refer you to specific volumes in the *Main Set*.

Illustration 6A.1
Canadian Encyclopedic Digest: Index (First Page)

INDEX KEY

This Index Key covers all titles published up to and including **Release 2010-1**.

References are to volumes, titles and paragraphs within those titles. For example, 1-5§44 refers to Volume 1, Title 5, paragraph 44. "(Supp.)" in the reference indicates material found in a supplement to the title.

A.L.E.R.T TESTING

See Constitutional Law; Criminal Law — Offences

ABANDONMENT

See Children; Contracts; Easements; Expropriation; Insurance; Landlord and Tenant; Mines and Minerals; Oil and Gas; Patents; Personal Property; Sale of Land

ABATEMENT

See Actions; Landlord and Tenant; Nuisance; Sale of Land; Specific Performance; Wills

ABDUCTION

See Children; Criminal Law — Offences; Family Law — Divorce

ABORIGINAL LAW

See also Burial and Cremation; Children; Constitutional Law; Customs and Excise; Execution; Executors and Administrators; Family Law — General; Federal and Provincial Taxation; Fish and Wildlife; Highways and Streets; Income Tax; International Law; Liquor Control; Motor Vehicles; Municipal and School Taxation; Prerogative Remedies; Public Health and Welfare; Timber

1

Illustration 6A.2
Canadian Encyclopedic Digest: Contents Key

THE KEY TO CED

LIST OF TITLES

The following is a list of the subject titles in CED (Ont. 4th), showing the
volumes in which they appear and their respective title numbers.

	Subject Title	Volume
1.	Aboriginal Law (3rd Ed.)	1
2.	Absentees	1
3.	Actions	1
4.	Administrative Law (3rd Ed.)	1
5.	Agency	2
6.	Agriculture	2
7.	Animals	2
8.	Annuities	3
9.	Arbitration	3
10.	Associations and Not-for-Profit Corporations	3
11.	Auctions	3
12.	Aviation	3
13.	Bailment	4
14.	Banking	4
15.	Bankruptcy and Insolvency (3rd Ed.)	5
16.	Barristers and Solicitors (3rd Ed.)	6
17.	Bills of Exchange	6
18.	Boundaries and Surveys	6
19.	Building Contracts	6
20.	Bulk Sales	7
21.	Burial and Cremation (3rd Ed.)	7
22.	Business Corporations	7
23.	Carriers	8
24.	Charities (3rd Ed.)	8
25.	Children	8
27.	Companies' Creditors Arrangement Act	9
29.	Condominiums	10
30.	Conflict of Laws	10
31.	Conspiracy	10
32.	Constitutional Law	11
33.	Construction Liens	11

Subject	Title	Volume
34.	Contempt of Court (3rd Ed.)	11
35.	Contracts	12 & 13
36.	Co-operatives	13
37.	Copyright	13
38.	Coroners and Medical Examiners (3rd Ed.)	14
39.	Costs (3rd Ed.)	14
40.	Courts	14
41.	Criminal Law — Defences	15
42.	Criminal Law — Offences	15 & 16
43.	Criminal Law — Procedure	17
44.	Crown	18
45.	Customs and Excise (3rd Ed.)	18
46.	Damages	19
47.	Debtor and Creditor (3rd Ed.)	19
48.	Deeds and Documents (3rd Ed.)	19
49.	Defamation	20
50.	Devolution of Estates	20
51.	Discovery	20
52.	Distress (3rd Ed.)	20
53.	Drainage	21
54.	Easements	21
55.	Education	21
56.	Elections	21
57.	Employment Insurance (3rd Ed.)	22
58.	Employment Law	22
59.	Environmental Law	23
60.	Equity	23
61.	Estoppel	23
62.	Evidence (3rd Ed.)	24
63.	Execution	25
64.	Executors and Administrators (3rd Ed.)	25
65.	Expropriation	25
66.	Extradition	26
67.	Family Law — Divorce (3rd Ed.)	26
68.	Family Law — General (3rd Ed.)	27
69.	Family Law — Property	28
70.	Federal and Provincial Taxation	29
71.	Firearms, Weapons and Explosives	29

1   February 2010   2

Canadian Encyclopedic Digest Fourth Edition, Key, Release February 2010. Reprinted by permission of Carswell, a division of Thomson Reuters Canada Limited.

As you can see from the above illustration, in the Contents Key there is a main heading entitled *Family Law – Property*. This subject is found in Title 69 in Volume 28. This is the title that could potentially apply to the Paul and Melody situation.

Illustration 6A.3
Canadian Encyclopedic Digest: Title Index (Family Property) (Ontario) Volume 28, Title 69

FAMILY LAW — PROPERTY

CED (4th) 6

Canadian Encyclopedic Digest Fourth Edition, Title Index. Reprinted by permission of Carswell, a division of Thomson Reuters Canada Limited.

Step 2: Go to the *Main Set* of volumes and look in the volumes that include your topics. Peruse the table of contents in that volume, locate the relevant topic and read the relevant paragraphs. Record citations of relevant cases and statutes.

Illustrations 6A.2 and 6A.3 are excerpts from the Contents Key and the Title Index that relate to the Paul and Melody situation. The Title Index refers the researcher to §338 of that title. The illustration below provides an example of the type of summaries contained in the CEDs. Once you find your topic you can read this information to gain an overview of the topic and record the citations of relevant statutes and cases. These statutes and cases will provide a springboard for further research. Some CED entries also provide some references to secondary sources.

Illustration 6A.4 shows the CED entry for Volume 28, Title 69, §388, the section which relates specifically to Paul and Melody's legal issue.

Step 3: Look at the front of the relevant title for the Supplement pages to see if the law has changed since the white pages were printed.

The CED is updated by supplements on coloured or shaded pages inserted at the front of a Title. Researchers should refer to these pages to see if the law has changed since the white pages were printed. Because Volume 28, Title 69, §388 was last updated in August 2009, there are not presently any supplementary pages to which the researcher can refer.

Illustration 6A.4
Canadian Encyclopedic Digest: Title 69 Family Law - Property, §388.

(iv) — Inheritances and Gifts

See Canadian Abridgment: FAM.III.5.c.ii Family law — Family property on marriage breakdown — Assets which may be excluded from property to be divided — Gifts and inheritances — British Columbia; FAM.III.5.c.xi Family law — Family property on marriage breakdown — Assets which may be excluded from property to be divided — Gifts and inheritances — Property acquired with donated services

§388 Where property has been acquired by inheritance or gift, it may be excluded from division as the property does not form part of the product of the marriage.[1] Where parents have advanced monies to their married children, the onus of proving that the monies were loans rather than gifts is on the person making that allegation.[2]

> 1   Family Relations Act, R.S.B.C. 1996, c. 128, s. 65(1)(d); *Bateman v. Bateman* (1979), 10 R.F.L. (2d) 63 (B.C. S.C.) (RRSP purchased with gift from mother); *Bandiera v. Bandiera* (1979), 13 B.C.L.R. 327 (B.C. S.C.) (inter vivos gift); *Caskey v. Caskey* (1979), 14 B.C.L.R. 193 (B.C. S.C.) (gift in form of loan at low interest rate taken into account); *Richardson v. Richardson* (1982), 32 R.F.L. (2d) 82 (B.C. S.C.); reversed on other grounds (1984), 43 R.F.L. (2d) 312 (B.C. C.A.) (husband's participation in litigation involving wife's inheritance not a "venture" within meaning of s. 45(3)(e) since no element of risk present; inheritance not family asset); *Barnard v. Barnard* (1987), 7 R.F.L. (3d) 163 (B.C. C.A.) (husband's use of inheritance as part of purchase price of property justifying unequal division); *Jasich v. Jasich* (1984), 40 R.F.L. (2d) 441 (B.C. S.C.) (inheritance kept intact and separate from family assets not constituting family asset); *Rushton v. Rushton* (1984), 38 R.F.L. (2d) 308 (B.C.

CED (4th)   412

Canadian Encyclopedic Digest, Fourth Edition. Reprinted by permission of Carswell, a division of Thomson Reuters Canada Limited.

Using the CED on Westlaw Canada

The CED is available online through Westlaw Canada. The electronic version includes both the Ontario and the Western editions and uses the same organizational structure and indexing as the print versions. Also, as with the print edition, researchers must be sure to check the currency of each title as the electronic version simply replicates the print version. When the print is out of date so is the electronic version. One advantage to searching the CED electronically is that the supplements are incorporated into the text, making one-stop searching easier. Another advantage is that in most cases there are direct links from the footnotes to the full text of the cases and legislation being referenced. One disadvantage is that you do not have access to the various finding tools available in the print version, which can make searching less efficient.

There are essentially two ways to search the CED electronically: by browsing the table of contents or by using the template to conduct a word search. It is best to scan the contents first to get a general sense of what is included in order to avoid becoming overwhelmed by the amount of information and the level of detail. It is also best to have a fairly good sense of your topic and how it is categorized before conducting an electronic search. Having said that, if you know your specific topic, there is no harm in doing a quick word search to see what you find and then going back to the more systematic approach. More instructions on how to search electronic sources are found in Chapter 5 (How to Find the Law and Legal Information).

HALSBURY'S LAWS OF CANADA

Generally speaking, *Halsbury's Laws of Canada* will be easier than the CED for the beginning researcher to use because it closely resembles a general encyclopedia. You simply select the appropriate volume based on the legal topic you are researching. The print volumes are updated by an annual paper supplement.

Each subject title is authored by a Canadian expert on the topic and is divided into logical divisions and then more detailed subheadings concerning that particular topic. Like the CED, each title and paragraph includes references to cases and legislation for further research. However, for additional help, each volume contains a detailed subject index and a glossary of relevant terms. Also included are abbreviations guides and consolidated tables of cases, statutes and statutory instruments. Some titles have tables of treaties and conventions, and tables of non-statutory materials when appropriate. One feature that differentiates *Halsbury's* from the CED is the list of additional recommended secondary sources.

If you are not sure where to locate specific information, consult the consolidated index. This index combines all the subjects from each individual topic index into one alphabetical list.

Step 1: Locate either the *Consolidated Index* or the *Subject Index* in the volume relevant to your area of research. These sources will refer you to specific volumes in the *Main Set*. The example used here relates to an immigration law situation.

Illustration 6A.5
Excerpt from Halsbury's Laws of Canada: Consolidated Index

CONSOLIDATED INDEX

CHRISTMAS DAY — *cont'd*
provincial — *cont'd*
· Nova Scotia, HHL-22
· Nunavut, HHL-26
· Ontario, HHL-28
· Prince Edward Island, HHL-32
· Saskatchewan, HHL-38
· Yukon, HHL-41

CHRISTMAS EVE
public servants, HHL-22

CHURCH *see* INTERMENT

CIRCULARS, HAD-58
see INFORMATION CIRCULARS

CITIZENSHIP AND NATIONALITY
ancestry, distinguished from, HDH-104
appeals, HIM-57
athletics programs, HDH-129
by birth
· born in Canada, HIM-33
· Canadian parentage, HIM-34
· second-generation applications,
  HIM-34
Charter, *see* CHARTER OF RIGHTS
citizenship status, HIM-9, HIM-32
contracts, personal services, HDH-128
definitions, HDH-120
dual citizenship, HIM-52
employment
· general, HDH-122
· harassment, HDH-130
general, HDH-118
loss of status, HIM-9, HIM-37, HIM-51
· procedure, HIM-56
· regaining citizenship, HIM-47
· renunciation, HIM-54
· revocation, obtained by fraud, HIM-55
· second-generation citizens, failure to
  apply, HIM-53
national origin, distinguished from,
  HDH-103
naturalization, *see* NATURALIZATION
non-profit institutions, HDH-127
offences
· contravention of *Citizenship Act*, HIM-58
· failure to comply with property
  restrictions, HIM-58
· forgery of citizenship certificate, HIM-58
· impersonation, HIM-58

Ontario
· exemptions, HDH-125
· landlord provisions, HDH-126
owner-occupied tenancies, HDH-124
police inquiries, HDH-123
prohibition against discrimination,
  HDH-119
religious institutions, HDH-127
  see also NATIONAL ORIGIN
rights of citizens, HIM-9

CITIZENSHIP CERTIFICATES
fraudulent use, HCR-157

CIVIC
Alberta, HHL-64
appointment, HHL-25
declaration, HHL-6, HHL-9,
  HHL-27, HHL-39
Manitoba, HHL-64
Ontario, HHL-64
Nova Scotia, HHL-64
Prince Edward Island, HHL-64
proclamation, HHL-22

CIVIL ACTIONS
abuse of process, HDE-234
breach of confidence, HDE-235
common law defamation
see also COMMON LAW
  DEFAMATION
· Charter application, HDE-15, HDE-18,
  HDE-19
· conduct of defendant, effect, HDE-208 –
  HDE-210
· conspiracy inapplicable, HDE-236
· damages, HDE-194 – HDE-228
· defences, HDE-7, HDE-59 – HDE-193
· elements, HDE-6, HDE-22 – HDE-58
· limitation periods, HDE-191 – HDE-193
· notice requirements, HDE-180 – HDE-190
· personal cause of action, HDE-44
· pleading, *see* PLEADING
· slander, HDE-230
dominant means of enforcement, HDE-2
intentional interference with economic
  relations, HDE-233
invasion of privacy, HDE-235
malicious falsehood, HDE-231
negligence, HDE-232
Québec *Civil Code*, HDE-8

Step 2: Go to the *Main Set* of volumes and look in the volume(s) that include your topics. Peruse the table of contents in that volume, locate the relevant topic and read the relevant paragraphs. Record citations of relevant cases and statutes.

Illustration 6A.6
Excerpt from Halsbury's Laws of Canada: Immigration Law
(Title Page)

Halsbury's
Laws of Canada
First Edition

Immigration and Citizenship

Contributed by

Lorne Waldman
LL.B., LL.M.
of the Ontario Bar

Waldman & Associates
Barrister and Solicitors

Contributing Editor
Mary K. McLean, B.A., LL.B.

LexisNexis·

Illustration 6A.7
Excerpt from Halsbury's Laws of Canada: Immigration Law (Table of Contents)

TABLE OF CONTENTS

Illustration 6A.8
Excerpt from Halsbury's Laws of Canada: Immigration Law
(HIM 33 – Citizenship by Birth)

▼ **HIM-33** ▼　　　　　　IMMIGRATION AND CITIZENSHIP

4.　(CAN) *Citizenship Act*, R.S.C. 1985, c. C-29, s. 3(1)(d).

5.　(CAN) *Citizenship Act*, R.S.C. 1985, c. C-29, s. 3(1)(d).

6.　(CAN) *Citizenship Act*, R.S.C. 1985, c. C-29, s. 3(1)(b). Note that second-generation application is required before age 28.

7.　Birth registration and second-generation application are required before age 28. As a result of the decision of the Supreme Court of Canada in *Benner v. Canada (Secretary of State)*, [1997] 1 S.C.R. 358, [1997] S.C.J. No. 26 (S.C.C.), there is no longer any distinction regarding the rights to citizenship based on birth between December 31, 1946 and February 15, 1977 to a Canadian mother or father.

8.　A declaration is required for minors. However, in *Benner v. Canada (Secretary of State)*, [1997] 1 S.C.R. 358, [1997] S.C.J. No. 26 (S.C.C.), the Court held that the distinction in this section of the *Citizenship Act* was inconsistent with s. 15 of the *Canadian Charter of Rights and Freedoms*, Part I of the *Constitution Act, 1982*, being Schedule B to the *Canada Act 1982* (U.K.), 1982, c.11, such that there is no longer any distinction in the application of the law regardless of the marital status of the mother at the time of birth.

9.　In light of *Benner v. Canada (Secretary of State)*, [1997] 1 S.C.R. 358, [1997] S.C.J. No. 26 (S.C.C.), it is likely that these people would have a direct claim to citizenship and would not have to seek it through naturalization. In *Benner v. Canada (Secretary of State)*, [1997] 1 S.C.R. 358, [1997] S.C.J. No. 26 (S.C.C.), the Court held that the distinction in this section of the *Citizenship Act* was inconsistent with s. 15 of the *Canadian Charter of Rights and Freedoms*, Part I of the *Constitution Act, 1982*, being Schedule B to the *Canada Act 1982* (U.K.), 1982, c.11, such that there is no longer any distinction in the application of the law regardless of the marital status of the mother at the time of birth.

10.　(CAN) S.C. 1946, c. 15.

2.　Citizenship By Birth

(1)　Persons Born in Canada (*Jus Soli*)[1]

▼ **HIM-33** ▼　**Right to citizenship.** The following persons are citizens:

1.　Persons born in Canada after February 14, 1977;[2]
2.　Persons born in Canada after December 31, 1946 and before February 15, 1977;[3] and
3.　British subjects born in Canada prior to January 1, 1947.[4]

Immigration status not relevant. It makes no difference what the citizenship or immigration status ("illegal" included) of the parents of the

Step 3: Check the Cumulative Supplement to see if the law has changed since the initial volumes were printed.

Illustration 6A.9
Excerpt from Halsbury's Laws of Canada Cumulative Supplement

<hr>

Title Update

IMMIGRATION AND CITIZENSHIP (HIM)
(Published December 2006)
Main title contributed by Lorne Waldman
Updates prepared by LexisNexis Canada Inc.

Covers developments in the law between June 30, 2006 and February 1, 2009

▼ HIM-33 ▼   Right to citizenship
Note 6
(CAN) *Citizenship Act*, R.S.C. 1985, c. C-29, s. 2(2)(a) amended by S.C. 2001, c. 26, s. 286 to be replaced as follows:

(a) a person is deemed to be born in Canada if the person is born on a Canadian vessel as defined in section 2 of the Canada Shipping Act, 2001, or on an aircraft registered in Canada under the Aeronautics Act and regulations made under that Act;

▼ HIM-34 ▼   Right to citizenship
In the text, add after 3.
4. On application, persons who were adopted by a citizen after February 14, 1977 while the person was a minor or adult child, subject to specific requirements, including that there was a genuine parental relationship and the adoption was not entered into primarily for the purpose of acquiring citizenship.[3.1]

Note 3
See *Taylor v. Canada (Minister of Citizenship and Immigration)*, [2007] F.C.J. No. 1478, 2007 FCA 349 (Fed. C.A.), revg [2006] F.C.J. No. 1328, 2006 FC 1053 (F.C.) (children of war brides born prior to 1947 not entitled to Canadian citizenship; *Canadian Charter of Rights and Freedoms* could not have retrospective effect in this instance).

Note 3.1
(CAN) *Citizenship Act*, R.S.C. 1985, c. C-29, s. 5.1, changed by 2007 c. 24 s. 2, in force December 23, 2007.

▼ HIM-38 ▼   Residence defined
Note 3
See *Zhao v. Canada (Minister of Citizenship and Immigration)*, [2006] F.C.J. No. 1923, 2006 FC 1536 (F.C.) (citizenship judge may adopt and apply one of several approaches developed by Federal Court to determine compliance with the residency requirement); *Ibrahim v. Canada (Minister of Citizenship and Immigration)*, [2007] F.C.J. No. 851 at para. 16, 2007 FC 633 (F.C.); *Haj-Kamali v. Canada (Minister of Citizenship and Immigration)*, [2007] F.C.J. No. 136, 2007 FC 102 (F.C.) (citizenship judge failed to identify legal test for residency

Using *Halsbury's Laws of Canada* on LexisNexis/Quicklaw

The electronic version of *Halsbury's Laws of Canada* is virtually identical to the print version. Each subject title includes not only the main contents of each volume but all the finding tools (the tables of cases, statutes, indexes, *etc.*) as well. The only tool not included is the cumulative table of cases. As with the CED on Westlaw Canada, *Halsbury's* can be both searched using keywords or browsed using drop down menus. The two advantages of using the electronic version are that there are links to the full text of any statutes and case law noted in the footnotes and that the entire database is searchable by keywords. The useful list of secondary sources also provides links to the full-text journal articles that are included in the LN/QL's journals database.

Appendix 6B: Checklist: How to Find Secondary Materials

Locating and reading secondary materials to gain an overview of the law is the best way to start your research. Generally, start with books or a legal encyclopedia, then move on to legal journals and periodicals.

As you locate materials, read generally at first, looking for particular keywords describing your topic. Make notes of relevant subject headings and record references to specific cases, statutes and other sources.

TEXTBOOKS

In the library

- ☐ Search a law library's electronic catalogue using keywords to generate a list of book titles. Note the subject headings assigned for this topic. Record the books' titles and call numbers.
- ☐ Locate these books in the library. Browse adjacent shelves for similar, relevant books. Check for similar call numbers in the library's "Reserve" area where the most current, highly used materials are kept.
- ☐ Scan each book's *Table of Contents* to get an overview of its arrangement and check its *Index* for your subject headings or keywords. Read generally at first. Record relevant cases, statutes, articles and books mentioned in the text and footnotes.
- ☐ Some researchers photocopy important pages with specific citations for cases and statutes or key quotations. Photocopying the book's title page too will save you time later, and make a note of its call number in case you have to find it again. For loose-leaf texts, note the date of the last release filed, since this indicates the currency of the information.

Online

- ☐ Some books are available in electronic format (e-books) through commercial providers such as LN/QL and WC (often in the law practice specific collections).
- ☐ Other publishers distribute some of their books in electronic format. These will be available through your library's catalogue. Check with publishers and online service providers or search their catalogues or lists on their websites. Note the title, author, publisher, and date of publication so that you can easily find the resource(s).

LEGAL ENCYCLOPEDIAS

In the library

- ☐ Locate either the *Canadian Encyclopedic Digest* (CED), Western or Ontario set, or go to *Halsbury's Laws of Canada*.
- ☐ If using the CEDs, start by looking in the first volume in the *Contents Key* or the *Index* to locate relevant subject titles. From there you can go to the volumes that cover your subject. Each title has its own Table of Contents — showing the subject headings and subheadings used — and an Index. Read generally at first. Note the currency date of the information and update the information you read by referring to the title's supplement. After you have focused your research, record relevant cases and statutes.
- ☐ If using *Halsbury's*, go to the Table of Contents to locate the subject headings and their subheadings as appropriate and read those sections, again, recording relevant cases and statutes.

Online

- ☐ The CED is also available through WC. You can browse its *Table of Contents*, or search the full text using keywords and the search template provided.
- ☐ *Halsbury's* is available through LN/QL and like the CED is both browsable and searchable.

LEGAL DICTIONARIES AND WORDS AND PHRASES

In the library

- ☐ Use the *Dictionary of Canadian Law*, 3d ed., by Dukelow (Thomson Carswell) or *Black's Law Dictionary* to define unfamiliar terms.
- ☐ Look at *Words and Phrases Judicially defined in Canadian Courts* (part of the *Canadian Abridgment*) to determine how courts have interpreted a particular phrase or term.

Online

- ☐ *Words and Phrases Judicially defined in Canadian Courts* is available on WC, or check out *Canadian Legal Words and Phrases* on LN/QL. These sources will provide links to the cases where the terms were interpreted.

LEGAL JOURNALS AND PERIODICALS

In the library

- ☐ Most law libraries have huge collections of journal articles. To locate articles, go to the legal periodical indexes — in print or electronic format. Search by subject (from your prior research), keywords, author, case name or statute title. In electronic indexes, read the search tips and use the advanced search template to construct a more defined search.

❑ The main legal periodical indexes are:

- *Index to Canadian Legal Literature* (ICLL) (online and in print as part of the *Canadian Abridgment*)
- *LegalTrac* (online)
- *Index to Legal Periodicals and Books* (ILPB) (online and in print)

❑ As you find relevant journal articles on your subject, note the subject headings assigned to them and follow these leads to find more relevant articles.

❑ If you locate a particularly relevant journal (*e.g.*, *Canadian Journal of Women and the Law*) it is a good idea to scan the Tables of Contents of recent issues of that journal for more articles.

Online

❑ LN/QL and WC have databases containing different types of secondary materials including journals, periodical indexes, newsletters, topical reports with commentary. Browse their database lists.

❑ A very comprehensive collection of full-text legal journals is the *Hein Online Law Journal Library* <http://www.HeinOnline.org>. Most law libraries subscribe to this service, which may be searched by author, title or keyword.

OTHER SOURCES OF SECONDARY MATERIALS

Other sources of legal information can be found through the following:

❑ Social Science Research Network
❑ Law Firm Newsletters
❑ Blogs and Wikis
❑ Listservs or electronic discussion lists
❑ Government websites
❑ Law Library websites

How to Find and Update Statutes 7

There is rarely a legal situation today that does not involve a statute, or government-made law. With the publication of statutes in electronic form, statute research has become much easier today than it was in the past. However, because not all statutes are in electronic form, and for other reasons explained below, most law students will, at some point, still need to find statutes in print in the law library.

This chapter provides an introduction to statutes and describes how to find, update and note up statutes using both the law library and the various electronic-based resources. It explains how statutes are published and how they become law, how to determine whether a statute is in force and how to cite a statute.

LEARNING OBJECTIVES

At the end of this chapter you will be able to:

- Describe how statutes are created and published
- Describe the four steps in any statute research
- Locate a statute by title, citation or subject
- Update a statute (*i.e.*, find revisions) and find out when a statute came into force
- Locate cases that have considered statutes (*i.e.*, note up a statute)
- Write a citation for a statute

ABOUT RESEARCHING STATUTES

Statute research involves locating and updating statutes and also locating cases that have interpreted or applied statutes. For example, a researcher confronted with a situation involving the dismissal of an employee would look for labour and employment statutes, determine whether they have been repealed or revised, and then search for cases that have considered or interpreted those statutes. Often cases that apply statutes add a new interpretation to a statute, so a researcher should always look for the most recent cases even if a statute is new.

The following also should be kept in mind when conducting statute research:

- Statutes work in combination with cases.
- There may be more than one applicable statute.

- There may be overlap between provincial and federal statutes.
- Statutes are revised regularly, so research must always be current.
- Cases interpret statutes and can affect the meaning of statutes.

Another important concept to remember is that legislation has mandatory authority **only** in its own jurisdiction. A person living or working in British Columbia cannot be held to the requirements of a Manitoba statute, although the Manitoba statute might have some persuasive authority if B.C. had no statute that addressed that particular legal issue but Manitoba did. Legislation in its own jurisdiction has "binding" or mandatory authority. Thus, legal researchers must be familiar with the laws of their own province or territory, along with any federal statutes that have a bearing on the issue at hand.

It is also important to know that there are "unofficial" and "official" versions of statutes available, either from commercial publishers or government websites. The unofficial can be very valuable since they are usually published ahead of the government print versions and often come in consolidated or noted-up versions. Each government now provides online access to current, in-force consolidated statutes. These statutes, however, (with the exception of those from the federal, Ontario and Quebec governments) are not considered to be official. For jurisdictions where the online version is not official, print versions are still required for use in court.

Finally, when researching statutes it is critical to know the timing of your legal issue. For example, when did the client act? This is because each statute is created on a particular date and becomes effective on a specific date. You must be sure that the statute you find is not an earlier or later version of that piece of legislation.

HOW LEGISLATION IS CREATED

In order to research legislation properly you must understand three fundamental things:

- the stages through which a statute passes, or how it is created;
- the manner in which legislation is published, officially and unofficially; and
- the main research aids designed to help you find, update and note up statutes.

The Stages of Legislation

As explained in Chapter 4 (Introduction to Law and Legal Materials), governments are constantly introducing or repealing statutes and thereby creating new law. Proposed legislation goes through a lengthy legislative process before becoming law. A provincial bill must be read three times in its legislature since provincial parliaments consist of single legislatures. A federal bill must be read three times in each house of Parliament (the Senate and the

House of Commons) and receive the consent of both houses before legislation can be effective.

A researcher must be able to trace the progress of legislation from bill to final statute and any revisions to that statute.

The five basic stages of the creation of statutes are as follows:

Bill/First Reading	➔	Second Reading	➔		Third Reading
➔ Royal Assent	➔	Coming into Force (by Proclamation or Delayed Effective Date)			

Bill (First Reading)

A statute is first introduced in a provincial legislature or the federal Parliament as a bill. At first reading, bills are assigned a number and then are usually sent to a committee to be debated. This first reading is merely a formality. A bill may be either a public bill, which deals with public policy, or a private bill, which affects individuals or institutions. A bill is debated at its second reading. At the third reading, the bill is reviewed in final form, with any changes that have been made in committee or as a result of debates.

Bills are made only when Parliament is in session, so laws are categorized by session — usually one or two years in length. Any bills that do not become law in a session die "on the order table" and must be reintroduced in the next session. Each session of Parliament is numbered after each election. For example, the 40th Parliament since Confederation in 1867 began in November 2008 after that federal election.

Because the Parliament of Canada consists of two houses — the House of Commons and the Senate — federal laws must be passed by each house. Each bill is read three times in the House of Commons and three times in the Senate. At the third reading, it is voted on and if passed receives Royal Assent by the Queen's federal representative, the Governor General. The Royal Assent date is printed on the front of every bill that is passed (see further discussion of assent below).

A statute introduced in the House of Commons is called a "commons" bill and a statute introduced in the Senate is called a "senate" bill. Each federal bill is assigned alpha-numeric numbers indicating where they were introduced (C = Commons; S = Senate) and when they were introduced in a particular session.

The legislation-making process is similar in all of the provinces since each of the provincial and territorial parliaments consist of one house. A statute is introduced as a bill and must receive three readings in the legislature and then given Royal Assent by the Queen's provincial representative (the Lieutenant Governor), before becoming law.

The "coming into force" CIF procedure for federal, provincial and territorial legislation is very similar, with most Acts coming into force by one of the ways mentioned below.

Royal Assent

Royal Assent is the symbolic acceptance by the sovereign and simply involves signing the statute by the Governor General (for federal statutes) or Lieutenant Governor (for provincial and territorial statutes). Royal Assent occurs after the bill goes through the procedure described above and is approved by both houses (federal) and by the legislature (provincial or territorial). However, not all statutes become law upon Royal Assent. As mentioned above, the effective date of some statutes may be delayed. This results in the statute coming into effect later, upon proclamation, or on a specified date. (See above discussion of "coming into force".)

For an example of the first page of a federal Act, see Appendix 7A. An example of the first page of a typical provincial Act appears in Appendix 7B.

How a Statute Comes into Force

Just because an Act receives Royal Assent does not mean it automatically has enforceability. There are several ways by which an Act may "come into force" (CIF):

Immediately: The Act may be entirely silent on the coming into force. In this case the Act is deemed to be in force "on assent", that is, on the exact day it received Royal Assent.

Retrospectively: Very occasionally, legislators make an Act come in force retrospectively, meaning it is deemed to have come into force at an earlier date than it actually received Royal Assent. An example of this would be a taxation Act that was enforced retroactively to allow a government to collect "back taxes". To locate this date you look at the last (or nearly last) section of the Act where it states a specified day of coming into force (a commencement clause). It is almost always a future date.

Delayed: If the last section of the Act states that the Act (or specific sections of the Act) shall come into force on "a day or days to be proclaimed by the Governor General, acting on behalf of the federal cabinet" this means the Act has a "delayed effective date". This is usually because a date could not be determined at the time of assent and usually occurs when complicated administrative arrangements must be carried out before it is possible for the government to actually enforce the Act. The effective date is postponed until such preparations are in place. Proclamations can be located in the federal or provincial tables of public statutes, which list the CIF date of statutes that are proclaimed into force.

Debates and Explanatory Notes

A bill at first reading contains explanatory notes that can be helpful to researchers when determining the intent of a statute. However, these notes are never cited in judicial decisions because they are not actually part of the law but they can be viewed by checking out the first reading bills either in print or online.

Once introduced, a bill may be debated and/or sent to a committee for further deliberations. These debates are often used by researchers to gauge government and opposition thinking at the time the bill is before Parliament.

HOW LEGISLATION IS PUBLISHED

Bills and statutes are published by the federal government and by each provincial and territorial government. In other words, there is one set of federal statutes published by the Canadian government and one set of statutes for each of the provinces and territories, published by their respective governments.

Within each set of statutes (provincial and federal) there are the following four main components:

Format	Stage
Bills (First Reading)	Merely proposed but not yet approved
First Printing (Gazettes)	First publication of statutes once they are passed (usually as individual paper Acts or several paper Acts softbound together)
Annual or Sessional Volumes	Formal bound set, usually published annually
Revised Statutes	Consolidation of statutes at a point in time

Bills (First and Third Reading)

Both provincial and federal bills can be obtained from the relevant legislatures via their websites and through the sale of print copies. In addition, some law libraries collect first and third reading bills in print for the purposes of comparison and historical research.

To make the contents of new statutes available as quickly as possible, the third reading of a bill is usually published after its passage through the Parliament or Legislature. Third reading bills are identical to the final version of the statute which will be formally published a few months later in a Gazette and then again later in the annual statutory volume(s) for that year.

The section below describes the various tools researchers can use to obtain copies of bills and track the progress of a bill from first reading to when it finally comes into force.

First Printing of Statutes (Gazettes)

After bills receive Royal Assent and thus become statutes, each one is assigned a chapter number. Then all the statutes from that year are collected together and printed. The chapter numbers assigned to federal statutes are consecutive numbers beginning with Chapter 1 in each new year. The statutes are numbered in the order in which they are passed into law. Thus, a federal statute about genetically modified foods might be Chapter 3 of a given year's statutes, and a statute about human rights might be Chapter 4 of that same year's statutes. The subject matter of the statutes has no logical relationship to the chapter number assigned.

Some provinces number their statutes in slightly different ways. For example, for brand new legislation, some use an alpha-numeric system, so that a new Act about farm animal health might be Chapter F-2. For amendments to existing Acts, they usually use the simple numeric designation. For example, an Act to amend an existing law about employment standards might be simply Chapter 45. Researchers will soon become familiar with the numbering system in place in their jurisdictions of interest.

Federal statutes are printed in the *Canada Gazette, Part III: Acts of Parliament*. Copies are available both in print and electronically (see Illustration 7.1). The print softbound publications fill the gap between the printing of the individual original statute and the publication of the hardbound volume of statutes. Because they are softbound, libraries receive them within a few months of Royal Assent.

Provincial statutes are published in various ways, including what is typically called the *Third Reading Bills* in print. Some government websites bypass providing third reading bills and instead, either publish the statute immediately on the web or provide a supplement to the first reading bill with any changes or amendments to that bill included.

Presently, the federal *Canada Gazette, Part III* and most of the provincial and territorial gazettes are on their respective government's websites. (See Appendix 7C: Legislation on Government Websites.) Illustration 7.1 gives the "look" of an opening page of the *Canada Gazette, Part III*.

Illustration 7.1
Cover Image of the *Canada Gazette, Part III*

Vol. 32, No. 3   Vol. 32, n° 3

Canada Gazette
Part III

Gazette du Canada
Partie III

OTTAWA, FRIDAY, JANUARY 22, 2010

Statutes of Canada, 2009

Chapters 27 to 34

Acts assented to from 24 June, 2009
to 15 December, 2009

OTTAWA, LE VENDREDI 22 JANVIER 2010

Lois du Canada (2009)

Chapitres 27 à 34

Lois sanctionnées du 24 juin 2009
au 15 décembre 2009

NOTICE TO READERS

The *Canada Gazette* Part III is published under the authority of the *Statutory Instruments Act*. The purpose of Part III is to publish public Acts as soon as is reasonably practicable after they have received Royal Assent in order to expedite their distribution.

Part III of the *Canada Gazette* contains the public Acts of Canada and certain other ancillary publications, including a list of Proclamations of Canada and Orders in Council relating to the coming into force of Acts, from the date of the previous number to the date shown above.

AVIS AU LECTEUR

La Partie III de la *Gazette du Canada*, dont la publication est régie par la *Loi sur les textes réglementaires*, a pour objet d'assurer, dans les meilleurs délais suivant la sanction royale, la diffusion des lois d'intérêt public.

La Partie III de la *Gazette du Canada* présente en outre certains textes complémentaires, comme la liste des décrets d'entrée en vigueur et des proclamations du Canada ultérieurs au numéro précédent.

With permission from Public Works and Government Services Canada. Not an official copy.

Annual or Sessional Volumes

At the end of each year or legislative session, all of the statutes from that year or session are collected and published in hardbound volumes called the "annual" or "sessional" volumes. Provincial sets of annual statutes are fairly similar to the federal set, although they go by slightly different titles. These volumes are received by libraries within a year after the end of the year or session. Often, they appear on the public websites of the various governments at the same time that they are distributed in print (see Appendix 7C: Legislation on Government Websites). Until the annual volume(s) are released, one can always refer back to the official versions published in the gazette of that jurisdiction (see previous sections).

Annual or sessional volumes also typically include helpful research tools such as tables of contents, tables of statutes and tables of proclamations. Each volume is identified by the year or session on its spine. Some sessions may span more than one year or there may be more than one session in a single year, although at the provincial and territorial levels, the modern trend is to stick strictly to publication by year. There may be one or several volumes per year, depending on the amount of legislation passed in that year.

Revised Statutes (Consolidations)

The federal government and most provincial governments periodically consolidate their statutes into a "revised" set of statutes in force. This involves reprinting all statutes that are still in force, that is, not repealed, and incorporating all amendments up to that time. The revisions effectively repeal and replace all prior legislation. They are essentially consolidations of all public statutes in effect at the time of publication. The federal government did this in 1886, 1906, 1927, 1952, 1970, and 1985. The most recent federal consolidation is the *Revised Statutes of Canada, 1985*.

The old annual volumes that contain statutes from before the consolidation are rarely used and remain in the library mainly for historical purposes (*e.g.*, to see a statute in its original form). Researchers should rarely have to consult the pre-consolidated version of a statute, although this does occur.

Illustration 7.2
Arrangement of Statutes in a Library

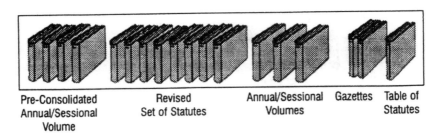

| Pre-Consolidated Annual/Sessional Volume | Revised Set of Statutes | Annual/Sessional Volumes | Gazettes | Table of Statutes |

For federal research, it is important to note that it took so long (four years) to produce the 1985 revision that the statutes that were amended or introduced between 1984 and 1988 were placed in supplements to the revised set. Therefore, the *Revised Statutes of Canada, 1985* consists of eight main volumes plus five supplements: one for each of the years from 1985 to 1988 and an Appendix volume. The main volumes and four supplements include all statutes enacted up to December 12, 1988. A researcher should always keep this problem in mind since this situation is true for most provinces also; many statutes continue to be passed while the revised set is being compiled.

Unofficial Annotated and Office Consolidations of Statutes

In a law library, you will find not only the official version of the consolidated statutes, but unofficial versions as well. These are usually published by commercial publishers and are compiled in a way that makes them useful to lawyers.

A few of the more popular statutes are published individually, with all current amendments incorporated into them. They often include the regulations and are in softcover. Examples include the Company Acts from various provinces and the *Criminal Code*. Some of these "desktop consolidations" are annotated with commentary from experts, citations to cases that have interpreted the statute, historical information on particular sections, and more.

Loose-leaf Editions of Statutes and Citators

There are several sets of commercially published loose-leaf editions of statutes. These are extremely useful tools because they are updated regularly by inserts so that you can avoid having to go through several volumes of statutes to determine which sections have been revised. As well, they are often annotated and include citations to cases that have considered a statute. These are called "annotations" or "statute citators". They are in both print and electronic form, although they are becoming less popular with the increasing number of statutes being made available by commercial online providers. The print and online versions of citators are discussed further below, under noting up statutes.

How to Read the Citation of a Statute

When a statute is published it is given a citation which consists of letters and numbers that indicate where the statute will be published and thus located. A full citation includes the title of a statute, the date it was brought into force (or revised), its location in the statute volumes and often a specific section number.

Titles are assigned to each statute when created and many are given short titles by which they are commonly known. Short titles can be useful when searching, since long titles are cumbersome. As an example, the *Act to extend the present laws of Canada that provide access to information under the control of the Government of Canada* is cited as the *Access to Information Act* (as per s. 1).

As for abbreviations, in a citation, if the abbreviation starts with an "R" then you know that the statute you are looking for is part of a revised (consolidated) set of statutes. If it starts with an "S" then you know the statute was published *after* the printed revised set and can be found in its original, as-passed version in the sessional or annual volume(s) for the year of passage. The remaining few first letters represent the jurisdiction.

Examples of Statute Abbreviations	
Abbreviation	**Full Title**
R.S.C.	*Revised Statutes of Canada*
S.C.	*Statutes of Canada*
R.S.O.	*Revised Statutes of Ontario*
S.O.	*Statutes of Ontario*

Armed with a proper citation you can, even without knowing a statute's title, easily retrieve that statute from the shelf or from any electronic database. For example, R.S.Y. 2002, c. 46 will lead you to Chapter 46 of the 2002 Revised Statutes of the Yukon, the *Corrections (Young Offenders) Act.*

RESEARCH AIDS FOR BILLS AND STATUTES

There are several places to locate research aids for legislation:

- In the library in print form in loose-leaf binders
- On government websites
- At a particular legislature (access by phone)
- Online through commercial providers

Most law libraries have print copies of federal and provincial bills and statutes (from their jurisdiction, at least) and research aids that explain what stage the bill and statute is at.

These research aids, including tables and indexes, not only help researchers locate bills and statutes, but also note any changes to the legislation and the various stages they may be at. With the introduction of web-based electronic indexes, using these tools has become much simpler.

Research Aids for Bills

Many bills may also be obtained directly from the federal and provincial government websites. Many of the print versions are also available online.

There are several publications that list the progress of a bill. The most current information can be found on most government websites (*e.g.*, in a "legislative digest" or a "progress of bills" table) or by phoning the relevant legislature's library or clerk's office. CanLII, LN/QL and WC do not provide access to any bills from any jurisdiction.

The following are some of the research aids that can assist researchers in locating bills and determining their status.

Research Aids for Federal Bills

Federal and provincial governments keep close track of the progress of bills and provide this information to the public through their online "progress of bills" reports.

The following are the various sources:

- *LEGISinfo* is the main federal service and is available online at <http://www2.parl.gc.ca/Sites/LOP/LEGISINFO/index.asp?Language=E>.

  This website provides:

  - the text of the bill at various stages;
  - government press releases and backgrounders (for government bills);
  - legislative summaries from the Parliamentary Information and Research Service;
  - important speeches at second reading;
  - votes; and
  - coming into force data.

LEGISinfo enables the researcher to know exactly which stage in the law-making process the bill has reached, whether it has been amended, what the amendments were, if it has been passed or if it died on the order table. The service also provides other background and contextual information.

- *Ottawa Letter*: Published by CCH Canadian, *Ottawa Letter* is a loose-leaf service and newsletter that contains information entitled "Progress of Legislation", which describes the progress of federal bills through Parliament. This is a useful source for determining the status of a bill in the House of Commons or the Senate. There is no electronic version *per se* but see instead the CCH Legislative Pulse below.

- *Canadian Legislative Pulse*: This online service from CCH Canadian allows researchers to check the current status and recent progress of legislation for all Canadian jurisdictions from one consolidated source. It includes links to full-text versions of bills from the government websites, customized e-mail updates on selected legislation changes on selected bills (based on the client's profile), and e-mail updates summarizing all legislative changes from across Canada. Having links to full text obviates the need for the researcher to obtain bills elsewhere.

- *Legislation: Legislation* is part of the *Canadian Abridgment* that may be bought on subscription. Each monthly issue shows the progress of new federal, provincial and territorial legislation, amendments to existing legislation and regulations that have been promulgated. This information cumulates into the *Legislation Annual*, which is a complete snapshot of all legislative and regulatory action for all Canadian jurisdictions. (Note: no full text of legislation is provided.) It is an excellent current and historical reference, especially for identifying bills that never went past first reading. It is not currently available online.

- *Order Paper and Notices*: Parliament's agenda, outlining what will happen to a bill that day. This is rarely used for research but is handy for tracking legislation. The *Order Paper and Notices* for the federal government can be found by linking from the Parliament of Canada website at <http://www2.parl.gc.ca/housechamberbusiness/ChamberSittings.aspx?View=N&Language=E&Mode=1&Parl=40&Ses=3>.

Research Aids for Provincial Bills

Each provincial legislature publishes services that can be used by researchers to determine the status of a bill. Each of these publications contains similar information, but some provinces provide separate "progress of bills" pages while others integrate this information with each bill as it appears on the site. Ontario, for example, provides the full text of each bill along with links to its Status, Debates, Explanatory Notes, Background Information and Acts Affected on its bills website. For some provinces you may need to locate the progress of bills page to research its status, while for others you simply need to locate the bill and then follow the links to locate both background and status information.

Current-session versions of many of these are now online and available to the public through the websites of provincial and territorial legislatures, although they may be archived at the end of a legislative session. (See Appendix 7C for a list of these websites.) The following are some of the titles used:

- *Orders of the Day* (sometimes called "Progress of Bills" or "Progress of Legislation"): A daily agenda of a provincial legislative assembly. It contains information on bills and the stage they are at.
- *Legislation and Legislation Annual*, part of the *Canadian Abridgment* (see above).
- *Canadian Legislative Pulse* (see above).
- *Votes and Proceedings*: A program of what happened on a particular day during a legislative sitting. The provincial and territorial parliamentary web pages will also have links to their agendas although each may be named differently; look for terms like "House Business" or "Documents and Proceedings".

Research Aids for Debates

Most of the more recent government debates can be located online.

As for Senate debates, the federal government created a series of online indexes from 1991 onward. These indexes provide an alphabetical subject list and an index by date for each session. They are in PDF format and do not provide links to the full-text debates. To locate the text of the debate the researcher must go to the Debates of the Senate of Canada (Hansard) and select the appropriate session.

As for House of Commons debates, these debates are completely electronic and fully linked to the full-text online debates. Links to these indexes are available through the Parliament of Canada website. Here are the websites:

- Senate debates index:
  <http://dsp-psd.pwgsc.gc.ca/Collection-R/Senate/index-e.html>).

- Senate debates :
  <http://www.parl.gc.ca/common/Chamber_Senate_Debates.asp?>

- House of Commons debates:
  <http://www.parl.gc.ca/common/index.asp?Language=E>.

Research Aids for Finding and Updating Statutes

There are two main tools designed for researching statutes: tables of public statutes and statute citators. Because citators are used not only to update statutes but to also locate cases that consider statutes (note up statutes), they will be discussed in the section below. There are also a few provincial statute subject indexes, but they are slowly being phased out.

Tables of Public Statutes

The main way to locate print statutes is by looking in the relevant federal or provincial table of public statutes. This way is freely available to anyone without having to purchase a commercial service or product.

By locating the title of your statute in the table (by year and chapter number) you can easily locate it in the main set of statutes, whether it is in the consolidated ("revised") set or in an annual volume.

Most provincial governments and the federal government publish comprehensive consolidated tables of public statutes. The tables are cumulative, alphabetical lists of all statutes in force and are constantly updated. Other important information is usually included in the tables, such as the date the statute came into effect and the way it was brought into effect (*e.g.*, by proclamation and on what date). The table also lists amendments to the statute.

The **federal table** is called the *Table of Public Statutes and Responsible Ministers* and is published in the final annual statute volume for each year. It is published in English (gold pages) and French (blue pages), making it easy to locate in the hardcover volume. It is also published in paperback format up to three times annually. For the past several decades, the minister responsible for enforcing each Act has been shown. An online version of this table can be found at <http://laws.justice.gc.ca/eng/TablePublicStatutes/index.html>.

The Federal *Table of Public Statutes* is just one of the four main publications of the federal government. The following publications accompany the hardbound set of federal statutes:

- *Canada Gazette, Part I*: Contains formal notices required by statute to be published.
- *Canada Gazette, Part II*: Contains new regulations (see Chapter 8).
- *Canada Gazette, Part III*: Contains new statutes and a table of proclamations.
- *Table of Public Statutes and Responsible Ministers*: A cumulative list showing the history of all federal public statutes, both those that are in force and those that have been repealed since the last printed revised set (see below).

Provincial and territorial tables of statutes have various titles and various frequencies of publication. Some are published on coloured paper for ease of locating.

As you can see, these tools combined provide all that a researcher needs to locate print-based statutes. These tools are regularly updated or supplemented and so it is critical for the researcher to be looking at the most recent version of each.

Statute Citators

If you are using print sources, the quickest way to locate, update and note up a statute is by looking in a commercially published loose-leaf statute set, sometimes known as a "statute citator". Although citators are not the official version of statutes, they will give you the proper title of the statute, the text of any revisions to that statute, and a few of the leading cases that have considered the statute. (Just to confuse matters slightly, the term citator can have two slightly different meanings. Unlike the commercial loose-leaf citators, the citators provided by the *Canadian Abridgment*, LN/QL and *WC* do not include the text of the revisions, but rather simply note up the case.)

Because the commercially published statute citators are not official you must confirm the information in the official set of statutes published by the relevant government. And, given the convenience, speed and economy of online consolidation, it is doubtful that most commercially produced loose-leaf sets will be continued much longer.

Here are a few examples of popular statute citators:

In Print

All Canada: *Canadian Statute Citations* (*Canadian Abridgment*), Thomson Carswell. This citator consists of a set of volumes listing federal, provincial and territorial statutes by title as well as those cases that have considered each statute. Statutes are listed alphabetically by jurisdiction (see Illustration 7.3).

Federal Statutes: *Canada Statute Service* (Canada Law Book) in loose-leaf format (see Illustration 7.4).

Provincial Statutes: There are also numerous provincial citators, since each province has its own set of statutes. The main legal publishers each have their own versions. However, at present there are no separate citators for the smaller provinces and the territories because of a lack of purchasers. There are commercially produced statute citators for British Columbia and Ontario only. The following are examples of a few British Columbia statute citators:

- *British Columbia Statute Service* (Canada Law Book), also on CD-ROM
- *British Columbia Decisions: Statute Citator* (Canada Law Book), also available online on BestCase

Online

CanLII, LexisNexis/Quicklaw, and Westlaw Canada have statute citators built into their legislation databases. Once you have located your chosen legislation it is often simply a matter of clicking the link to the citator and you will see a list of cases that have considered that particular statute. Because these statutes are already current and consolidated, you will not see the changes and amendments to the statute featured separately.

Illustration 7.3
Canadian Statute Citations
(*Canadian Abridgment*, Carswell)

ILLUSTRATION

Statutes
This sample is taken from the Canada section of the statutes:

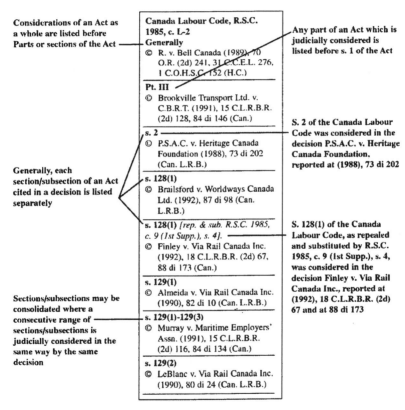

Considerations of an Act as a whole are listed before Parts or sections of the Act

Any part of an Act which is judicially considered is listed before s. 1 of the Act

Generally, each section/subsection of an Act cited in a decision is listed separately

S. 2 of the Canada Labour Code was considered in the decision P.S.A.C. v. Heritage Canada Foundation, reported at (1988), 73 di 202

Sections/subsections may be consolidated where a consecutive range of sections/subsections is judicially considered in the same way by the same decision

S. 128(1) of the Canada Labour Code, as repealed and substituted by R.S.C. 1985, c. 9 (1st Supp.), s. 4, was considered in the decision Finley v. Via Rail Canada Inc., reported at (1992), 18 C.L.R.B.R. (2d) 67 and at 88 di 173

Canada Labour Code, R.S.C. 1985, c. L-2
Generally
© R. v. Bell Canada (1989), 70 O.R. (2d) 241, 31 C.C.E.L. 276, 1 C.O.H.S.C. 152 (H.C.)

Pt. III
© Brookville Transport Ltd. v. C.B.R.T. (1991), 15 C.L.R.B.R. (2d) 128, 84 di 146 (Can.)

s. 2
© P.S.A.C. v. Heritage Canada Foundation (1988), 73 di 202 (Can. L.R.B.)

s. 128(1)
© Brailsford v. Worldways Canada Ltd. (1992), 87 di 98 (Can. L.R.B.)

s. 128(1) *[rep. & sub. R.S.C. 1985, c. 9 (1st Supp.), s. 4].*
© Finley v. Via Rail Canada Inc. (1992), 18 C.L.R.B.R. (2d) 67, 88 di 173 (Can.)

s. 129(1)
© Almeida v. Via Rail Canada Inc. (1990), 82 di 10 (Can. L.R.B.)

s. 129(1)-129(3)
© Murray v. Maritime Employers' Assn. (1991), 15 C.L.R.B.R. (2d) 116, 84 di 134 (Can.)

s. 129(2)
© LeBlanc v. Via Rail Canada Inc. (1990), 80 di 24 (Can. L.R.B.)

Canadian Statute Citations. Reprinted by permission of Carswell, a division of Thomson Reuters Canada Limited.

Illustration 7.4
Canada Statute Citator (Canada Law Book)

CANADA

STATUTE

CITATOR

R.S.C. 1985

VOLUME 3

Canadian Heritage Languages Act to Customs Tariff

Legal Editor
Adela Rodriguez, B.Sc., LL.B.

Production Editor
Christine Schpuniar

CANADA LAW BOOK
A Division of The Cartwright Group Ltd.
240 EDWARD STREET, AURORA, ONTARIO, L4G 3S9
www.canadalawbook.ca

DEC. 2009

CITIZENSHIP ACT
R.S.C. 1985, Chap. C-29
Amended R.S.C. 1985, c. 28 (1st Supp.), s. 49
Amended R.S.C. 1985, c. 30 (3rd Supp.), s. 11
Amended R.S.C. 1985, c. 44 (3rd Supp.)
Amended R.S.C. 1985, c. 28 (4th Supp.), s. 36
Amended 1992, c. 21, ss. 6 to 8; brought into force June 30, 1992 by SI/92-126, *Can. Gaz., Part II*, July 15, 1992
Amended 1992, c. 47, s. 67; brought into force August 1, 1996 by SI/96-56
Amended 1992, c. 49, s. 124; brought into force February 1, 1993
Amended 1993, c. 28, Sch. III, s. 18; in force April 1, 1999
Amended 1995, c. 5, s. 25(1)(e); brought into force May 13, 1995 by SI/95-65, *Can. Gaz., Part II*, May 31, 1995
Amended 1995, c. 15, s. 23; brought into force July 10, 1995 by SI/95-76, *Can. Gaz., Part II*, July 12, 1995
Amended 1997, c. 22, ss. 1 to 3; brought into force May 20, 1997 by SI/97-64, *Can. Gaz., Part II*, June 11, 1997
Amended 1999, c. 31, s. 42; in force June 17, 1999
Amended 2000, c. 12, ss. 74 to 77; ss. 74, 75 brought into force July1, 2003 by SI/2003-118, *Can. Gaz., Part II*, June 18, 2003; ss. 76, 77 to come into force as provided by these sections
Amended 2000, c. 24, s. 33; brought into force October 23, 2000 by SI/2000-95, *Can. Gaz., Part II*, November 8, 2000
Amended 2001, c. 26, s. 286; brought into force July 1, 2007 by SI/2007-65, *Can. Gaz. Part II*, June 27, 2007
Amended 2001, c. 27, ss. 227.1 to 232; brought into force June 28, 2002 by para. (*f*) of SI/2002-97, *Can. Gaz., Part II*, June 14, 2002
Amended 2002, c. 7, s. 131; brought into force April 1, 2003 by SI/2003-48, *Can. Gaz., Part II*, April 9, 2003
Amended 2002, c. 8, ss. 182(1)(*j*), 183(1)(*d*); brought into force July 2, 2003 by SI/2003-109, *Can. Gaz., Part II*, June 4, 2003
Amended 2003, c. 22, s. 149; brought into force April 1, 2005 by para. (*b*) of SI/2005-24, *Can. Gaz., Part II*, April 6, 2005
Amended 2005, c. 10, s. 14; brought into force April 4, 2005 by SI/2005-29, *Can. Gaz., Part II*, April 20, 2005
Amended 2005, c. 17, s. 1; in force May 5, 2005
Amended 2007, c. 24, ss. 1 to 3.1; in force December 22, 2007
Amended 2008, c. 14, ss. 1 to 12 and 13(2) to (4); in force April 17, 2009 as provided by s. 14

Administered by the Department of Citizenship and Immigration

Generally

NOTE: SI/94-86 (P.C. 1994-1122, June 30, 1994), *Can. Gaz., Part II*, July 27, 1994, designates the Minister of Citizenship and Immigration as Minister of this Act.

NOTE: 1997, c. 22, s. 10 provides as follows:

10. If, before section 1 of this Act comes into force, a legal proceeding has been commenced with respect to an investigation under subsection 19(4) of the *Citizenship Act*, a final decision in that proceeding that the Review Committee must cease its investigation is deemed to be a decision of the Review Committee under subsection 19(4.1) of that Act, as enacted by subsection 1(2) of this Act.

HOW TO LOCATE, UPDATE AND NOTE UP STATUTES

Now that you understand how the law is made and published in Canada and you are familiar with some of the tools, you are ready to locate statutes. If, from your secondary research, you already know the title or the citation of a statute it will be fairly easy to locate both in paper and online. If not, you will need to search for the statute by subject or topic, which is more difficult.

Statutes are generally easy to find because each of the governments that create them also print them (usually through the Queen's Printer) and publish them on their websites. However, before jumping online, you may want to consider conducting a search in the library. Here are a few things to consider.

Electronic versus Paper

Although computers have revolutionized statute research, some legal research may involve finding statutes in paper form, in a law library. The statutes in print are still the only sources that are considered official in most of the provinces with federal, Ontario and Quebec statutes online being the exceptions. Not only that, but the complete historical versions of statutes are still not available from either CanLII, government websites, or the commercial databases, so it is highly likely that you will have to consult statutes in print at some point while doing legal research.

Learning about the print versions can also improve your understanding of the location, layout and organization of the electronic versions. For example, many of the electronic statute databases are organized much like statute volumes on the shelves of a library. One database may contain a consolidated set of statutes with all changes integrated. Another may contain the original statutes, without showing any recent revisions.

For this reason (as we will emphasize throughout this book) you must always be sure what is contained in each of the databases. Most databases have a hyperlink (*e.g.*, "Info" button) which describes the ever-changing database contents.

Advantages of Electronic Statutes

Having said that, computers have revolutionized statute research in three key ways:

- Statute databases can be searched by a simple keyword command. However, researchers should be aware that a simple keyword search, unless carefully planned, may retrieve too many results because keyword searching will find *every* instance of a word in *every* statute. Unless you know the specific word or words that define the concepts you are looking for, you will have a difficult time locating the statute and waste time filtering through unwanted results.
- The electronic form of statutes can be kept fairly current because no time is needed to print, publish and distribute the statutes.

- The electronic version may be consolidated on a continuing basis — meaning that changes can be incorporated right into the statute so you do not have to search through several supplements and revisions to locate amendments.

One additional way in which computers have revolutionized statute research is that they have made locating the regulations that are associated with a particular statute seamless. We cover regulations in Chapter 8, as well as in this chapter in those cases where statutes and regulations can be researched together.

THE FOUR STEPS IN STATUTE RESEARCH

To determine whether a statute is relevant and whether it is still "good law" you need to:

- Locate the statute (by title, citation or subject)
- Find out whether the statute is in force (what is its effective date?)
- Find out whether the statute has been amended (update it)
- Find cases that have considered the statute (note it up)

Each of these steps is described here.

Step 1: Locate the Statute

A statute can be located by the title, by the citation or by subject.

Locating a Statute by Title

If you know the title or name of a particular statute, the statute is fairly easy to locate. You can either:

- conduct an electronic search for the title in one of the many statute databases (commercial and public non-fee collections);
- search in the library shelves in a Statute Citator (such as the *Canadian Abridgment*). It will provide you with the citation of your statute, amendments and cases that considered it; or
- search in the library shelves in an index of statutes (usually called the *Tables of Public Statutes*). It will provide you with the statute citation and any updates so you can find the volume that contains your statute.

Locating a Statute by Citation

If you know the citation of a particular statute, the statute will be fairly easy to find. You can either:

- conduct an electronic search in one of the many statute databases (commercial and public non-fee collections); or
- look in the library shelves in various volumes of statutes. Go to the volume whose date corresponds with that mentioned in your citation.

The citation provides information about where to locate a statute. It is simply an abbreviated reference used to help locate statutes. A full citation includes the title of a statute, the date it was brought into force (or revised), its location in the statute volumes and often a specific section number. A search for R.S.Y. 2002, c. 46 will take you to Chapter 46 of the 2002 Revised Statutes of the Yukon, which is the *Corrections (Young Offenders) Act*.

Locating a Statute by Subject

If you do not know the title or citation of the statute you are looking for, you will need to search by subject. The best way to begin such a search is by reading about your topic generally in secondary materials and commentaries, and refining your search. After that you can more effectively conduct an electronic search for the statute by title.

The most helpful secondary materials are the *Canadian Encyclopedic Digest* (CED), *Halsbury's Laws of Canada* and textbooks. These secondary materials are essentially explanations and commentaries about the law and are described in detail in Chapter 6 (How to Find Secondary Materials). They provide an overview of the law and direct the researcher to specific cases and statutes.

Step 2: Find Out Whether the Statute is in Force

As mentioned above, some statutes are not in force immediately. In other words, if no date is stated, then the Act is deemed to have come into force on assent. If the last section mentions a delayed date or a proclamation, then the Act has to be proclaimed.

To locate a proclamation, look in the Federal or provincial *Table of Public Statutes*, which lists the CIF (coming into force information) of the statute. Find your statute and locate the statutory instrument or regulation that brought the Act into effect (although it is really just the proclamation of the Act). Then confirm your findings by locating the specified regulation (see Chapter 8, How to Find and Update Regulations) to ensure the statute was actually "in force" on the day the client's legal issue commenced.

Step 3: Find Out if the Statute Has Been Amended (Update It)

It is very important to determine whether and how a statute has been amended. A key section that you are relying on may have been amended or repealed, which would seriously damage your legal argument. And there is always the possibility that an entire statute has been repealed or replaced with a new statute.

To locate any amendments to your statute you can use any of the following:

- **Public websites:** With electronic services, amendments are usually incorporated into the text of the consolidated statutes (on an ongoing basis). If not, you will need to find a *Table of Public Statutes* that lists the CIF (coming into force) information.

- **Commercial provider:** Conduct an electronic search for your statute in the relevant statute database. Commercial providers usually incorporate amendments and are fairly up-to-date.
- **In the library:** Find the relevant index of statutes (usually called the *Tables of Public Statutes*). It will direct you to the volume that contains your statute. Or go to one of the print-based statute citators (such as the *Canadian Abridgment*) and look in the alphabetical list.

There are two ways to find out how a statute has been amended: the official way and the unofficial way.

The Official Way: In the Table of Public Statutes

To find out if a statute has been amended (or repealed), it is fairly easy to look in the relevant federal or provincial *Table of Public Statutes*, either online or in print. Most of these tables provide the citation of the statute, amendments and coming into force (CIF) information. Others give the CIF information in separate "proclamation" tables or schedules. This method of updating a statute always works, regardless of jurisdiction, because *all* Canadian jurisdictions have some kind of tables. The drawback is that some government-produced tables may not be quite as up-to-date as commercial versions. But for some research, timeliness is not necessarily that critical, especially if your research involves some issue that happened in the relatively distant past.

Researchers need to become familiar with the layout and contents of the tables of their jurisdictions of interest. Some provinces no longer publish these tables but publish a list of legislative changes instead. In these situations it is best to use electronic sources. These tables of statutes and proclamations are usually linked from government websites that display provincial consolidated statutes. See Appendix 7C for a list of such sites.

Illustration 7.6 below (an excerpt from the Federal *Table of Public Statutes*) shows how statutes are listed alphabetically and how their location is indicated by the year, volume and chapter number of the statute. The table also lists amendments to each section. At the bottom is convenient CIF information for the original Act itself and each change to each section. Researchers must get into the habit of noting not only the changes to sections of interest, but also the CIF information.

The Unofficial Way: In Statute Citators

The unofficial way to locate amendments to a statute is by using a commercially published statute citator. The loose-leaf print versions of citators will list all statutes and provide the text of their amendments. Citators are a wonderful starting point, but all of the information must be confirmed because they are not considered official and may have errors.

Researchers should note that there are almost no remaining printed statute citators for the smaller provinces and the territories because of lack of sufficient numbers of purchasers. Also, citators are not free, as are government-produced tables. With the advent of online citators (see below), all jurisdictions now have electronic statute citators. CanLII recently introduced a new release which provides a citator function for each jurisdiction to the public at no cost.

Illustration 7.5
Cover Page of a Federal Table of Statutes

TABLE OF PUBLIC STATUTES AND RESPONSIBLE MINISTERS
(UPDATED TO DECEMBER 31, 2009)*

TABLE OF PUBLIC STATUTES AND RESPONSIBLE MINISTERS
SHOWING
ALL THE CHAPTERS OF THE REVISED STATUTES, 1985, WITH THEIR AMENDMENTS AND CERTAIN OTHER PUBLIC ACTS AND THEIR AMENDMENTS
UPDATED TO DECEMBER 31, 2009*

This Table is available in electronic form on the Justice Laws Web site at http://laws-lois.justice.gc.ca (see the left navigation menu), where it is updated regularly.

In the Table, Acts in the following categories are listed alphabetically under those headings:
Agreements   Income Tax, Estate Tax, Succession Duty, and related tax matters
Agreements — Trade, Commerce and related matters
Bridges, Electoral Districts, Provincial Boundaries, and Treaties of Peace.

Immediately under the title of each Act is the equivalent title, printed in italics, of the Act in the other official language. This will assist users in finding the Act in the French version of this Table.

The name of the minister who has responsibility for the administration of the Act is listed under the title of the Act. Where a minister is expressly designated in an Act as the minister responsible, that minister's name is given. If a minister is designated by order in council, the registration number of the designation order (SI) is included. Where no minister has been specifically designated, either in the Act or by order in council, the name of the minister who introduced the bill in Parliament is given. It should also be noted that this Table does not necessarily reflect changes in ministerial responsibilities resulting from orders made under the *Public Service Rearrangement and Transfer of Duties Act*.

The section references in bold face under an Act indicate the provisions of that Act that have been added or amended. Users should refer to the coming into force (CIF) entry for each amendment at the end of the list of amendments to an Act. CIF dates are given in day-month-year order (e.g. 05.01.06 is 5 January, 2006).

The term SOR or SI is a reference to Statutory Orders and Regulations or Statutory Instruments as published in the *Canada Gazette*, Part II. CIF refers to the date of coming into force. (E) indicates an amendment to the English version only and (F) indicates an amendment to the French version only.

To subscribe to this publication, to change the address of your current subscription or for information about your subscription, please contact: **Publishing and Depository Services, Public Works and Government Services Canada, Ottawa, Ontario K1A OS5 (Tel.: 613-941-5995; Orders only: 1-800-635-7943; Email:** Publications@pwgsc-tpsgc.gc.ca; **Internet:** http://www.publications.gc.ca).

Any comments or inquiries concerning the contents of this Table should be directed, preferably in writing, to:

Chief Legislative Editor
Department of Justice
284 Wellington Street, Room 3115 SAT   Tel.: 613-957-0026
Ottawa, Ontario K1A 0H8   Fax: 613-957-7866
                                               Email: Tabl@justice.gc.ca

---

*There are a certain number of public Acts, passed before January 1, 1985, that were not consolidated in the Revised Statutes of Canada, 1927, 1952, 1970 or 1985. As those Acts are still in force, they are included in this Table. There are also a number of sections (or parts thereof) in Acts passed before January 1, 1985, that were not consolidated in the Revised Statutes of Canada, 1927, 1952, 1970 or 1985. Those provisions may be found in Schedule A to the Revised Statutes of Canada, 1927 (p. 4283 of Volume IV), Schedule A to the Revised Statutes of Canada, 1952 (p. 5967 of Volume V (Supplement)), Schedule A (Reprinted) to the Revised Statutes of Canada, 1970 (p. 397 of the 2nd Supplement, replacing what was Schedule A in the 1st Supplement), Schedule A (Continued) to the Revised Statutes of Canada, 1970 (p. 435 of the 2nd Supplement) and the Schedules to the Revised Statutes of Canada, 1985 (Appendix I in the "Appendices" volume and the Schedules at the end of the 1st to 4th Supplements). In each Schedule the sections (or parts thereof) that were not consolidated are shown as exceptions in the third column entitled "Extent of Repeal."

Illustration 7.6
Excerpt from a Federal Table of Public Statutes

Citizenship Act — R.S., 1985, c. C-29

(Citoyenneté, Loi sur la)

Minister of Citizenship and Immigration (SI/94-86)

s. 2, R.S., c. 28 (4th Supp.), s. 36(2) (Sch., item 2); 1992, c. 21, s. 6; 2000, c. 12, s. 74; 2001, c. 26, s. 286, c. 27, s. 227.1; 2002, c. 8, par. 183(1)(*d*); 2008, c. 14, s. 1
s. 3, 1995, c. 5, s. 25(1)(*e*); 2007, c. 24, s. 1; 2008, c. 14, ss. 2 and 13(2)
s. 4, 2008, c. 14, s. 3
s. 5, R.S., c. 44 (3rd Supp.), s. 1; 1992, c. 21, s. 7; 2000, c. 12, s. 75; 2001, c. 27, s. 228; 2003, c. 22, s. 149(E); 2008, c. 14, s. 4
s. 5.1, added, 2007, c. 24, s. 2; 2008, c. 14, s. 13(3)

...

CIF, R.S., c. 28 (1st Supp.), s. 49 proclaimed in force 30.06.85 *see* SI/85-128

...

CIF, 1992, c. 1, s. 144 (Sch. VII, item 22)(F) in force on assent 28.02.92
CIF, 1992, c. 21, ss. 6 to 8 in force 30.06.92 *see* SI/92-126
CIF, 1992, c. 47, s. 67 in force 01.08.96 *see* SI/96-56

...

CIF, 1997, c. 22, ss. 1 to 3 and 10 in force 20.05.97 *see* SI/97-64
CIF, 1999, c. 31, s. 42 in force on assent 17.06.99
CIF, 2000, c. 12, ss. 76 and 77 in force on assent 29.06.2000; ss. 74 and 75 in force 01.07.2003 *see* SI/2003-118
CIF, 2000, c. 24, s. 33 in force 23.10.2000 *see* SI/2000-95
CIF, 2001, c. 26, s. 286 in force 01.07.2007 *see* SI/2007-65
CIF, 2001, c. 27, ss. 227.1 to 232 in force 28.06.2002 *see* SI/2002-97
CIF, 2002, c. 7, s. 131 in force 01.04.2003 *see* SI/2003-48
CIF, 2002, c. 8, ss. 182 and 183 in force 02.07.2003 *see* SI/2003-109
CIF, 2003, c. 22, s. 149 in force 01.04.2005 *see* SI/2005-24
CIF, 2005, c. 10, s. 14 in force 04.04.2005 *see* SI/2005-29
CIF, 2005, c. 17 in force on assent 05.05.2005
CIF, 2007, c. 24 (assent: 22.06.2007), ss. 1 to 3.1 in force 22.12.2007 *see* s. 4
CIF, 2008, c. 14, s. 13 in force on assent 17.04.2008; ss. 1 to 12 in force 17.04.2009 *see* s. 14

This information reads as follows:

Top Line — The *Citizenship Act* (Canada) can be found in the *Revised Statutes of Canada, 1985* in c. C-29. Therefore, the proper citation for this statute is: *Citizenship Act*, R.S.C. 1985, c. C-29.

Line 6 — Section 5 of the *Citizenship Act* was amended in the *Revised Statutes of Canada, 1985*, Chapter 44 (3rd supplement), by s. 1; in 1992, Chapter 21, by s. 7; in 2000, Chapter 12, by s. 75; in 2001, Chapter 27, by s. 228; in 2003, Chapter 22, by s. 149(E) and in 2008, Chapter 14, by s. 4.

If you look at the CIF (coming into force) references (bolded above), you can see that these amendments came into effect on 30.06.92, 29.06.2000, 01.07.2003, 28.06.2002, 01.04.2005, 17.04.2008 and 17.04.2009, respectively.

As a final step and to ensure that your statute is completely up-to-date, check the current session bills to see if there are any more recent amendments to statutes (*i.e.*, those published after the date of publication of the most recent table of statutes). You can locate current session bills on the websites from the various legislatures. Look very closely for the date that the information was updated. If it is a few days old, it is best to update even further by speaking to a law librarian, who can usually provide you with contact information for the clerk of the appropriate legislature.

Locate the Amending Statute

Armed with the citation of the amending statute, a researcher can locate the amending statute(s). Amending statutes may amend more than one statute, so you may have to locate the specific sections that amend your particular statute. For example, if you look up the first amendment to s. 5 of the *Citizenship Act* (in c. 44 (3rd supplement) of the *Revised Statutes of Canada, 1985*), you will see that the title of the statute is *An Act to amend the Citizenship Act (period of residence)*. Section 1 of that Act amends the *Citizenship Act*.

You can ensure that the amendment is effective by looking up the regulation that brought the amendment into effect. For example, you can see from the *Table of Public Statutes and Responsible Ministers* above that the first amendment to s. 5 of the *Citizenship Act* came into effect on 15.02.88 (that is, February 15, 1988) by proclamation (published as a statutory instrument numbered SI/88-32). Again, researchers rarely need to look at the actual written proclamation since it is verifiable by consulting various government-produced tables.

Step 4: Find Cases That Considered the Statute (Note It Up)

The way in which a court interprets a statute is as important to statutory research as locating the statute itself. Cases tell a researcher how a statute has been interpreted by the courts and whether it is consistent with the Constitution and other statutes. Therefore, locating cases that have considered statutes is a vital part of statute research. This step is called noting up a statute.

To locate cases that have considered your statute you can do any of the following:

- **Public (no-fee) websites:** None of the government sites keep track of cases that considered statutes. On CanLII, however, you can note up a statute by clicking on the "Noteup" link. This will provide you with links

to the cases that have considered the statute that you are researching, but only those cases that are included in the CanLII database
- **Commercial providers:** Conduct an electronic search for your statute in the relevant statute database. From inside this statute you can usually use the "citation" function to be hyperlinked to a list of cases that considered your statutes. Or you can go directly to the *Statute Citator* database if there is one.
- **In the library:** Find one of the print-based Statute Citators (such as in the *Canadian Abridgment's Canadian Statute Citations*) and look in the alphabetical list.

The following section explains how to use electronic statutes, then describes how to find, update and note up statutes for each of the main providers of statutes, namely:

- *CanLII* (The Canadian Legal Information Institute);
- Federal, provincial and territorial government websites;
- Westlaw Canada;
- LexisNexis/QuickLaw

When Using Electronic Statutes

LexisNexis/Quicklaw and *Westlaw Canada* have databases of statutes and regulations for the federal, provincial and territorial governments. The two services are almost identical in terms of content, although they have different types of interface and varying search tools and updater features.

CanLII and the government sites are free services while LexisNexis/Quicklaw and Westlaw Canada are accessible for a fee. As law firms are becoming more aware of the cost of using electronic databases, they often encourage researchers to take advantage of free sources before using the commercial databases.

No matter what online service you are using, it is critical that you find out exactly what is in each database and how current the information is. Always use the service provider's information tools (often a hyperlink or button) to check the coverage and currency of the database before you do a search. To conduct absolutely up-to-date research you may need to search in print sources or even phone the legislature. Here is a quick checklist to use when searching statutes online:

- Note the date of the most recent consolidation (*i.e.*, which amendments have been incorporated into the text?).
- Look for the "in force" information (when did the regulation come into effect?).
- Look for the date up to which the whole database is current.
- Update further if necessary offline.

For any online statutes the following information pertains:

- Most online statutes are consolidated versions, so any amendments have been incorporated into the text. Therefore updating is only necessary from the most recent consolidation.

- There are essentially two ways to find a statute online. You can either conduct a **word search** from a template (full-text search) or you can **browse** the alphabetical lists of regulations and the lists of empowering statutes (like in print).

How to Find Statutes Using CanLII

CanLII (<http://www.CanLII.org>) is the best free source for all consolidated current federal, provincial and territorial statutes and regulations.

CanLII gets all its information from government and researchers, and the website is updated fairly frequently so the information is fairly accurate, but the versions provided are still not considered official for the purposes of the courts. In addition to providing the text of current statutes, CanLII adds value by providing currency, in-force and amendment information.

Step 1: Locate the Statute

From the landing page (the default search page at Illustration 7.7) you are given the option of conducting a word search of the whole database ("Search all CanLII Databases") or to limit your search to a particular jurisdiction (by selecting that jurisdiction from the menu on the left).

In the template you can either do a full-text word search (Field 1) or enter the information about your case (*e.g.*, statute name / case name / citation / docket number in Field 2) to limit your search.

For example, if you know the **citation** (2001, S.O. 2001, c. 32) enter this information in Field 2. This search field is very forgiving, so a search for *2001 SO 2001 c32* will yield the same results as a search for the properly punctuated *2001, S.O. 2001, c. 32*. You can then narrow your search further (in Field 4) by selecting either Legislation, Courts, or Boards and Tribunals.

If you know your jurisdiction (*e.g.*, the *Ontarians with Disabilities Act*), you can select the link for that jurisdiction, and then follow the "Statutes and Regulations" link. You can then either **browse** the alphabetical list (arranged by short title), or you can conduct a **word search**.

If you are searching by **subject**, it is best to use Field 1 (a full-text search), making sure you limit your search to legislation only. CanLII does not provide a subject index.

Illustration 7.7
CanLII Default Search Page

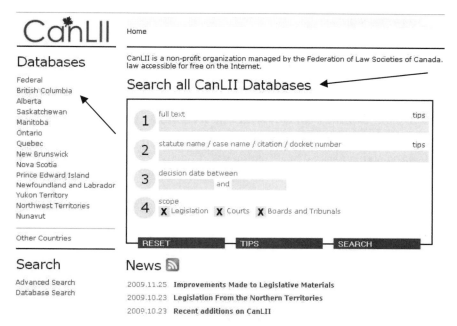

Reproduced by permission of CanLII.

Steps 2 and 3: Find Out Whether the Statute Is in Force and If it Has Been Amended

Once you have located your statute, you will see not only the text of the statute but links to previous versions, if they are available.

To ensure the statute is **current** and **in force,** read the currency information that appears at the beginning of the text of each statute. CanLII provides the date on which the statute came into force as well as the date the database was last updated. If you are doing historical research, CanLII provides the ability to compare current and previous versions of a statute on one screen.

To make sure you are completely current you will still have to check current session bills for very recent and pending amendments. To do this, go to the website for the appropriate legislature and search for bills that amend your statute. These websites provide the full text of each bill and information on its status or progress through the house.

Step 4: Find Cases That Have Considered the Statute (Note It Up)

To **note up** the statute (*i.e.*, to see if it has been considered in the courts), once you have located the statute click the "Noteup" tab and then the search button. Links to cases that have considered that statute will be displayed. You can limit your search to a particular section of the Act if necessary. Be aware that noting-up on CanLII is not comprehensive as this feature is limited to cases included in this database.

Locate Regulations

To locate **regulations** by title or enabling statute, select your jurisdiction and follow the "Statutes and Regulations" link to the lists of regulations organized alphabetically by title and by the title of the enabling statute. (See Chapter 8 for a complete description of how regulations are made and how to find them in print.)

How to Find Statutes on Government Websites

Each government website provides access to current, in-force consolidated statutes and regulations. Some of the sites also supply links to recent volumes of the annual statutes which are the original source of the legislation that appears in the current consolidation.

Even though these statutes come from government websites, in most cases, (with the exception of those from the federal, Ontario and Quebec governments) they are not considered official and therefore cannot be presented in a court of law. For these jurisdictions, print versions are still required.

If you are looking for a shortcut to government websites, the Bora Laskin Law Library provides a list entitled *Internet Sources of Canadian Legislation and Parliamentary Material* which has links to the Federal, Provincial and Territorial Parliaments & Assemblies, Debates, Bills, Statutes, Regulations, Gazettes, Journals and Votes & Proceedings at <http://www.law-lib.utoronto.ca/resources/locate/canleg.htm>. (See also Appendix 7C: Legislation on Government Websites.)

Step 1: Locate the Statute

All government websites provide alphabetical lists of statutes by short titles so most statute research involves browsing through lists of statutes. Therefore, you will likely need to know the short title of your statute before you start.

Some governments allow for title or full-text searching (see Illustration 7.8). If the site provides full text, read the information on the site about how to conduct a search before you start.

If you know the **title** of the statute, browse for it using the alphabetical list provided. You may be able to search for a **citation** or **subject** if the website allows full-text searching. Searching by subject, however, is the least efficient way of locating applicable legislation.

Steps 2 and 3: Find Out Whether the Statute Is In Force and If It Has Been Amended

To ensure that the statute is **current** and **in force**, you will need to check the currency dates provided.

Some websites provide the currency information as part of the statute. Others provide a link to a legislative history page which provides currency and in force information as well as alerting the researcher to pending amendments. Others simply highlight the currency date on the main page of the site and some provide links to a Table of Public Statutes or Acts. To ensure each statute is up-to-date, check current session bills for very recent and pending amendments. The website for each legislature provides the full text of each bill and information on its status or progress through the house.

Step 4: Find Cases That Have Considered the Statute (Note It Up)

To **note up** the statute, you will need to use a commercial provider or print source since government websites do not provide this information.

To Locate Regulations

To locate **regulations**, look under the name of the enabling statute. Regulations are generally appended to the enabling statute but they might also be located in a separate regulations page.

Illustration 7.8
Government of British Columbia Website
Statutes and Regulations of British Columbia

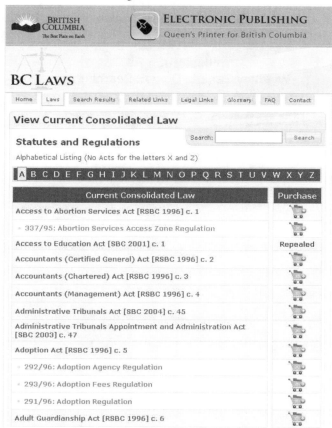

As you can see in the illustration, each consolidated statute, with its corresponding regulations, is listed and is available in electronic form. The currency date, that is, the date of the most recent consolidation, is usually shown at the top of the text of each Act once you have clicked the link. It is important to the researcher to know how recently the text has been consolidated (also referred to as "revised"). The historical tables or legislative changes may be listed below each statute, or changes may be in a separate table.

How to Find Statutes Using *Westlaw Canada*

Westlaw Canada provides unofficial consolidations of in-force statutes and their amendments. It also provides 2,500 of the "most frequently consulted regulations". Since not all regulations are included in this database, researchers must be aware that a regulation search in Westlaw Canada may not be complete. The database also includes rules of court for every jurisdiction except Quebec.

The currency information is provided below the title of each statute so you are able to find out when the database was last updated. Westlaw Canada also includes legislative concordances for family law, personal property security acts, rules of civil procedure and securities acts. These concordances allow the researcher to locate all legislation on a particular topic from all jurisdictions in Canada.

Illustration 7.9
Westlaw Canada Default Search Page

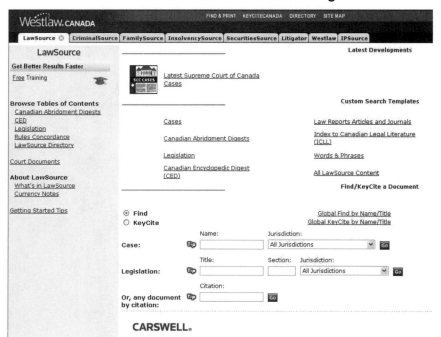

Reprinted by permission of Carswell, a division of Thomson Reuters Canada Limited.

Step 1: Locate the Statute

On the landing page (LawSource) you are given three options:

- go to the "Custom Search Template" and click on "Legislation";
- go to "Find/Keycite a Document" and use the template to conduct a global database search; or
- go to the "Browse Tables of Contents" (in left margin) and click on "Legislation". This will take you to a list of statutes, organized by jurisdiction and alphabetically. From there you are linked to the full text.

If you know the **title, citation or subject**, it is best to use the "Custom Search Template" and the *Legislation* database and search in the templates provided.

On the *Legislation* search page you will be given the choice of either using the template or conducting a more specific word search using "Terms and Connectors" — with Boolean operators and proximity searching or "Natural Language" (phrase your search in the form of a question). Check to make sure you are doing it properly by clicking the "Searching Tips" link.

Either way, you will see the search results are similar. Each individual section of the statute has its own page. If you found the statute through a word search you can click the Next or Previous links to navigate through the document. If you found it through the Table of Contents, each individual section will have a direct link.

Steps 2 and 3: Find Out Whether the Statute Is In Force and If It Has Been Amended

The **currency** date of each statute is indicated at the top of each page. In addition, the text includes amendments that are not yet in force, clearly identified with gray highlighting, so that the researcher can be aware of pending changes to the legislation. The database does not, however, provide information about the date on which the statute originally came into force.

Westlaw Canada does not have a database of current bills, so you will need to find the most recent amendments or updates since the *Legislation* database was last updated by going to the appropriate government website. The website for each legislature provides the full text of each bill and information on its status or progress through the house.

Step 4: Find Cases That Have Considered the Statute (Note It Up)

To **note up** a statute (*i.e.*, to check to see if it has been considered in the courts) you can use the citation feature called *Keycite Canada.*

When you have located the section of the statute you are interested in, click on the "Related Info" tab and then select the "Citing References" link, which will provide a list of cases, with links to the full text, which have considered each section of your statute.

You can also note up the statute directly by entering its title or citation into the *Keycite* section of the main search page. *Keycite* will note up previous revisions as well as court rules and regulations. Once you have noted up the statute you can use the "Limit Citing References" feature to narrow your search down to cases that include a particular word or concept. *Keycite Canada* may also include references to relevant commentary if available.

To Locate Regulations

To locate **regulations**, you can use the *Legislation* search template if you know the title of the regulation. If you do not know the title of the regulation but know the title of the enabling statute, you should browse the *Legislation* Table of Contents by jurisdiction and the title of the statute. Regulations can be noted up the same way you note up statutes using *KeyCite Canada*.

How to Find Statutes Using LexisNexis Quicklaw

LexisNexis/Quicklaw also provides unofficial current consolidations of statutes and regulations from all jurisdictions in Canada. The regulations collection in this database is more complete than the collection in Westlaw Canada. It includes all regulations from June 2002 onwards for all jurisdictions. In addition, LN/QL provides point-in-time versions of statutes from the federal government and the provinces of Ontario, Alberta and British Columbia. Point-in-time versions enable researchers to view all the versions of a particular section of a statute up until the current version or any whole statute as it was at a particular date. Always check the currency information, which is provided above the title of each statute, in order to see whether the statute is up-to-date.

Illustration 7.10
LexisNexis/Quicklaw Default Search Page

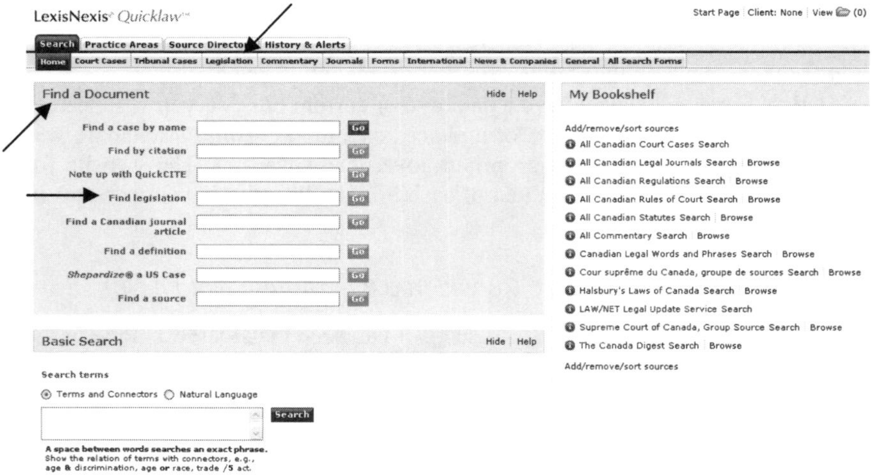

Step 1: Locate the Statute

From the landing page you are given the following options:

- use the "Find a Document" template and insert your search terms into "Find Legislation"; or
- click the "Legislation" tab (on the top) and use the search template provided.

If you know the **title** or **citation** of the statute, select the *Legislation* Tab and search *All Canadian Statutes and Regulations* or any of the jurisdiction-specific databases by title or citation. When using the *All Canadian Statutes and Regulations Database*, you can limit your search by jurisdiction and section number as well as selecting point-in-time versions of statutes from Canada, Alberta, British Columbia and Ontario.

If you are searching by **subject**, go to the *All Canadian Statutes* database and search the full text using terms and connectors as appropriate. For more information on searching, click on the "View Connectors" link.

If you know the **jurisdiction** and title of a statute, browse the *Current Consolidations* (on the left after clicking on the Legislation tab) database which is in order by jurisdiction and then by title. The link to this database appears on the left hand side of the screen that you see.

Steps 2 and 3: Find Out Whether the Statute Is in Force and If It Has Been Amended

As with Westlaw Canada, each individual section has its own page. The title page provides both currency and citation information. Each page also gives the effective (in-force) date for the statute. To ensure **currency**, check current session bills for recent or pending amendments using the appropriate government's website.

Step 4: Find Cases that Considered the Statute (Note It Up)

To **note up** your statute, check judicial consideration using *QuickCite Statutes* but be aware that *Quickcite* only notes up cases from 1992 (2005 for Quebec) and only notes up the most recent revision. Generally *QuickCite* is not as comprehensive as *Keycite Canada*.

To Locate Regulations

To locate **regulations** separately, you can search or browse *All Canadian Regulations* or any of the jurisdiction specific regulations databases. Or you can use the *All Canadian Statutes and Regulations* database to search statutes and regulations together.

CITATION OF A STATUTE

A citation provides information about where to locate a source. Therefore, the fundamental rule in all citation is to include enough information in the citation to enable a reader to locate the material referred to. There is a reason why citations take the form they do, and researchers should be aware of the logic underlying citation, as well as the precise rules of citation itself.

There are three parts to the citation of a statute:

1. Title
2. Location
3. Section Number

Example:

Powers of Attorney Act, R.S.O. 1990, c. P.20, as am. by S.O. 1992, c. 32, s. 24; 1993, c. 27, Sched.

Title

The title of the statute is obviously a critical part of a statute citation. Statutes may have very similar titles, so precision is important. It is acceptable to refer to a short title if there is one. This short title is often stated in the first section of a statute.

The title must be *italicized* and any quotations or references to years in the title must appear in the citation exactly as they do in the title. For example, statutes may have a date in the title that distinguishes them from other statutes with the same name. The title must be italicized or underlined. In the above example, this is *not* the case.

Location

Statutes are labelled by the year they were brought into effect (or revised) and a specific chapter number. Each statute is published in an annual or sessional volume. The following abbreviations describe the volumes and chapter designation:

- Statutes = S. (*i.e.*, annual or sessional volumes)
- Revised Statutes = R.S. (*i.e.*, consolidated volumes)
- R.S.B.C. = *Revised Statutes of British Columbia*
- R.S.C. = *Revised Statutes of Canada*
- c. = chapter

Section Number

If you refer to a specific section in a statute, you must refer to that section in the citation. The following abbreviations are used to describe section numbers:

- s. = one section
- ss. = several sections

Amendments

Although statutes are usually assumed to undergo amending over time, and likewise are often repealed over time, you may choose to specify a specific statute that amended or repealed another one, particularly if the amendment or repeal is crucial to your presentation or argument. If you choose to identify the repealing or amending Act, add its citation to the end of the primary citation, as shown below. Otherwise, the title of the amending statute is simply omitted in the citation. Use these abbreviations:

- as amended = as am.; *or* as am. by citation to amending Act
- repealed by = as rep.; *or* as rep. by citation to repealing Act
- an Act that amends an earlier Act = amending
- an Act that repeals an earlier Act = repealing

Punctuation

Some basic rules of punctuation in statute citation are as follows:

- Use periods after abbreviations.
- Use commas after the title and the year.
- Use commas before notations (*i.e.*, as am. by).

Electronic Citations

If the statute is taken from an Internet source, it is recommended that you add that information to the citation, for the ease of readers trying to locate that statute. If a commercial online system was used, add the abbreviation for the provider (*e.g.*, LN/QL or WC). If an Internet site was used, after the citation (above), add a comma and then the word "online" followed by a colon. Add the name of the website followed by the name of the specific part of the site, then the URL (Uniform Resource Locator) in angled brackets. For example:

Strata Property Act, S.B.C. 1998, c. 43, online: LN/QL

Labour Relations Regulation, B.C. Reg. 7/93, online: Queen's Printer (Revised Statutes and Consolidated Regulations) < http://www.bclaws.ca/>

If you are citing a regulation from a website which is considered an official source, use the regular citation format and omit citing to the electronic source.

SELF TEST

The answers to these questions are found at the back of the book in the "Answers to Self Tests" section.

1. Where on the Internet could you locate a statute?
2. How are statutes arranged in a library?
3. What is a table of statutes?
4. Name two commercial providers that provide access to electronic statutes.
5. What is a statute citator?

SAMPLE EXERCISES — FINDING AND UPDATING STATUTES

Objectives

At the end of this exercise you should to be able to:

- Locate a statute and its amendments in print
- Determine the effective date of a statute
- Locate cases that have considered a statute
- Properly cite a statute

Instructions

- Do background reading on how to locate, update and cite statutes.
- Keep a record of all of the steps and time taken to complete the exercise.

Provincial Statutes

Read the following fact pattern and answer the following questions. Assume the research situation occurred in your province.

Fact Pattern

Mr. Chapps

Mr. Chapps has recently acquired the property of his dreams. After years of saving he finally was able to purchase an old farmhouse on a piece of property overlooking a lake. He moved into the farmhouse last month and has just begun to renovate.

Two days ago, he received a letter from the Minister of Municipal Affairs. The letter stated, "This letter will serve as notice of expropriation." It went on to explain that Mr. Chapp's property was going to be expropriated so that the city could build a sewage treatment plant on it. Mr. Chapp is very upset and wants to know what he can do to fight the expropriation.

1. Before entering the library, brainstorm for possible legal subject areas. List about five words relating to the above research situation that you might search for in the library.

    Words:

2. Using either a provincial subject index or a table of statutes, find a statute relevant to your research situation. Give the proper citation to the most recent consolidation of that statute.

    Citation:

Amendments

3. Use the most recent table of statutes or table of legislative changes to determine whether the consolidated statute you found in Q. 2 above has ever been amended. Locate one amendment to s. 2 of that Act and give the full citation of the amending statute. Locate that statute and record the name.

    Citation:

    Coming into Force:

4. Look at the table of legislative changes from Q. 3 above. Does it provide effective dates of legislation? If yes, what was the effective date (CIF) of s. 1 of the amending statute you found in Q. 3 above?

    Date of CIF:

Statutes Judicially Considered

5. Using the *Canadian Abridgment, Canadian Statute Citations*, locate your statute and record:

    a. A case name that considered the statute:
    b. Section number of the statute that was considered:
    c. Volume and date of the citator:

Federal Statutes

1. Give the proper citation for the following federal statute: S.C. 1990, c. 22.

    Citation:

Amendments

2. Using the most recent federal *Table of Public Statutes and Responsible Ministers*, determine whether the statute from Q. 1 above was amended. Note the amendment to s. 46 and record the citation. Locate the amending statute and give the full citation, including the name of the statute, and explain how and when it came into effect.

    Citation:

Statutes Judicially Considered

3. Locate the *Canadian Abridgment, Canadian Statute Citations* (Carswell) and the *Canada Statute Citator* (Canada Law Book). Find your statute in both sources and record the name of a case that has considered the statute. Record the section number of the statute that has been considered by the case. If the statute has not been judicially considered, state this.

   a. Case name:
   b. Section number:
   c. Name of citator:

Electronic Resources

1. Using Westlaw Canada or LexisNexis/Quicklaw, locate a case from 2000 that has considered British Columbia's *Good Samaritan Act*, R.S.B.C. 1996, c. 172.

2. Using CanLII, locate and cite the statute that identifies the mineral emblem for the province of Newfoundland and Labrador.

ANSWERS TO SAMPLE EXERCISES

Note: Amendments occurring after the publication of this text will not be shown in these answers.

Provincial Statutes

(British Columbia was used to answer this question.)

1. Words: municipal affairs; property; expropriation; sewage treatment.
2. Citation: *Expropriation Act*, R.S.B.C. 1996, c. 125.

Amendments

3. The most recent *Table of Legislative Changes* (changes in force) dated Jan. 1, 2005-Dec. 31, 2008 states that amendments were made to s. 1 (and other sections) of the *Expropriation Act*. The first amendment to s. 1 was made by 2004-61-1. If you look up this statute in the annual volume for 1994, c. 61, s. 1, you find the *Expropriation Amendment Act, 2004*, S.B.C, c. 61. Section 1 of that Act amends the *Expropriation Act*.

4. Yes, it does give effective dates. Date of CIF: March 18, 2005.

Statutes Judicially Considered

5. a. *Okanagan Opal Inc. v. British Columbia (Minister of Transportation & Highways)* (2007), 92 L.C.R. 239, 58 R.P.R. (4th) 232, 2007 CarswellBC 1215, BCSC 754 (B.C.S.C.)

   b. Generally

    c. *Canadian Statute Citator (Canadian Abridgment)* — BC Volume A-E (October 2003-September 2008)

Federal Statutes

1. *Plant Protection Act*, S.C. 1990, c. 22.

Amendments

2. Yes, the statute has been amended. For example, s. 21 was amended twice by S.C. 1997, c. 6, s. 82 and by S.C. 2005, c. 38, s. 123. The *Table of Public Statutes* shows that S.C. 1997, c. 6, s. 82 came into force 01.04.1997 and S.C. 2005, c. 38, s. 123 came into force on 12.12.2005. (You could confirm this by merely going to the statute, but that is not necessary. The table is official.)

Statutes Judicially Considered

3. *Canadian Statute Citations* (Carswell)

    a. *Adams v. Borrel* (2008), 336 N.B.R. (2d) 223, [2008] N.B.J. No. 327, 2008 NBCA 62, 2008 CarswellNB 424, 2008 CarswellNB 425, 297 D.L.R. (4th) 400, 60 C.C.L.T. (3d) 161, 862 A.P.R. 223, (N.B.C.A.)

    b. Generally

    c. *Canadian Statute Citations (Canadian Abridgment)* (October 2006 to September 2009) Vol. Canada J to Z / International.

Canada Statute Citator (Canada Law Book):

    a. *Rodd v. Canada (Minister of Agriculture)* (2005), 2005 FC 1625.

    b. s. 58

    c. *Canada Statute Citator*, Vol. 7 (June 2006)

Electronic Resources

1. *Stevenson v. Clearview Riverside Resort*, 2000 CarswellOnt 4888, [2000] O.J. No. 4863 (Ont. S.C.J. Dec. 21, 2000).

2. *Mineral Emblem Act*, R.S.N.L. 1990, c. M-13.

Appendix 7A: Sample Federal Statute and Legislative History

The following is an example of the first page of a typical federal statute.

57-58 ELIZABETH II

CHAPTER 10

An Act to amend the Customs Act

[Assented to 11th June, 2009]

Her Majesty, by and with the advice and consent of the Senate and House of Commons of Canada, enacts as follows:

R.S., c. 1 (2nd Supp.)

CUSTOMS ACT

1998, c. 19, s. 262(1)

1. Subsection 2(4) of the French version of the *Customs Act* is replaced by the following:

Délégation

(4) Le ministre peut autoriser un agent ou une catégorie d'agents à exercer les pouvoirs et fonctions, y compris les pouvoirs et fonctions judiciaires ou quasi judiciaires, qui lui sont conférés en vertu de la présente loi.

2001, c. 25, s. 11

2. (1) Paragraph 11.3(*a*) of the Act is replaced by the following:

(*a*) has been authorized by the Minister; or

(2) Section 11.3 of the Act is renumbered as subsection 11.3(1) and is amended by adding the following:

Amendment, etc., of authorization

(2) The Minister may amend, suspend, renew, cancel or reinstate an authorization.

2001, c. 25, s. 11

3. (1) The portion of subsection 11.4(1) of the Act before paragraph (*a*) is replaced by the following:

Presentation and reporting — when leaving customs controlled area

11.4 (1) Subject to subsection (2), every person who is leaving a customs controlled area shall, if requested to do so by an officer,

57-58 ELIZABETH II

CHAPITRE 10

Loi modifiant la Loi sur les douanes

[Sanctionnée le 11 juin 2009]

Sa Majesté, sur l'avis et avec le consentement du Sénat et de la Chambre des communes du Canada, édicte :

LOI SUR LES DOUANES

L.R., ch. 1 (2ᵉ suppl.)

1. Le paragraphe 2(4) de la version française de la *Loi sur les douanes* est remplacé par ce qui suit :

1998, ch. 19, par. 262(1)

(4) Le ministre peut autoriser un agent ou une catégorie d'agents à exercer les pouvoirs et fonctions, y compris les pouvoirs et fonctions judiciaires ou quasi judiciaires, qui lui sont conférés en vertu de la présente loi.

Délégation

2. (1) L'alinéa 11.3*a*) de la même loi est remplacé par ce qui suit :

2001, ch. 25, art. 11

a) est autorisée par le ministre;

(2) L'article 11.3 de la même loi devient le paragraphe 11.3(1) et est modifié par adjonction de ce qui suit :

(2) Le ministre peut modifier, suspendre, renouveler, annuler ou rétablir une autorisation.

Modification, suspension, etc.

3. (1) Le passage du paragraphe 11.4(1) de la même loi précédant l'alinéa *a*) est remplacé par ce qui suit :

2001, ch. 25, art. 11

11.4 (1) Sous réserve du paragraphe (2), la personne qui quitte une zone de contrôle des douanes doit, à la demande de tout agent :

Présentation et déclaration — en quittant une zone de contrôle des douanes

Since 2003, the federal Queen's Printer has been supplying a legislative history that is bound adjacent to each statute in the annual statutory volumes. This history gives the original bill number and all of the steps through which the bill went, in both the House of Commons and the Senate. Thus, the researcher has all the necessary background information pertaining to the progress and passage of the legislation.

The following is an example of a page from the Legislative History describing the various readings of this statute.

LEGISLATIVE HISTORY / HISTORIQUE

An Act to amend the Customs Act – Bill S-2
(Introduced by: Leader of the Government in the Senate)
Loi modifiant la Loi sur les douanes – Projet de loi S-2
(Déposé par : Le leader du gouvernement au Sénat)

House of Commons / Chambre des communes		Senate / Sénat	
Bill Stage / Étape du projet de loi	**Date**	**Bill Stage / Étape du projet de loi**	**Date**
First Reading / Première lecture	2009-04-27	First Reading / Première lecture	2009-01-29
Debate(s) at Second Reading / Débat(s) à la deuxième lecture	2009-05-04 2009-05-05	Debate(s) at Second Reading / Débat(s) à la deuxième lecture	2009-02-03 2009-02-24 2009-02-25 2009-03-03
Second Reading / Deuxième lecture	2009-05-05	Second Reading / Deuxième lecture	2009-03-03
Committee / Comité	Public Safety and National Security / Sécurité publique et nationale	Committee / Comité	National Security and Defence / Sécurité nationale et défense
Committee Meeting(s) / Réunion(s) du comité	2009-05-26	Committee Meeting(s) / Réunion(s) du comité	2009-03-30
Committee Report / Rapport du comité	2009-05-26	Committee Report / Rapport du comité	2009-03-31
Debate(s) at Report Stage / Débat(s) à l'étape du rapport	2009-05-28	Debate(s) at Report Stage / Débat(s) à l'étape du rapport	2009-03-31 2009-04-01 2009-04-02 2009-04-21
Report Stage / Étape du rapport	2009-05-28	Report Stage / Étape du rapport	2009-04-21
Debate(s) at Third Reading / Débat(s) à la troisième lecture	2009-05-28	Debate(s) at Third Reading / Débat(s) à la troisième lecture	2009-04-22 2009-04-23
Third Reading / Troisième lecture	2009-05-28	Third Reading / Troisième lecture	2009-04-23
Royal Assent: June 11, 2009, Statutes of Canada, 2009, chapter 10 **Sanction royale : Le 11 juin 2009, Lois du Canada (2009), chapitre 10**			

Appendix 7B: Sample Provincial Statute

The following is an example of the first page of a typical provincial statute.

ELECTION AMENDMENT ACT, 2008

CHAPTER 41

Assented to May 29, 2008

HER MAJESTY, by and with the advice and consent of the Legislative Assembly of the Province of British Columbia, enacts as follows:

Election Act

1   *Section 1 of the Election Act, R.S.B.C. 1996, c. 106, is amended by repealing the definition of* "conduct".

2   *The following section is added to Part 1:*

Act does not inhibit government or members

3.1   (1) For greater certainty, nothing in this Act affects an officer, director, employee or agent of one of the following bodies in the doing of an act necessary for carrying out the proper function of the body:

      (a) the government as reported through the consolidated revenue fund;

      (b) a government corporation within the meaning of the *Financial Administration Act* other than one that is a government corporation solely by reason of being, under an Act, an agent of the government;

      (c) a corporation or organization that, under generally accepted accounting principles, is considered to be controlled by

          (i) the government as reported through the consolidated revenue fund, or

         (ii) a government corporation within the meaning of the *Financial Administration Act* other than one that is a government corporation solely by reason of being, under an Act, an agent of the government.

     (2) For greater certainty, nothing in this Act affects a member of the Legislative Assembly in the doing of an act necessary for the performance of the member's duties.

3   *Section 12 (1) is amended by adding the following paragraph:*

      (d) to ensure that this Act is enforced.

4   *Section 18 is amended*

  (a) by repealing subsection (1) (b) and substituting the following:

      (b) one or more deputy district electoral officers, who are to assist the district electoral officer. ,

1

Appendix 7C: Legislation on Government Websites

Although much legislation can be linked through CanLII (<www.canlii.org>), not all bills and gazettes are available through that site. Sometimes you may want to go directly to the original government website, especially if you are looking for progress of bills, and names, e-mail addresses and telephone numbers of government officials and members of the legislature.

Jurisdiction	Description	
Federal	URL:	<http://laws.justice.gc.ca/en/index.html>
	Contains:	Official Current Consolidated Statutes and Regulations
		Annual Statutes from 2002 onward
	Browsable:	Alphabetically by title
	Searchable:	Searches full text
		Simple and Advanced searches are available
	Regulations:	Accompany the text of the enabling statute
Alberta	URL:	<http://www.qp.alberta.ca/Laws_Online.cfm>
	Contains:	Current Consolidated Statutes and Regulations
	Browsable:	Alphabetically by title
	Searchable:	No full-text searching
		Can Search by title or Chapter or regulation number
	Regulations:	Are listed alphabetically rather than by association with their enabling statute
British Columbia	URL:	<http://www.bclaws.ca/>
	Contains:	Current Consolidated Statutes and Regulations
	Browsable:	Alphabetically by title
	Searchable:	Simple full-text searching available
	Regulations:	Are included in the alphabetical list under the name of the enabling statute
Manitoba	URL:	<http://web2.gov.mb.ca/laws/index.php>
	Contains:	Continuing Consolidation of the Statutes of Manitoba (CCSM), Municipal Acts and Private Acts
	Browsable:	Alphabetically by title
	Searchable:	Simple title-only searching available
	Regulations:	Links to regulations accompany the enabling statute

Jurisdiction	Description
New Brunswick	URL: <http://www.gnb.ca/0062/acts/> Contains: Current consolidated statutes Annual volumes of statutes and regulations from 2000 Browsable: Alphabetically by title Searchable: Simple full-text search available Regulations: Links to regulations accompany the enabling statute on the alphabetical list
Newfoundland and Labrador	URL: <http://www.assembly.nl.ca/legislation/default.htm> Contains: Current consolidated statutes Annual volumes of statutes from 1991 Browsable: Alphabetically by title Searchable: No searching available Regulations: Links to regulations accompany the enabling statute
Northwest Territories	URL: <http://www.justice.gov.nt.ca/Legislation/SearchLeg&Reg.shtml> Contains: Current consolidated statutes Browsable: Alphabetically by title Searchable: Advanced full-text search available Regulations: The Statutes and Regulations list provides links to regulations under the name of the enabling Act
Nova Scotia	URL: <http://www.gov.ns.ca/legislature/legc/acts.htm> Contains: Statutes at Large 1758-1835 Annual Statutes from 1995 Current consolidated statutes Browsable: Consolidated statutes are listed alphabetically by title Searchable: Full-text search is available Regulations: Available from the Registry of Regulations <http://www.gov.ns.ca/just/regulations/index.htm>
Nunavut	URL: <http://www.justice.gov.nu.ca/apps/authoring/dspPage.aspx?page=STATUTES+AND+REGULATIONS+PAGE> Contains: Annual Statutes from 1999 Current consolidated statutes and regulations Browsable: Consolidated statutes are listed alphabetically by title Searchable: Full-text search is available Regulations: The Statutes and Regulations list provides links to regulations under the name of the enabling Act This site provides a disclaimer that all legislation is not available as an up-to-date consolidation.

Jurisdiction	Description	
Ontario	URL:	<http://www.e-laws.gov.on.ca/index.html>
	Contains:	Annual Statutes (or source law) and regulations from 2000
		Official versions of current consolidated statutes and regulations
	Browsable:	Consolidated statutes are listed alphabetically by title
	Searchable:	Full-text search of consolidated statutes and regulations is available
	Regulations:	The Statutes and Regulations list provides links to regulations under the name of the enabling Act
Prince Edward Island	URL:	<http://www.gov.pe.ca/law/statutes/index.php3> <http://www.gov.pe.ca/law/regulations/index.php3>
	Contains:	PDFs of Office Consolidations of current statutes
	Browsable:	Statutes are listed alphabetically by title with links to regulations if you go to the regulations page
	Searchable:	There are separate search engines for statutes and regulations
	Regulations:	The regulations list provides links to both the statutes and regulations under the name of the enabling Act
Québec	URL:	<http://www3.publicationsduquebec.gouv.qc.ca/loisreglements.en.html>
	Contains:	Annual statutes from 1986
		Current compilation of Québec laws and regulations
	Browsable:	Statutes are listed alphabetically by title
	Searchable:	Full-text keyword search is available
	Regulations:	The alphabetical list provides links to the corresponding regulations under the name of the enabling Act
Saskatchewan	URL:	<http://www.publications.gov.sk.ca/deplist.cfm?d=1&c=42>
	Contains:	Current consolidated statutes
	Browsable:	Statutes are listed alphabetically by title
	Searchable:	Searching is not available
	Regulations:	Linking to the statute from the alphabetical list leads to a page with includes links to all the relevant statutes

Jurisdiction	Description
Yukon Territory	URL: <http://www.gov.yk.ca/legislation/> Contains: Annual statutes from 2003 Current consolidated statutes Browsable: Statutes are listed alphabetically by title Searchable: Searching is not available Regulations: Links to regulations are included in the alphabetical list This site also provides a link to CanLII which provides much easier access to currency and in-force information

Appendix 7D: Checklist: How to Find, Update, and Note Up Statutes

All statute research involves four steps: locating the statute (by title, citation or subject); finding the effective date of the statute; finding amendments to it (updating it); and finding cases that have considered it (noting it up). You can research statutes in a law library, through a public (no-fee) online service or through an online commercial service. Each of these services is described here.

FINDING STATUTES IN THE LIBRARY

Step 1. Locate the statute in a library

To search by title: If you know the title of a statute, go to the most recent federal or relevant provincial table of statutes (often called a Table of Public Statutes). Find your title in the alphabetical list and record its citation and any amendments.

To search by citation: If you know the citation, go to the statute volumes for the appropriate jurisdiction and look in the relevant year, volume and chapter number.

To search by subject: Read secondary sources to find keywords, topics and statute citations. Try reading law textbooks or encyclopedias such as *Halsbury's Laws of Canada* (in print and on LN/QL); the *Canadian Encyclopedic Digest* (CED) (in print or on WC). Check their currency. Once you have learned more about your topic, use that information to scan the tables of public statutes (print or electronic) or conduct a keyword search in any of the electronic sources (see below).

Step 2. Find out when the statute came into effect in a library

You can determine whether a statute has come into force ("CIF") by finding its commencement provision(s) usually listed in a table of public statutes such as the federal *Table of Public Statutes* (in print and at <http://laws.justice.gc.ca/en/publaw/index.html> or in provincial tables of proclamation.

Step 3. Update a statute in a library

Official way: To determine whether your statute has been amended or repealed, go to the relevant tables of statutes and look in the alphabetical list. Each statute is listed with all its amendments and when they came into force. If the statute has been repealed you will see that information as well. Check current session bills for the most recent amendments.

Unofficial way: You may also look in commercial statute citators (print and online), which usually include amendments and judicial considerations.

Step 4: Note up a statute in a library

To find cases which have considered your statute, look in a statute citator. Some examples of statute citators are: *Canada Statute Citator* (Canada Law Book) and *Canadian Statute Citations* (part of *Canadian Abridgment*, Carswell). Check each for currency and update from there.

FINDING STATUTES ON PUBLIC (NO-FEE) ONLINE SOURCES

There are only a few no-fee (free) online providers of legislation. The most comprehensive is CanLII, but public sites and governments sites also provide access to statutes. Each has its own databases and templates in which to locate and update statutes. Noting up is not possible through the government websites but is available through CanLII.

CanLII: <http://www.canlii.org> provides access to most current Canadian statutes, with revisions incorporated (consolidated versions).

Step 1. Locate the statute

Locate the statute by searching by title, citation or subject using the search templates.

Steps 2 and 3. Find out when the statute came into effect and update it

Look for the "in force" information and the "currency date" in the statute you have found. It is usually written on each statute. Since most electronic versions of statutes are consolidated the minute revisions to the statute come into effect, there is no need to "update" them unless the consolidated version is out-of-date. If the electronic version is not consolidated, then you must look in other databases that contain the revisions, such as databases of gazettes.

Step 4: Note up the statute

Some public (no-fee) services provide information on cases that have interpreted statutes. CanLII allows the noting-up of statutes from all Canadian jurisdictions. However, since the cases in CanLII usually go back only to the late 1990s or early 2000s, you will not get every case, but only those from recent years.

Public websites: Some university and courthouse library websites provide links to other sites where statutes can be found.

Government websites: Current electronic full-text statutes are available (usually consolidated) on government websites. Most sites list the statutes by title and some allow full-text searching. (See Appendix 7C: Legislation on Government Websites).

FINDING STATUTES ON COMMERCIAL ONLINE SOURCES

Both LN/QL and WC have collections of all federal, provincial and territorial consolidated statutes.

Step 1. Locate the statute

If you know the citation, enter it into the citation search box in the main search template. If you know the title, locate the statute by browsing the list of statutes or conducting a keyword search in the templates. To search by subject, once you are familiar with the terms and concepts, use those to conduct a keyword search using the appropriate search template.

Steps 2 and 3. Find out when the statute came into effect and update it

Look for the "in force" information and the date of the consolidation — usually written on the top of electronic statutes. Since most electronic versions are consolidated, it is only necessary to update them from the date of the consolidation. If the electronic version is not consolidated then you must look in other databases that contain the revisions, such as databases of gazettes.

Step 4: Note up the statute

Both LN/QL and WC have powerful electronic statute citators that not only locate statutes but hyperlink them to cases that have considered these statutes. In WC, once you are looking at your statute you can use *KeyCite Canada* for links to cases that have considered the statute as well as to secondary material relevant to that statute. Alternatively, you can go directly to *KeyCite Canada* and search for your statute. In LN/QL, use *QuickCite Statutes* but be aware that *QuickCite Statutes* only updates from 1992 (2005 for Quebec) and only notes up the most recent revision.

How to Find and Update Regulations

8

Regulations, rules, and municipal bylaws are similar to statutes in that they are laws created by a particular authority. Unlike statutes, they are not created by the legislature, but are created by a delegated authority. They are sometimes called delegated or subordinate legislation.

This chapter explains how regulations are published and describes a step-by-step technique for finding regulations in a law library and online. It also explains how to cite regulations.

LEARNING OBJECTIVES

At the end of this chapter you will be able to:

- Describe how regulations are made
- Locate, update and note-up a regulation
- Provide a proper citation for a regulation
- Describe what a municipal bylaw is
- Explain how to locate bylaws

HOW REGULATIONS ARE MADE AND PUBLISHED

Legislatures are continually making subordinate legislation or regulations. These regulations provide the "flesh on the bones" of statutes. People come into contact with regulations daily; for example, a regulation may state how many metres one must stay back from an emergency vehicle while driving on a highway, or how many litres of waste may be legally disposed of in a waterway. Regulations spell out the details of subject matter covered in their "enabling" statute.

There are three types of subordinate legislation: regulations, rules and proclamations. Unlike statutes, in order for regulations to become law they need only be "passed" by the authority described (and usually specifically named) in the statute (a government ministry, board, agency or department) "filed or deposited", and published.

Passed: Regulations are passed by the executive arm of governments. For example, they are usually prepared by a department or agency of government and then passed by the Lieutenant Governor in Council (provincial or territorial cabinet) or the Governor in Council (federal cabinet) without the need for approval in the House of Commons.

Filed: Federal regulations are effective when filed with the clerk of the Privy Council. Provincial regulations are effective on the date deposited with a government office such as the registrar of regulations. These dates are specified in the regulation.

Published: Because regulations do not go through the House of Commons or the Senate, or through provincial or territorial legislatures, and do not go through readings like bills, they are only published once — in the official gazettes (provincial, territorial or federal).

Rules, regulations and proclamations are published in sets called regulations. They can be found in law libraries, usually right beside the statutes for each particular jurisdiction. When first published, regulations appear in the federal or provincial softbound gazettes. Federal regulations are published in the *Canada Gazette, Part II*. After a number of gazettes have accumulated, they are usually hardbound. Provincial and territorial gazettes follow this same pattern; the issues come out periodically — usually weekly — and then the issues are gathered and bound.

Periodically, governments consolidate their regulations. The federal government and some provinces have consolidated their regulations into "revised" sets, much like the revised versions of statutes. An example of a consolidation is the 1978 federal government consolidation of all federal regulations: the *Consolidated Regulations of Canada, 1978* (*C.R.C. 1978*). The *C.R.C. 1978* incorporates all regulations and amendments to the regulations up to the date of publication.

Thus, on the library shelves there are usually four parts to each set of federal regulations:

- A consolidated set of regulations. The federal set is called the *Consolidated Regulations of Canada, 1978* (18 volumes).
- Annual or sessional regulations. The federal set consists of the *Canada Gazette, Part II*, hardbound for each year.
- Current regulations. The federal version is the *Canada Gazette, Part II*, which includes the most recent regulations, in paper form.
- An index. The federal *Canada Gazette, Part II* includes the most recent *Consolidated Index of Statutory Instruments*. This index can be found online at: <http://laws.justice.gc.ca/en/IndexStatutoryInstruments>.

Provincial regulations usually follow a similar pattern to the above. Some have consolidated their regulations from time to time. Others simply have bound their gazette (often called the *Royal Gazette*) into annual volumes. They may or may not have indexes, and some of the indexes are cumulative while others are not.

A few provinces and territories have loose-leaf sets of consolidated regulations. These are very useful because amendments to the regulations are inserted directly into the set and you avoid looking in several volumes for amendments to the regulations. Some of the more popular regulations (for the larger, more populous provinces) are published by commercial publishers and annotated. These annotated sets usually include the relevant statute and revisions to both the statute and the regulations, and refer to cases that considered the statute or the regulations.

A new publication from Thomson Carswell, part of the *Canadian Abridgment*, is entitled *Regulations Judicially Considered.* It does for regulations what the Carswell statute citator does for statutes, that is, it identifies cases from all Canadian jurisdictions that have considered or interpreted regulations. It is available by subscription and is a welcome addition to the legal research field. Regulations can also be updated on Westlaw Canada using KeyCite*Canada.*

RULES OF COURT

Researchers should be aware of a certain type of regulation known as "a rule" or "rules of court". Rules set out the requirements and policies that must be met in order to present cases to the various courts and tribunals. Rules also give guidance to practitioners about court deadlines, procedures and various forms.

For provinces and territories, these are enabled under a statute usually called a *Judicature Act* or a *Courts Act*. At the federal level, the enabling Acts are the *Supreme Court Act* and the *Federal Courts Act*, as well as the Acts that have established federal administrative tribunals such as the Competition Bureau.

Another new publication from Thomson Carswell, again part of the *Canadian Abridgment*, is entitled *Rules Judicially Considered.* It does for rules what the other Carswell citators do for statutes and regulations (see above) — it identifies cases from all Canadian jurisdictions that have considered or interpreted court or tribunal rules. Rules can also be updated on Westlaw Canada using KeyCite*Canada.*

HOW TO READ A REGULATION

It is important to be able to read a regulation so you can find out quickly how it impacts the law and when it came into effect. A regulation typically consists of the following five parts:

- regulation number (*e.g.*, SOR/93-246 (federal), or B.C. Reg 91/80 (provincial or territorial);
- date of filing or deposit (*e.g.*, 11 May 1993, or March 21, 1980);
- title (and sometimes the short title);
- enabling statute (*e.g.*, *Citizenship Act*, s. 27, or *Name Act*, s. 13); and
- how it was brought in (PC: federal Privy Council; OC: provincial or territorial Order in Council).

The parts of regulations can be seen in Illustrations 8.1 and 8.2, which are excerpts from a federal and a provincial regulation.

Illustration 8.1
A Federal Regulation
(The Citizenship Regulations, SOR/93-246)

Registration

SOR/93-246 11 May, 1993

CITIZENSHIP ACT

Citizenship Regulations, 1993

P.C. 1993-943 11 May, 1993

His Excellency the Governor General in Council, on the recommendation of the Minister of Multiculturalism and Citizenship, pursuant to section 27 of the Citizenship Act, is pleased hereby to revoke the Citizenship Regulations, C.R.C., c. 400, and to make the annexed Regulations respecting Citizenship, in substitution therefor.

REGULATIONS RESPECTING CITIZENSHIP

Short Title

1. These Regulations may be cited as the *Citizenship Regulations*, 1993

Illustration 8.2
A B.C. Regulation
(The Name Act Regulation, B.C. Reg. 91/80)

B.C. Reg. 91/80 Filed March 21, 1980

Effective June 1, 1980

O.C. 617/80

Name Act

NAME ACT REGULATION

[includes amendments up to B.C. Reg. 110/97]

Fees

1 Under the *Name Act* the fee

(a) on filing an application for a Change of Name shall be $137 for the applicant and $27 for each person who is listed in the application as a person whose name will be changed by reason of a change of name of the applicant, which fees include the issuance of one certificate of Change of Name for the applicant and each listed person and the cost of publication of the certificates in the Gazette following approval of the application.

(b) for a search of one registration of Change of Name shall be $27 for each 3 year period or part of a 3 year period covered by the search,

(c) for each certificate of Change of Name shall be

(i) $27 including the fee for a search covering one 3 year period, or

(ii) $60 including, where same day search service is offered and requested, the fee for a search that same day covering one 3 year period, and

(d) for copies of documents supporting an application for Change of Name shall be $50.

[am. B.C. Regs. 326/84; 73/87; 121/88; 111/90; 133/91; 87/92; 79/94; 132/95; 554/95; 110/97.]

[Provisions of the *Name Act*, RSBC 1996, c. 328, relevant to the enactment of this regulation: section 17]

EMPOWERING STATUTE

All regulations are made under the authority of a statute. Therefore you must know the statute under which the regulation is made. Since law-making power is delegated through statutes, each regulation must have an empowering, or enabling, statute, which authorizes an executive arm of the government to create regulations. This is evidenced by an "enabling section", which describes who has the power to make regulations and the matters about which regulations can be made. One might think of the relationship between a statute and a regulation as that of a parent to a child; the child holds on to the parent and does not function independently of the parent.

The following is an example of such an enabling section.

Illustration 8.3
An Enabling Section
(From the Federal *Citizenship Act*)

---

27. The Governor in Council may make regulations
(*a*) prescribing the manner in which and the place at which applications are to be made and notices are to be given under this Act and the evidence that is to be provided with respect to those applications and notices;
(*b*) fixing fees for

    (i) the making of any application under this Act,

    (ii) the issuing of any certificate under this Act,

    (iii) [Repealed, 2008, c. 14, s. 12]

    (iv) the provision of any certified or uncertified copy of a document from the records kept in the course of the administration of this Act or prior legislation,

    (v) the administration of any oath, solemn affirmation or declaration filed, made, issued, delivered or administered pursuant to this Act or the regulations, or

    (vi) any search of the records referred to in subparagraph (iv);
(*c*) providing for the remission of fees referred to in paragraph (*b*);
(*d*) providing for various criteria that may be applied to determine whether a person

    (i) has an adequate knowledge of one of the official languages of Canada, or …

HOW TO FIND AND UPDATE REGULATIONS

To determine whether a regulation is "good law", you need to find it and update it. There are three steps to finding and updating regulations:

- Find the title and citation of the regulation
- Find the regulation
- Update the regulation

The following section describes each of these steps as it relates to each of the main providers of regulations:

- A law library;
- CanLII (The Canadian Legal Information Institute);
- Federal, provincial and territorial government websites;
- Westlaw Canada; and
- LexisNexis/Quicklaw.

Computers have revolutionized regulation research. Because there are several available full-text electronic versions of both federal and many provincial and territorial regulations, searches are fairly straightforward. Therefore, if you know the name of the relevant statute under which your regulation was made, you will likely be able to find the regulation through one of these electronic sources.

An advantage of electronic regulations is that you do not need to know the related statute. You can simply do a search for a word in the statute or a word in the regulation. However, be aware that these databases are huge and it can be very difficult to isolate the particular regulations that you may be looking for.

Westlaw Canada and LexisNexis/Quicklaw both have electronic collections of federal, provincial and territorial regulations and rules. Both services strive to stay up-to-date with regulations and rules as soon as they are published. As with statutes, usually the commercial online providers are ahead of government websites in terms of timeliness because, as value-added providers, they actually monitor the government's daily activities more closely than the government itself does.

You can search by scanning the table of regulations or by conducting a word search using the template provided. Keep in mind, however, that the electronic version is still not viewed by all courts as the official version, so you may need to locate the official print version in order to confirm that the electronic version of the regulation is current and accurate.

How to Find Regulations in a Law Library

Step 1: Find the Title of the Regulation

Since all regulations are made pursuant to a statute, the easiest way to locate the title and citation of a regulation is through the title of the relevant statute. And finding the title of the statute is made easy because most governments publish two helpful tables:

- one table that lists all *regulations* alphabetically by title and their corresponding statutes (called a concordance); and
- one table that lists all *statutes* alphabetically by title and their corresponding regulations.

These tables are usually consolidated and therefore include all regulations in force at the time of publication and all their amendments. They are called different things in each province but federally they are called the *Consolidated Index of Statutory Instruments* (Illustration 8.4), Table I and Table II:

Table I: *Table of Regulations, Statutory Instruments (other than Regulations) and Other Documents.* All regulations and their corresponding statutes are listed. (The abbreviation SI stands for "Statutory Instrument". The SI number is merely a way of numbering and organizing regulations chronologically for publishing.) (See Illustration 8.5)

Table II: *Table of Regulations, Statutory Instruments (other than Regulations) and Other Documents Arranged by Statute.* (The abbreviation SOR stands for "Statutory Orders". The SOR number is merely a way of numbering and organizing these other types of documents chronologically for publishing.) (See Illustration 8.6)

This handy index is also online at: <http://laws.justice.gc.ca/en/IndexStatutory Instruments>. Carswell also publishes the *Canadian Regulations Index*, which is a very useful research tool if you know the name of the relevant statute. It is in loose-leaf form and lists all regulations made pursuant to each federal statute.

In these tables you will find the citation of each regulation and other documents (that is, the Statutory Orders (SORs) and Statutory Instruments (SIS) pertaining to each statute).

Each province has comparable twin tables. In British Columbia they are found in the Consolidated Regulations of British Columbia:

1. The *Regulation/Act Concordance* is found in the front of the *Consolidated Regulations of British Columbia* (C.R.B.C. Volume I). It lists all regulations and corresponding statutes. (See Illustration 8.7)

2. *Table of Contents* or *Index* of Current B.C. Regulations. Both list all statutes of British Columbia and their corresponding regulations. (See Illustrations 8.8 and 8.9)

So whether you are looking for federal or provincial regulations, you will start by looking at the two tables that list regulations and statutes. If you know only the title of the **regulation**, you would look in a *concordance* (*e.g.*, Table I), and if you know the title of the **statute**, you would look in a table of statutes (*e.g.*, Table II).

Illustration 8.4
Cover Image of the Canada Gazette, Part II
(*Consolidated Index of Statutory Instruments*)

Canada Gazette

Part II

Gazette du Canada

Partie II

CONSOLIDATED INDEX

OF STATUTORY

INSTRUMENTS

INDEX CODIFIÉ

DES TEXTES

RÉGLEMENTAIRES

JANUARY 1, 1955 TO DECEMBER 31, 2009

DU 1ᵉʳ JANVIER 1955 AU 31 DÉCEMBRE 2009

© Her Majesty the Queen in Right of Canada, 2010
Published by the Queen's Printer for Canada, 2010

ISSN 0045-4206

© Sa Majesté la Reine du Chef du Canada, 2010
Publié par l'Imprimeur de la Reine pour le Canada, 2010

Illustration 8.5
"Table II"
(Federal Table of Regulations — Listed by Statute)

59

II—TABLE OF REGULATIONS, STATUTORY INSTRUMENTS (OTHER THAN
REGULATIONS) AND OTHER DOCUMENTS ARRANGED BY STATUTE

DECEMBER 31, 2009

. . .

CHILDREN'S SPECIAL ALLOWANCES ACT [S.C. 1992, c. 48]
(ALLOCATIONS SPÉCIALES POUR ENFANTS (LOI))
Children's Special Allowance Regulations, SOR/93-12
[Allocations spéciales pour enfants — Règlement]
s. 3, SOR/99-326, s. 1
s. 4, SOR/97-35, s. 1
s. 6, SOR/97-35, s. 2(E); SOR/99-326, s. 2
s. 6.1, added, SOR/99-326, s. 3; SOR/2003-161, s. 1
s. 9, SOR/97-35, s. 3
CITIZENSHIP ACT [R.S. 1985, c. C-29]
[CITOYENNETÉ (LOI)]
Citizenship Regulations, SOR/93-246
[Citoyenneté — Règlement]
Former Title: Citizenship Regulations, 1993
Long Title, replaced, SOR/2009-108, ss. 1 and 25
s. 1, repealed, SOR/2009-108, ss. 2 and 25
s. 2, *"bureau de la citoyenneté"*, SOR/2009-108, ss. 3(F) and 25
s. 2, **"citizenship court",** repealed (E), SOR/2009-108, ss. 3 and 25
s. 2, **"citizenship office",** added (E), SOR/2009-108, ss. 3 and 25
s. 2, **"Hague Convention on Adoption",** added,
SOR/2007-281, s. 1
s. 3, SOR/94-442, s. 1; SOR/2009-108, ss. 4 and 25
s. 3.1, added, SOR/2009-108, ss. 5 and 25
s. 4, SOR/2009-108, ss. 6 and 25
s. 5, repealed, SOR/2009-108, ss. 7 and 25
s. 5.1, added, SOR/2007-281, s. 2; SOR/2009-108, ss. 8 and 25
s. 5.2, added, SOR/2007-281, s. 2; SOR/2009-108, ss. 9 and 25
s. 5.3, added, SOR/2007-281, s. 2; SOR/2009-108, ss. 10 and 25
s. 5.4, added, SOR/2007-281, s. 2; SOR/2009-108, ss. 11 and 25
s. 5.5, added, SOR/2007-281, s. 2; SOR/2009-108, ss. 12 and 25
s. 6, repealed, SOR/2009-108, ss. 13 and 25
s. 7, SOR/2009-108, ss. 14 and 25
s. 7.1, added, SOR/2009-108, ss. 15 and 25
s. 8, SOR/2009-108, ss. 16 and 25
s. 10, SOR/2009-108, ss. 17 and 25
s. 11, SOR/94-442, s. 2; SOR/2009-108, ss. 18 and 25
s. 12, SOR/94-442, s. 2
s. 13, repealed, SOR/94-442, s. 2
s. 14, SOR/94-442, s. 2
s. 15, SOR/94-442, s. 3
s. 16, repealed, SOR/2009-108, ss. 19 and 25
s. 18, repealed, SOR/2009-108, ss. 20 and 25

s. 19, SOR/2009-108, ss. 21(E) and 25
s. 20, SOR/2009-108, ss. 22(E) and 25
s. 22, SOR/94-442, s. 4
s. 30, replaced, SOR/2009-108, ss. 23 and 25
s. 32, added, SOR/95-122, s. 1
s. 33, added, SOR/95-122, s. 1
Schedule, SOR/95-122, s. 2; SOR/97-23, s. 1; SOR/2007-281, s. 3;
SOR/2009-108, ss. 24 and 25
Foreign Ownership of Land Regulations, SOR/79-416
[Propriété de terres appartenant à des étrangers — Règlement]
s. 12, SOR/80-156, s. 1
s. 22, SOR/80-156, s. 2
s. 23, SOR/79-514, s. 1
s. 25, SOR/82-544, s. 1
Schedule, SOR/79-514, s. 2; SOR/80-156, s. 3; SOR/82-544, s. 2

Example 1: Federal Regulations

As you can see, the regulations (SOR and SI) pertaining to each statute are listed underneath each statute. If the regulation was made before 1978, it will have a reference to C.R.C. 1978 (the consolidated set of regulations). When reading these tables you will want to record the number and year of all of the relevant regulations and their citations. For example, the first regulation under the *Citizenship Act* is the *Citizenship Regulations, 1993*, SOR/93-246.

Illustration 8.6
"Table I"
(Federal Table of Regulations — Listed by Regulation)

I — TABLE OF REGULATIONS, STATUTORY INSTRUMENTS (OTHER THAN REGULATIONS) AND OTHER DOCUMENTS DECEMBER 31, 2009

This Table provides a reference to regulations, statutory instruments (other than regulations) and other documents that have been made under statutory or other authority and that were in force at any time during the current calendar year. The instruments are listed alphabetically according to their title showing the authority under which they were made and are listed in Table II. For instruments no longer in force, that were published in the *Canada Gazette* Part II, reference should be made to the Consolidated Index of December 31st of the year in question.

Abandonment of Branch Lines Prohibition Orders	**Acting Customs Excise Enforcement Officers Exclusion Approval Order**	**Affiliated Persons (Insurance Companies) Regs**
Canada Transportation Act	Public Service Employment Act	Insurance Companies Act
Abatement of Duties Payable Regs	**Additional Legislative Powers Designation Order**	**Affiliated Persons (Trust and Loan Companies) Regs**
Customs Act	Northwest Territories Act	Trust and Loan Companies Act
Abbotsford Airport Zoning Regs		
Aeronautics Act	**Adjudication Division Rules**	**African Development Bank Privileges and Immunities Order**
Aboriginal Communal Fishing Licenses Regs	Immigration Act	Foreign Missions and International Organizations Act
Fisheries Act	**Adjustment Assistance Benefit Regs**	
Aboriginal Peoples of Canada Adaptations Regs (Firearms)	Appropriation Acts	**African Development Fund Privileges and Immunities Order**
Firearms Act	**Adjustment Assistance Regs (Textile and Clothing Workers)**	Foreign Missions and International Organizations Act
Accelerated Elimination of Customs Duties	Appropriation Acts	**Age Guideline**
Customs Tariff	**Administration of Labour Market Development Services Divestiture Regs**	Canadian Human Rights Act

Example 2: Provincial Regulations

If you know the name of the provincial statute, look in the table that lists the statutes and all the corresponding regulations. In British Columbia this is called the Regulation/Act Concordance and is found in the front of the *Consolidated Regulations of British Columbia* (C.R.B.C.). It lists all regulations and corresponding statutes. Other provinces and territories have similar tables.

Illustration 8.7
Cover Image of the Consolidated Regulations of
British Columbia (Volume 8)

Province of British Columbia

CONSOLIDATED

REGULATIONS OF

BRITISH COLUMBIA

A consolidation of regulations
of general public interest
published under the authority of
the *Regulations Act*

VOLUME 8

Queen's Printer for British Columbia
Victoria, 1999

Illustration 8.8
B.C. Regulation Act/Concordance
(List of Regulations by Title)

REGULATION / ACT CONCORDANCE

REGULATION	ACT
Motor Vehicle Fees Regulation	Motor Vehicle
Motor Vehicle Prohibition Regulation	Wildlife
Motorcycle Safety Helmet Exemption Regulation	Motor Vehicle
Mountain Pine Beetle Salvage Area under section 14.1 of the Act – notice	Forest
Multilateral Instrument 11-101 *Principal Regulator System*	Securities
Multilateral Instrument 11-102 *Passport System*	Securities
Multilateral Instrument 62-104 *Take-Over Bids and Issuer Bids*	Securities
Municipal Act Fees Regulation No. 1	Local Government
Municipal Finance Authority Regulation	Municipal Finance Authority
Municipal Liabilities Regulation	Community Charter
Municipal Sewage Regulation	Environmental Management
Municipal Tax Regulation	Community Charter
Mushroom Composting Pollution Prevention Regulation	Environmental Management
Mushroom Industry Development Council Regulation	Farming and Fishing Industries Development
Muskwa-Kechika Management Plan Regulation	Muskwa-Kechika Management Area Benefits Agreement Implementation
Musqueam Reconciliation, Settlement and Benefits Agreement Implementation Regulation	Musqueam Reconciliation, Settlement and Benefits Agreement Implementation
Mutual Fund Trustee Exemption Regulation	Financial Institutions
Name Act Regulation	Name
Nanaimo and South West Water Supply Service Regulation	Nanaimo and South West Water Supply
Nanaimo Regional District Regulation	Local Government
National Instrument 13-101 *System for Electronic Document Analysis and Retrieval (SEDAR)*	Securities
National Instrument 14-101 *Definitions*	Securities
National Instrument 21-101 *Marketplace Operation*	Securities
National Instrument 23-101 *Trading Rules*	Securities
National Instrument 24-101 *Institutional Trade Matching and Settlement*	Securities
National Instrument 31-102 *National Registration Database*	Securities
National Instrument 33-102 *Regulation of Certain Registrant Activities*	Securities
National Instrument 33-105 *Underwriting Conflicts*	Securities
National Instrument 33-109 *Registration Information*	Securities
National Instrument 35-101 *Conditional Exemption from Registration for United States Broker-Dealers and Agents*	Securities
National Instrument 41-101 *General Prospectus Requirements*	Securities
National Instrument 43-101 *Standards of Disclosure for Mineral Projects*	Securities
National Instrument 44-101 *Short Form Prospectus Distributions*	Securities
National Instrument 44-102 *Shelf Distributions*	Securities
National Instrument 44-103 *Post-Receipt Pricing*	Securities
National Instrument 45-101 *Rights Offerings*	Securities
National Instrument 45-102 *Resale of Securities*	Securities
National Instrument 45-106 *Prospectus and Registration Exemptions*	Securities
National Instrument 51-101 *Standards of Disclosure for Oil and Gas Activities*	Securities
National Instrument 51-102 *Continuous Disclosure Obligations*	Securities
National Instrument 52-107 *Acceptable Accounting Principles, Auditing Standards and Reporting Currency*	Securities
National Instrument 52-108 *Auditor Oversight*	Securities
National Instrument 52-109 *Certification of Disclosure in Issuers' Annual and Interim Filings*	Securities
National Instrument 52-110 *Audit Committees*	Securities

Illustration 8.9
Index of Current B.C. Regulations
(List of Regulations by Statute Title)

INDEX OF CURRENT B.C. REGULATIONS

These regulations are all technically in effect, but not all are in active use. Most, but not all, have been published in the B.C. Gazette, Part II. Regulations made under a repealed Act but which are still in use are listed under the replacement Act. Some regulations which were previously listed no longer meet the definition of "regulation" under the present *Regulations Act*, R.S.B.C. 1996, c. 402, and so have been deleted from this index. Symbols used are as follows:

* = not published
# = published in Part I Gazette

Citations such as "1985-55-42" signify the year, chapter and section of the statute cited.

B.C. Reg.

ACCESS TO ABORTION SERVICES ACT c. 1, R.S.B.C. 1996

Abortion Services Access Zone Regulation			337/95
amended	*385/98*	*277/2000*	*106/2002*

. . .

MUNICIPALITIES ENABLING and VALIDATING ACT c. 261, R.S.B.C. 1960

Prescribed Rates – District of Kent	380/2002

MUNICIPALITIES ENABLING and VALIDATING ACT (NO. 2) c. 61, S.B.C. 1990

Community Airport Bodies Regulation	167/99
Partnering Agreements Regulation	126/2000

MUNICIPALITIES ENABLING and VALIDATING ACT (NO. 3) c. 44, S.B.C. 2001

Community Port Authorities Regulation	194/2002

MUSEUM ACT c. 12, S.B.C. 2003

Museum Fees Regulation			286/95
amended	*166/96*	*140/97*	*257/97*	*56/99*
	283/99	*254/2002*		

MUSKWA-KECHIKA MANAGEMENT AREA ACT c. 38, S.B.C. 1998

Muskwa-Kechika Management Plan Regulation	53/2002

NAME ACT c. 328, R.S.B.C. 1996

Name Act Regulation			91/80
amended	*326/84*	*73/87*	*121/88*	*111/90*
	133/91	*87/92*	*79/94*	*132/95*
	554/95	*110/97*		

As you can see in Illustration 8.9, *The Name Act* has one regulation (the Name Act Regulation) and it has been amended many times. You can locate the original regulation (*e.g.*, B.C. Reg. 91/80) and each amendment by the number and year of the regulation (*e.g.*, B.C. Reg. 326/84 and others). You will note in the original regulation (Illustration 8.10), it was originally called the Change of Name Act Regulation.

In later consolidated versions, such as the one from the government website (Illustration 8.11), it is called the Name Act Regulation and all the amendments have been included.

Step 2: Find the Regulation

In the library, regulations are found in large bound volumes in sets by jurisdiction. Regulations are published by their number and date and can be located by finding the number and date of your regulation in a volume.

Federal regulations are located in either the consolidated set (the *Consolidated Regulations of Canada, 1978*), or in the *Canada Gazette, Part II* issues that have been published since the 1978 consolidation. Likewise, provincial and territorial regulations are numbered according to their own jurisdictional numbering scheme.

For example, here is an excerpt from British Columbia Regulation 91/80 (made pursuant to the *Name Act*). Note that it repeals a 1967 regulation.

Illustration 8.10
A British Columbia Regulation
(from print set in library)

B.C. Reg. 91/80   Filed March 21, 1980

CHANGE OF NAME ACT
[Section 14]

Order in Council 617, Approved and Ordered March 20, 1980

On the recommendation of the undersigned, the Lieutenant-Governor, by and with the advice and consent of the Executive Council, orders that, effective June 1, 1980, Order in Council 3437, approved November 7, 1967 (B.C. Reg. 253/67), be repealed and the following regulation be made.

CHANGE OF NAME ACT REGULATIONS

1. Under the *Change of Name Act* the fee

    (*a*) on filing an application for a Change of Name shall be $25, which fee includes the issuance of one certificate of Change of Name and cost of publication of the certificate in the Gazette following approval of the application,

    (*b*) for a search of one registration of Change of Name shall be $2 for each three-year period or part of a three-year period covered by the search, and

    (*c*) for each certificate of Change of Name shall be $5, including the fee for a search covering one three-year period.

K. R. MAIR
Minister of Health

W. R. BENNETT
Presiding Member of the Executive Council

. . .

apl -- 3506

Illustration 8.11
A British Columbia Consolidated Regulation
(from government website)

Name Act -- NAME ACT REGULATION   Page 1 of 1

This is not the official version.

B.C. Reg. 91/80   Filed March 21, 1980
O.C. 617/80   effective June 1, 1980

Name Act

NAME ACT REGULATION

[includes amendments up to B.C. Reg. 110/97]

Fees

1 Under the *Name Act* the fee

(a) on filing an application for a Change of Name shall be $137 for the applicant and $27 for each person who is listed in the application as a person whose name will be changed by reason of a change of name of the applicant, which fees include the issuance of one certificate of Change of Name for the applicant and each listed person and the cost of publication of the certificates in the Gazette following approval of the application.

(b) for a search of one registration of Change of Name shall be $27 for each 3 year period or part of a 3 year period covered by the search,

(c) for each certificate of Change of Name shall be

(i) $27 including the fee for a search covering one 3 year period, or

(ii) $60 including, where same day search service is offered and requested, the fee for a search that same day covering one 3 year period, and

(d) for copies of documents supporting an application for Change of Name shall be $50.

[am. B.C. Regs. 326/84; 73/87; 121/88; 111/90; 133/91; 87/92; 79/94; 132/95; 554/95; 110/97.]

[Provisions of the *Name Act*, R.S.B.C. 1996, c. 328, relevant to the enactment of this regulation: section 17]

Note that the consolidated regulation includes all of the amendments up to B.C. Reg. 110/97 and is not an official version.

Illustration 8.12
A B.C. Regulation that amends a Regulation
(from print version in library)

B.C. Reg. 110/97, deposited March 27, 1997, pursuant to the **NAME ACT** [Section 13 (1)]. Order in Council 359/97, approved and ordered March 26, 1997.

On the recommendation of the undersigned, the Lieutenant Governor, by and with the advice and consent of the Executive Council, orders that, effective April 1, 1997, section 1 (a) of B.C. Reg. 91/80, the Name Act Regulation, is amended by striking out "$125" and substituting "$137". — J. K. MACPHAIL, *Minister of Health and Minister Responsible for Seniors;* G. CLARK, *Presiding Member of the Executive Council.*

You will note in Illustration 8.12 that the regulation that amends another regulation simply changes the fee charged for a name change from $125 to $137. The fee charged in 1980 was $25.

Step 3: Update the Regulation

When updating regulations you will notice that most of the online versions are consolidated. In other words, the amendments are incorporated into the text. If it is consolidated, you must still record the consolidation date and update from that date to the present. You can do this by:

- checking a gazette (in print or online);
- checking recent print publications from legislative bodies (usually found in a law library);
- checking commercial updates (*e.g.*, Thomson Carswell's *Legislation*);
- checking the appropriate government website;
- going through a commercial online provider (*e.g.*, LexisNexis/Quicklaw); or
- speaking to a law librarian or call the Library of Parliament.

For library research of federal regulations, you need to look in the index of each of the softcover editions of the *Canada Gazette, Part II* that have come out **after** the most recent *Consolidated Index of Statutory Instruments* (see Chapter 7 for a full description of statutory research tools).

For provincial amendments to regulations, you need to look at the most current softcover editions of the provincial gazettes (often there is an index included) and the most recent legislative digests (above).

An excellent new online service for updating regulations (as well as statutes) from all Canadian jurisdictions is CCH Canadian's *Legislative Pulse* (described in detail in Chapter 7). This commercial online service makes updating very quick and thorough. However, even this service may not be entirely up-to-date, so be sure to update in the library from the currency date noted in the electronic version.

How to Find Regulations Using Electronic Sources

For all electronic regulations the following information pertains:

- Most online regulations are consolidated versions and the amendments have been incorporated into the text. Therefore updating is only necessary from the most recent consolidation.
- There are essentially two ways to find a regulation online. You can either conduct a word search from a template (full-text search) or you can browse the alphabetical lists of regulations and the lists of empowering statutes (like in print).
- Here is a quick checklist to use when looking at any online service:
  - Notice the date of the most recent consolidation (*e.g.*, which amendments have been incorporated into the text?).
  - Look for the "in force" information (when did the regulation come into effect?).
  - Look for the date up to which the whole database is current.
  - Update further if necessary offline.

Using CanLII to Find Regulations

CanLII (<http://www.canlii.org>) is the best free source for all consolidated current federal, provincial and territorial regulations. Here are the essential steps you will need to take:

- From the landing page select your jurisdiction.
- Follow the "Statutes and Regulations" link to the lists of regulations.
- There are two lists; one is organized alphabetically by the title of the regulation and the other by the title of the enabling statute.
- Browse for the one you are looking for.
- If you do not know the statute or regulation name you can do a full-text word search of the appropriate database (*e.g.*, the Ontario Statutes and Regulations database).
- Click on the link in your search results and you will be taken directly to the appropriate regulation.
- CanLII also provides the ability to compare current and previous versions of each regulation.
- To note up the regulation, click the "Note-Up" tab at the top of the screen and then the search button. Links to cases that have considered your regulation will be displayed. (Noting-up on CanLII is not comprehensive as with the commercial databases, as this feature is limited to only cases included in the CanLII databases.)

Using Government Websites to Find Regulations

Government websites provide the most recent consolidations of both statutes and regulations. Each government website has a unique interface and its own search tools. Generally, however, regulations are linked to statutes, so if you know the name of your statute, research will be easier through the statute. (See Appendix 7C: Legislation on Government Websites to find out whether searching is available in your jurisdiction.)

Here are the basic steps to take:

- Go to the government webpage and locate statutes or legislation.
- If you know the title of the enabling statute, search for it in a template.
- A word search may not be possible since some government websites are not full-text searchable.
- Clicking on search results will take you directly to the appropriate regulation.
- To note up the regulation, you will need to use a commercial provider or print source like Thomson Carswell's *Legislation* (part of the *Canadian Abridgment* set) since government websites do not provide this information.

Using Westlaw Canada to Find Regulations

Westlaw Canada provides access to 2,500 of the "most frequently consulted regulations" only. This means that a regulation search in Westlaw Canada may not be complete. The database also includes rules of court for every jurisdiction except Quebec.

To find a regulation you can either browse through a list of statutes or you can conduct a word search. Here are the basic steps to locating and updating a regulation in WC:

When browsing through regulations or statutes (Illustration 8.13):

- From the landing page go to "Table of Contents" (in left margin).
- Select All TOCS; select *Canada*; and select *Legislation*.
- Then select your jurisdiction (*e.g.*, Federal) and "Regulations".
- Browse the lists by the name of the enabling Act to find the title of your regulation.
- It will link you to the regulation.
- Note up your regulation by using the *KeyCite Canada* citator.

When word searching in regulations (Illustration 8.14):

- From the landing page go to LawSource.
- Find "search Legislation" and enter your search terms in the template.
- Note up your regulation by using the *KeyCite Canada* citator.

Illustration 8.13
Westlaw Canada Regulations Table of Contents

Table of Contents

Selected Databases

Canadian Federal Regulations (CANFED-REG) ⓘ

All TOCs > Canada > Legislation > Federal (English) > **Regulations** ⓘ

☐ ⊟ Canada Federal Regulations
☐   ⊞ Access to Information Act
☐   ⊟ **Aeronautics Act**
☐   ⊞ Can. Reg. 96-433 - Canadian Aviation Regulations
☐   ⊞ Can. Reg. 2009-231 - Ottawa Macdonald-Cartier International Airport Zoning Regulations
☐   ⊞ Can. Reg. 2009-298 - Vancouver 2010 Aviation Security Regulations [Repealed]
☐   ⊞ Agricultural Products Marketing Act
☐   ⊞ Air Travellers Security Charge Act
☐   ⊞ Assisted Human Reproduction Act
☐   ⊞ Bank Act
☐   ⊞ Bankruptcy and Insolvency Act
☐   ⊞ Canada Agricultural Products Act
☐   ⊞ Canada Business Corporations Act
☐   ⊞ Canada Cooperatives Act
☐   ⊞ Canada Corporations Act
☐   ⊞ Canada Deposit Insurance Corporation Act
☐   ⊞ Canada Disability Savings Act
☐   ⊞ Canada Education Savings Act
☐   ⊞ Canada Labour Code

Reprinted by permission of Carswell, a division of Thomson Reuters Canada Limited.

Illustration 8.14
Westlaw Canada Legislation Search Template

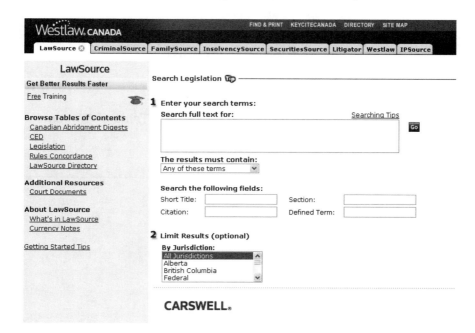

Reprinted by permission of Carswell, a division of Thomson Reuters Canada Limited.

Using LexisNexis/Quicklaw to Find Regulations

LexisNexis/Quicklaw's *Regulations* database includes all regulations from June 2002 onwards for all jurisdictions. Please note: regulations cannot be noted up using LexisNexis/Quicklaw.

To find a regulation you can either browse through a list of statutes or conduct a word search. Here are the basic steps to locating and updating a regulation in LN/QL.

When browsing through regulations or statutes (Illustration 8.15):

- From the landing page go to "Legislation".
- Under "current consolidations" (in left-hand menu), select "Browse".
- Enter your search terms in the template, which will do a global search of the "All Canadian Statutes and Regulations database" or any other database you select.
  or
- Select a particular jurisdiction from the list of jurisdictions (databases) and then search using the search template.
  or
- Browse the lists to find the title of the enabling Act, under which you will see a list links to regulations. Select the one you are looking for and you will be linked directly to the regulation.

When word searching in regulations (Illustration 8.16):

- From the landing page go to "Legislation".
- Under "current consolidations" (in left tab) select "Search".
- Enter your search terms in the template.
- Select your source (database), the "All Canadian Regulations" database or the "All Canadian Statutes and Regulations" database, for example, and insert other narrowing terms.

Illustration 8.15
Browsing the LexisNexis/Quicklaw Legislation Table of Contents

LexisNexis® *Quicklaw*™

| Search | Practice Areas | Source Directory | History & Alerts |

| Home | Court Cases | Tribunal Cases | Legislation | Commentary | Journals | Forms | International | News & Companies | General | All Search Forms |

Current Consolidations

Current Consolidations
> Search
> **Browse**

How do I...?

Find a section of a statute?
Find a former version of a section of an act?
Note up legislation?

View tutorials

Sources contained within "[All Canadian Statutes and Regulations]"
NOTE: Click any active link to browse an individual source.

Quick Search [＿＿＿＿＿＿＿] **Search**

- ❶ + Alberta Regulations
- ❶ + Alberta Statutes
- ❶ + British Columbia Regulations
- ❶ + British Columbia Statutes
- ❶ + Canada Income Tax Act and Application Rules
- ❶ + Canada Regulations
- ❶ + Canada Statutes
- ❶ + Constitutional Acts of Canada
- ❶ + Constitutional Documents of Canada
- ❶ + Documents constitutionnels du Canada
- ❶ + Loi de l'impôt sur le revenu et ses Règles d'application
- ❶ + Lois constitutionnelles du Canada
- ❶ + Lois du Canada
- ❶ + Lois du Nouveau-Brunswick
- ❶ + Lois du Québec
- ❶ + Manitoba Regulations
- ❶ + Manitoba Statutes
- ❶ + New Brunswick Regulations
- ❶ + New Brunswick Statutes
- ❶ + Newfoundland and Labrador Regulations

Illustration 8.16
LexisNexis/Quicklaw Legislation Search Template

LexisNexis® *Quicklaw*™

| Search | Practice Areas | Source Directory | History & Alerts |

Home | Court Cases | Tribunal Cases | **Legislation** | Commentary | Journals | Forms | International | News & Companies | General | All Search Forms

Current Consolidations

Current Consolidations
› **Search**
› Browse

Current Consolidations

QuickCITE™ Statute Citator

All Legislation

Related Searches

International Legislation (Common Law)
International Legislation (Civil Law)

How do I...?

Find a section of a statute?

Find a former version of a section of an act?
Note up legislation?

View tutorials

Search terms [   ] [**Search**]

A space between words searches an exact phrase.
Show the relation of terms with connectors, e.g.,
age & discrimination, age or race, trade /5 act.
View connectors...

Search Term Equivalents

☑ Singular and plural   ☑ Masculine and feminine

Sources [*All Canadian Statutes and Regulations ▾] ⓘ
Find more sources...

+ **Show document segments**

Jurisdiction [All Jurisdictions   ▾]

Legislation title [   ]

Citation [   ]

Provision [   ]
Number
(section /   Enter the legislation section or article number
article / rule)

Legislation type [All   ▾]

Select Version ⦿ Current Version (all jurisdictions)
○ All Versions (Point-in-Time sources only)
○ In Effect (Point-in-Time sources only) [On ▾] [ ] [▾] [ ]

Point-in-Time is only available for statute sources from Canada, B.C., Alberta and Ontario.

A WORD ABOUT MUNICIPAL BYLAWS

The Constitution does not mention legislative powers of municipalities. Municipal law-making powers are delegated provincial powers. These powers are delegated through statute and give municipalities the powers to create bylaws (also called ordinances). Typically, each municipality has a governing (enabling) statute (often called a *Municipalities Act* or a *Cities and Towns Act*) which describes the areas in which municipalities have powers to make bylaws.

The process by which bylaws are adopted is different than that of statutes or regulations. Usually the method of adoption is outlined in the enabling statute or another bylaw.

Some bylaws require that certain procedures be followed prior to their introduction. These include such procedures as public hearings or public votes. Bylaws usually require three readings; however, all three readings are often conducted in one sitting of municipal council. The committee work is usually done prior to the bylaw being introduced and there is usually "reconsideration" of the bylaw at least one day after third reading.

Municipal bylaws may be found cited as primary authority in case law. However, because law students tend to focus primarily on case law, they are often unfamiliar with municipal law when they graduate.

At present, there is no commercial online service or public website that provides full-text, or even a comprehensive listing, of the bylaws and ordinances of Canadian municipalities. As more references are made to them in judicial decisions, demand for such an online service will likely grow. In the meantime, the only way to find and read municipal bylaws is either on the website of the municipality in question or at a local public or law library. Public libraries are often designated as an "official public depository" for municipal legislation.

EFFECTIVE DATES OF STATUTES (VIA REGULATIONS)

As mentioned in Chapter 7 (How to Find and Update Statutes), some statutes require proclamation in order to come into force (CIF). Such proclamations officially appear in the form of a regulation from the jurisdiction. In actual fact, a researcher would never need to actually find and read the proclamation because, as stated in Chapter 7, legislatures publish "proclamation tables" either as separate documents or bound into annual statutory volumes.

These tables include information about when statutes were proclaimed and provide citations for the regulations that brought them into effect. One example of such a table is the *Canada Gazette, Part III*, entitled *Proclamations of Canada and Orders in Council Relating to the Coming into Force of Acts.*

Illustration 8.17
Federal Table of Proclamations (*Canada Gazette, Part III*)

PROCLAMATIONS OF CANADA AND ORDERS IN COUNCIL RELATING TO THE
COMING INTO FORCE OF ACTS — 9 JULY, 2009 TO 31 DECEMBER, 2009

	Date in force	Canada Gazette Part II
Arctic Waters Pollution Prevention Act, An Act to amend the, S.C. 2009, c. 11, the Act, in force	1 Aug., 2009	SI/2009-72 Vol. 143, p. 1716
Bankruptcy and Insolvency Act, the Companies' Creditors Arrangement Act, the Wage Earner Protection Program Act and chapter 47 of the Statutes of Canada, 2005, An Act to amend the, S.C. 2007, c. 36, subsection 1(1), sections 3 and 6, subsection 9(3), section 12 and 13, subsections 14(2) and (3), 15(2) and (3), 16(2) and (3) and 17(2), sections 19 to 22, 34, 35, 37, 42, 44, 46 to 48 and 50, subsection 51(1), sections 55 to 57, subsection 58(2) and section 67, in force	18 Sept. 2009	SI/2009-68 Vol. 143, p. 1711
Budget Implementation Act, 2008, S.C. 2008, c. 28,		SI/2009-66
subsection 101(1) and sections 106 and 112, in force..................	1 Aug., 2009	Vol. 143, p. 1709 SI/2009-116
sections 125 and 129, in force...................................	1 Jan., 2010	Vol. 143, p. 2662
Canada–Peru Free Trade Agreement Implementation Act, S.C. 2009, c. 16, the Act, in force	1 Aug., 2009	SI/2009-67 Vol. 143, p. 1710
Criminal Code (identity theft and related misconduct), An Act to amend the, S.C. 2009, c. 28, the Act, in force..............	8 Jan., 2010	SI/2009-120 Vol. 143, p. 2665
Criminal Code (organized crime and protection of justice system participants), An Act to amend the, S.C. 2009, c. 22, the Act, in force....	2 Oct., 2009	SI/2009-92 Vol. 143, p. 1958
Energy Efficiency Act, An Act to amend the, S.C. 2009, c. 8, the Act, in force..............................	21 Sept., 2009	SI/2009-93 Vol. 143, p. 1960
Financial institutions and to provide for related and consequential matters, An Act to amend the law governing, S.C. 2007, c. 6, subsection 186(1), sections 257, 263, 271, 275, 276, 278, 285 to 287, 292 and 296 to 298, subsection 309(2), section 445, subsection 446(1) and section 447, in force..........................	1 Jan., 2010	SI/2009-112 Vol. 143, p. 1441
Maanulth First Nations Final Agreement Act, S.C. 2009, c. 18, the Act, other than sections 10, 11 and 18, in force..................	1 April 2011	SI/2009-108 Vol. 143, p. 2047
Marine Liability Act and the Federal Courts Act and to make consequential amendments to other Acts, An Act to amend the, S.C. 2009, c. 21, sections 11, 13, 17 and 19 to 23, in force on the day that is the first day on which both of the following are in force in Canada:		
(a) the International Convention on Civil Liability for Bunker Oil Pollution Damage, 2001, and		
(b) the Protocol of 2003 to the International Convention on the Establishment of an International Fund for Compensation for Oil Pollution Damage, 1992:		
which day is 2 January, 2010....................................	2 Jan., 2010	SI/2009-102 Vol. 143, p. 2661

Some print tables of proclamation are cumulative and some are not. As seen in the example, this table of proclamation covers only one period: July 9, 2009 to December 31, 2009. Therefore, in this example, each table must be searched in each of the successive annual volumes. In other words, you must look at the table in the volume of the year in which the statute was given Royal Assent, **as well as all subsequent volumes**, until you finally find the date of the proclamation.

You will note that you are referred to the volume and page number of the *Canada Gazette, Part II* or a volume and page number of a provincial or territorial gazette, rather than to a regulation number.

Finally, you must find the actual regulation. If you have the regulation number, you can go directly to the volume of regulations or statutory instruments and locate the regulation by date and regulation number.

For the most recent information on statutes coming into force, look in the softcover volumes of the federal or provincial gazettes, or contact the legislative library. Alternatively, use Thomson Carswell's *Legislation* (monthly) or the online CCH Canadian *Legislative Pulse*, both of which give very current coming into force dates.

CITATION FOR REGULATIONS

The citation of regulations is fairly straightforward.

Federal Regulations

The title of a federal regulation is the short title, which is often stated in the regulation. Although it is not necessary to state the title of the regulation in the citation, it is good practice to do so, to confirm for your readers that they are reading the correct regulation. Those published in the *Consolidated Regulations of Canada, 1978* can be cited as follows: *Civil Service Insurance Regulations*, C.R.C., c. 401. Note you do not need to put the date in because the **only** C.R.C. that has ever been published is dated 1978.

Those published after the consolidation (*i.e.*, in the *Canada Gazette, Part II*) include both the SOR or SI number and the page reference. They are cited as follows: *Foreign Ownership of Land Regulations*, SOR/79-416, 2113. This means SOR number 416, published in 1979, at page 2113.

Provincial Regulations

The proper way to cite provincial regulations is by the name of the province (abbreviated) and the regulation number, for example: B.C. Reg. 91/80. This means this was the 91st regulation made in British Columbia in 1980 and it can be located in the 1980 volume of regulations. Note again that the title of the regulation is not necessary, but it is always good to state it, for the sake of clarity.

Electronic Citation

If the regulation is taken from an electronic source it is necessary to add that information to the citation. If a commercial online system was used, add the abbreviation for the provider (*e.g.*, LN/QL). If an Internet site was used, after the citation (above) add a comma and then the word "online" followed by a colon. Add the name of the website followed by the name of the specific part of the site, then the URL (Uniform Resource Locator) in angled brackets. If you are citing a regulation from a website which is considered an official source, use the regular citation format and omit citing to the electronic source.

SELF TEST

The answers to these questions are found at the end of the book in the "Answers to Self Tests" section.

1. What is a regulation?
2. Explain how regulations become law.
3. What is a consolidation of regulations?
4. How do you locate regulations?

SAMPLE EXERCISES — FINDING REGULATIONS

Objectives

At the end of this exercise you should be able to:

- Locate a federal regulation
- Locate a provincial regulation
- Use tables or indexes to update regulations
- Cite a regulation

Instructions

- Do background reading on how to locate and cite regulations.
- Keep a record of the time taken to complete the exercise.

Provincial Regulations

Answer questions 1 to 4 for the following regulation:

Bicycle Safety Helmet Exemption Regulation (B.C.)

1. Record the proper citation for the statute that authorizes this regulation.

    Citation:

2. Record the basic citation of the regulation.

    Citation:

3. Record the citation for any amendments to the regulation.

    Amendments:

4. Find the regulation and record the date of deposit or date of filing.

    Date of deposit or date of filing:

Federal Regulations

Answer questions 1 to 4 for the following regulation:

Honey Regulations (Canada)

1. Record the proper citation for the statute that authorizes this regulation.

    Citation:

2. Record the basic citation of the regulation.

    Citation:

3. Record the citation for the very first listed amendment to s. 2 of that regulation.

    Citation:

4. Find the regulation and record the P.C. (Privy Council) number for that amendment.

    P.C. number:

Electronic Sources

1. Using the Department of Justice website, locate and answer questions a. – d. for the following regulation:

    Olympic and Paralympic Marks Regulations

    a. Record the proper citation for the statute that authorizes this regulation.

        Citation:

    b. Record the basic citation of the regulation.

        Citation:

c. Record the citation for the very first listed amendment to that regulation.

Citation:

d. Find the regulation and record the P.C. (Privy Council) number for that amendment.

P.C. number:

2. Using Westlaw Canada or CanLII, locate a Supreme Court case that considered the following regulation:

School Regulation, B.C. Reg. 265/89

ANSWERS TO SAMPLE EXERCISES

Provincial Regulations

1. *Motor Vehicle Act*, R.S.B.C. 1996, c. 318.

2. B.C. Reg. 261/96.

3. B.C. Reg. 305/99.

4. Date of deposit for Reg. 261/96 is September 20, 1996.

Federal Regulations

1. *Canada Agricultural Products Act*, R.S.C. 1985 (4th Supp.), c. 20.

2. C.R.C. Vol. II, c. 287.

3. Section 2 was amended by SOR/91-524, s. 1.

4. P.C. number 1991-1631, Sept. 5, 1991.

(From Index volume Jan. 1, 1955 - Dec. 31, 2009)

Electronic Sources

1.
a. *Olympic and Paralympic Marks Act*, S.C. 2007, c. 25.

b. SOR/2007-294.

c. None.

d. P.C. 2007-1924 December 13, 2007.

2. *Trinity Western University v. British Columbia College of Teachers*, [2001] 1 S.C.R. 772.

Appendix 8A: Checklist: How to Find and Update Regulations

Regulations are found both in libraries and online in electronic format. All regulations are made pursuant to statutes and can be found in all law libraries in volumes next to the statutes. Current regulations (also called statutory orders and regulations (SOR) or statutory instruments (SI) are found in both current and consolidated sets. They are accompanied by an index of regulations (or statutory instruments) as follows:

- For **federal regulations**, this index is entitled *Consolidated Index of Statutory Instruments*. It is published quarterly as part *of Canada Gazette, Part II.*
- For **provincial and territorial regulations**, the index has various titles. In British Columbia the *Index of Current B.C. Regulations* lists regulations under the titles of their enabling statutes.

FINDING REGULATIONS IN THE LIBRARY

Step 1: Find the Title of the Regulation

In the library, go to the relevant volumes and locate the consolidated tables of regulations. You can look for the regulation by searching under the name of the enabling statute or by searching for the title of the regulation itself as described here.

One handy tool is *Legislation* (part of the *Canadian Abridgment*), a monthly publication which lists federal, provincial and territorial regulations that have been issued as well as their issuance date, SI or SOR number or regulation number, and enabling statute. *Legislation* has been in publication since 1989.

If You Know the Title of the Regulation But Not Its Enabling Statute

If you know the title of the *regulation*, but not the enabling statute's name, you will need to use a specific table that lists regulations by their title, for example:

- For **federal** regulations, this table is included in the *Consolidated Index of Statutory Instruments* and is entitled Table I: *Table of Regulations, Statutory Instruments (other than Regulations) and Other Documents*. Simply look up the title of the regulation there, *e.g., Foreign Ownership of Land Regulations, Letter Definition Regulations, etc.*

- For **provincial and territorial** regulations, the specific tables have various titles. In British Columbia it is called the *Regulation/Act*

Concordance and is located in volume 1 of the *Consolidated Regulations of British Columbia*.

Record the number and year of your regulations and their citations. Note the index date, since you will need to update from that date forward.

If You Know the Title of the Statute But Not the Name of the Regulation

If you know the title of the enabling *statute*, look for a different table that lists statutes and their corresponding regulations.

- For **federal** regulations, this table is included in the *Consolidated Index of Statutory Instruments* and is entitled Table II: *Table of Regulations, Statutory Instruments (other than Regulations) and Other Documents Arranged by Statute*.

- For **provincial and territorial** regulations, this index or table has various titles. In British Columbia it is called the *Index of Current B.C. Regulations*. Regulations are listed under the name of their enabling statute.

Record the number and year of all the relevant regulations and their citations. Note the index date so you can update from that date forward.

Step 2. Find the Regulation

- You can find regulations in the shelves in a law library. They are arranged chronologically by number. The citation of the regulation tells you both the year and the number to look for in each of the annual volumes.

- As for the numbering of regulations, most provincial regulations consist of the regulation number, then the year (*e.g.*, *Bee Regulation*, B.C. Reg. 373/88). Federal regulations include the regulation number, gazette date and page (*e.g.*, SOR/79-416, date 13/06/79, page 2113). SOR and SI numbers consist of the year and regulation number, *e.g.*, SOR/2002-345 or SI/79-23. Remember that for federal regulations, C.R.C. refers to the *Consolidated Regulations of Canada, 1978* — the last official print consolidation of federal regulations.

Step 3. Update the Regulation

- To locate the most recent amendments to regulations, look in the index or table of contents of *each* of the softcover issues of the jurisdictional gazette published after the most recent consolidated index or table (as described above).

- For federal regulations, these are the bi-weekly issues of the *Canada Gazette, Part II*. For provincial or territorial regulations, read the printed jurisdictional gazette. Or, for all jurisdictions, use Carswell's *Legislation* monthly issues.

- To update further, look at electronic gazettes online from the various provincial governments.

- To be absolutely up-to-date, you should contact the office of the minister named in the enabling statute and ask if there have been any very recent updates that have not been published.

FINDING REGULATIONS ONLINE

Electronic versions of regulations can be found on most government websites and on most commercial online services. Therefore, if you know the name of the relevant statute under which your regulation was made, you will be able to find the regulation through one of these electronic sources.

When updating regulations using electronic sources, you will see that most of the online versions state whether the regulations database is consolidated (whether the amendments have been incorporated into the text). If it is consolidated, record the consolidation date then check the appropriate gazette (either online or in paper form) for any amendments to the regulations since the consolidation date.

When using electronic sources you must still be familiar with the print sources to find the official version of the regulation and to confirm that the electronic version of the regulation is current and accurate.

Public (no-fee) providers: The federal government website and most provincial government websites include full-text regulations. CanLII (<http://www.canlii.org>) and law libraries also either list regulations or provide links to the originating parliament or legislature. The federal list is called the *Consolidated Index of Statutory Instruments*, and you can go directly to it online (<http://www.gazette.gc.ca/rp-pr/p2/2009/2009-03-31-c1/html/index-eng.html>). On these sites, you can usually either browse a title list or search by keyword in a search template. A list of government sites is in Appendix 7C.

LN/QL and WC: Both providers have databases containing federal, provincial and territorial regulations. Within regulations databases, you can browse a title list or perform a keyword search of the full text. WC enables the researcher to note up the statute using *KeyCite Canada.* LN/QL does not have this feature.

Be aware that each database has limitations. LN/QL only provides regulations from June 2002 onwards, while WC provides access to 2,500 of the "most frequently consulted regulations". Thus you may still need to consult the paper versions of the regulations to ensure your search is complete.

How to Find and Update Cases 9

Case law research involves locating relevant cases, seeing whether these cases have been appealed (updating) and locating later cases that have considered those cases (noting up). Thousands of cases are decided each year provincially, federally and internationally. In order to locate these judicial decisions, researchers must become familiar with how cases are published, how they are arranged in law libraries and databases, and the tools available to assist in locating them.

This chapter describes what cases are, how to read cases, and how cases are published in reports and displayed online. It then describes step-by-step how to locate cases, and explains how to cite cases.

LEARNING OBJECTIVES

At the end of this chapter you will be able to:

- Read a case and define its parts
- Describe how cases are published and name a few case reports
- Locate a case by case name, citation or subject in a law library or online
- Update and note up a case
- Use proper case citation

WHAT IS A CASE?

A case is a decision of a judge or a tribunal. It is the written outcome of a dispute that has been tried in a court or an administrative tribunal. Since Canadian judges are required to follow previously decided similar cases, these cases must be made available to the judges and the public. Cases form a very significant part of the common law in Canada.

HOW TO READ A CASE

The ability to read a case is critical to legal analysis but also equally important to the task of locating *relevant* cases. If you can read cases quickly and accurately, you can efficiently detect those cases that are relevant and exclude those that are not.

Reading cases involves some skill. Most cases follow a particular format and, after reading several cases, the researcher should be able to find relevant information quickly without getting bogged down in irrelevant information.

At the most basic level, researchers should be familiar with the format of published cases. A description of this format is provided in Appendix 9A. This format is also important for computer research since you can narrow down your search by asking the computer to search only certain locations in the text of reported cases (*e.g.*, the parties or the date).

HOW CASES ARE PUBLISHED

The system of common law and the doctrine of precedent require that judges follow past judgments to the extent that they are similar and binding. Therefore, in a common law system, it is very important that judgments be written and published. This process is called case reporting.

Although many cases are in electronic form, computers are not always the most effective or efficient method of finding cases. Not only are electronic cases not recognized by all courts, but not all cases are in electronic form. In addition, it helps to understand the print-based system since many of the computer databases are similar to their paper compilations in the library. For example, the same cases from the *Dominion Law Reports* (print version) are also on BestCase (electronic service by Canada Law Book).

WHAT ARE CASE REPORTS?

Case reports are sets of books containing decided cases. Case reports are also called case reporters, law reports or case reporting series.

Various commercial publishers and government bodies collect the decisions of courts and administrative bodies, and assemble and publish them for resale. There are over 100 distinct case reports in Canada. It is important to know that **not all cases are reported in print**. Usually only those that change or clarify the law are reported. Some are collected and placed in databases of "unreported" cases while others are not collected or published at all.

Each "case report" consists of many volumes of bound books, which are arranged in chronological order on the library shelves. Each hardbound volume contains many cases. As you can imagine, there are thousands of volumes of case reports, containing millions of cases, on the shelves of law libraries. Each case has a set of keywords and a headnote or summary of the issues at the top. These headnotes are written by editors and occasionally include case comments and references to other cases. These headnotes are less commonly found in electronic versions of cases unless the cases were originally published in paper copy. This is changing as online editors recognize the value added by this service.

When locating cases, particular attention should be paid to the publishers (usually corporations or governments) of legal materials. Although it may seem strange to the new researcher, the way in which cases are published directs much of legal research. This is because each publisher decides which cases are published, how they are categorized, and how they are indexed. In order to locate cases, therefore, researchers should be aware of the different publishers' indexing systems.

WHICH CASES ARE IN CASE REPORTS?

Cases are organized and published in a number of ways. There is no single complete set of *all* decided cases in Canada. Cases from different jurisdictions and on different subjects are published in different case reports. This is one of the main reasons why legal researchers need research aids to assist them in locating cases.

Although computer research can eliminate some of this problem, at present there is no single database that contains all decided cases. The same case can often be found in several case reports. Those who collect the cases in case reports (or databases) usually provide detailed lists of the types of cases they publish. It is always a good idea for new researchers to check and ensure that the cases they are looking for are in that particular report (or database). The following are some examples of case reports.

Federal Case Reports

There are three case reports that publish cases from the two Canadian federal courts: the *Supreme Court Reports* (S.C.R.), the *National Reporter* (N.R.), and the *Federal Courts Reports* (F.C.R. (formerly F.C.)). The *Supreme Court Reports* is the official reporter for the Supreme Court and contains only Supreme Court of Canada decisions. The *National Reporter*, from Maritime Law Book, publishes all of the judgments of the Supreme Court of Canada, the Federal Court of Appeal, and some decisions from the Federal Court (the trial court of the federal court system). The *Federal Courts Reports* is the official reporter of the Federal Courts of Canada and contains all of the decisions of the Federal Courts (which typically involve matters of taxation, immigration and other areas of federal jurisdiction).

General Case Reports

The only case report that publishes cases from all the provinces as well as the two federal courts is the *Dominion Law Reports* (D.L.R.). It is the best-known case report in Canada. It is available in most law libraries and online through BestCase.

Provincial Case Reports

Most provinces have their own set of case reports that include court decisions from that particular province and cases that are important to the law of that province. Examples include the *British Columbia Law Reports* (B.C.L.R.) and the *Ontario Reports* (O.R.). These case reports are published by private publishers and are generally recognized by courts, practitioners and the law society of the province as "semi-official" reports for that jurisdiction in the absence of any sets published by the government itself.

Regional Case Reports

Regional case reports include cases from regions of Canada. For example, the *Western Weekly Reports* (W.W.R.) includes cases only from the Western provinces and the *Atlantic Provinces Reports* (A.P.R.) includes cases only from the four Atlantic provinces.

Subject Case Reports

Over the past 30 years or so, there has been an increase in case reports that only include cases on particular subjects. This is because lawyers tend to specialize and will often only purchase case reports containing cases that are relevant to their particular specialty. *Canadian Criminal Cases* (C.C.C.) and *Canadian Cases on Employment Law* (C.C.E.L.) are examples of such subject-specific reports.

Administrative Tribunal Case Reports

The decisions of administrative tribunals are published in separate reports from those of cases decided by judges. Reports that include court cases do not, as a rule, include decisions of administrative bodies because they are not *per se* part of the common law (*i.e.*, law of general applicability made by judges). An example of an administrative tribunal case report is the *Canadian Labour Relations Board Reports* (C.L.R.B.R.). It includes labour tribunal decisions from across Canada. Tribunal decisions traditionally have been published "in house" by the board, commission or tribunal rendering the decision. Obtaining print copies of such decisions has been difficult until recently because they were not widely disseminated. One exception is the *Canadian Human Rights Reporter* (C.H.R.R.) which is privately published (see Chapter 5) and widely purchased in print and online. Recently, many administrative tribunals have begun to post their decisions on their websites. Searching the Web via an Internet search engine will likely lead you to the decisions of any administrative tribunal that you are researching.

Digests of Cases

There are some so-called case reports that include only digests or summaries of cases. Researchers typically use these reports to keep current on cases as they come out or to locate recent cases.

Digests are useful not only because they are very current but also because they enable you to decide quickly whether the case is worth reading in full. Most practising lawyers subscribe to digest services in order to stay current on the law. The digests are organized by subject area, so a busy lawyer only needs to read those summaries that are relevant to his or her practice area.

For example, *All Canada Weekly Summaries* (A.C.W.S.), available in print or on *BestCase*, consists of digests of cases that will ultimately be published in full in *Dominion Law Reports* (D.L.R.).

The most comprehensive set of Canadian digested cases is the *Case Digests*, (part of the *Canadian Abridgment,* published by Carswell). The digests are collected in a multiple-volume set and sorted by a subject classification scheme. In order to locate digests you need to figure out the classification for your particular topic.

All of the commercial online providers have digest databases, with hyperlinks to full-text versions of the case (where available online), which simplifies research.

THE FORMAT OF CASE REPORTS

Usually, case reports have tables of cases and subject indexes in each volume to assist in locating cases quickly. Some also have other aids for research, such as annotations of cases and statute indexes. When looking at a new case report, a researcher should try to become acquainted with the available research aids and the format of the particular case report.

Many case reports have been divided into several series (*e.g.*, 1st, 2d, and 3d series). For example, *Dominion Law Reports* has several series. This means that the numbering of the volumes begins over again every so often. In each series, the volumes are numbered consecutively for many years. At some point, the publishers decide to begin the numbering again and call it a new series. For example, a 2d series will begin once the numbering in the first series becomes unmanageable. A 2d series is not a second edition or reprinting of the cases in the first series, but rather a continuation of the set with new volume numbers that start over again at Volume 1. The series number is important for locating cases.

Other case reporters, the *Supreme Court Reports* for example, do not use consecutive volume numbers but rather begin each year with volume one. These reporters are usually cited with the year in square brackets and followed by the volume number.

Most cases are published in case reports as soon as they are issued by the courts. However, this process of publication may take some time. Case reports may not be received in hard copy by law libraries until about four to six months after the decisions are written. Therefore, it is always important to check for most recent cases online or directly through the courts.

What Is NOT a Case Report?

Beginning legal researchers often are confused about this question. During the course of a trial, many types of documents are prepared and collected in the court's file for that case. These may include briefs, pleadings and evidentiary materials prepared by or collected by both sides and presented to the court. They do not form part of any judicial decision. To obtain copies of these types of documents, you must obtain them from the clerk at the courthouse where the case was heard. They are not collected by law libraries anywhere, although recently companies like Westlaw Canada are beginning to provide online collections of certain court documents including motions, applications and appeal facta and briefs (*e.g.*, Westlaw's *Litigator* service).

One particularly interesting type of material is a transcript, which is a word-for-word account of everything that was said by all parties during a trial. The rules for retention of transcripts vary by jurisdiction and may be obtained from the court clerk. Often, if a lawyer decides to appeal a case he or she will want to look at transcripts or other materials associated with the case at any lower levels. Journalists and historians may also have an interest in these types of materials.

A Word about "Unreported" Cases

Since the mid-1980s, many decisions that have not been chosen for printing in case reports have been put into online databases by various information providers. (See Chapter 5 for names of providers.) Courts have also been increasingly willing to share electronic versions of their decisions with online providers so that more law is more easily accessible to everyone.

It is imperative for the legal researcher to understand that these "unreported" cases are valid Canadian decisions and may certainly be cited as authority. The only distinctions between them and "reported" decisions is that the latter show up in print and the former are simply online. In addition, reported cases are carefully edited, typographical errors and errors in citation are corrected and the editors may contact the judge for clarification or to confirm that the information is accurate when necessary.

Some decisions may stay in the grey area of "not yet reported" for some period of time. Usually, if a decision has not been included in a printed reporter after approximately two years, it will remain "unreported" forever and therefore only available online, if at all.

Jury Trials

When a trial is conducted by a jury, the judge does not render a decision but rather requires the jury to do so. Hence, there is no written decision in a jury trial because the jury does not have to justify its reasons for deciding a case a certain way. There will be a docket file in the courthouse where the trial occurred, stating the outcome of the trial and the sentence rendered, but no written judicial decision will exist. Should the case be heard by an appellate court, that panel of judges will produce a written decision which would appear in print or online, or in both formats.

HOW TO FIND, UPDATE AND NOTE UP CASES

There is no simple way to find relevant cases. It is an art as well as a skill. The main rule to keep in mind is to be systematic. If you proceed in a systematic way and record your steps as you go, it is unlikely that you will get off track or duplicate steps. Ideally, you should have a strategy or plan of attack before you enter the library. Developing a research plan is discussed in Chapter 12.

Before beginning your search, you should ask yourself the following questions. The answers will help you narrow down the sources you will look at.

- Do you want the full text of a case?
- Do you just want the citation of the case?
- Do you want a summary or digest of the case?
- Do you want a reported or a not-yet-reported case?
- Do you want a list of all the cases related to your case?
- Do you want the history of your case (*e.g.*, appeals)?

No matter what case you are looking for, it must not only be located, but updated and noted up. In other words, there are three steps to conducting any case law research:

Step 1: Locate the case.
Step 2: Make sure the case is still good law (update it).
Step 3: Find other cases that have considered the case (note it up).

In terms of locating a case, you can find it by its case name, by citation or by its subject. If you know its name or citation, an online search or search of tables of cases will quickly produce results. However, if you know only the subject, other tools must be used. No matter what method you employ, once you find a case you must update it (find any subsequent history of any appeals) and note it up (find later cases that have referred to your original case).

The rest of this chapter shows you how to find, update and note up cases using each of the main providers of case law, namely:

- A law library collection
- Free services (CanLII, court websites and RawLaw)
- Commercial services (LN/QL, Westlaw and BestCase)

A Word on Free Electronic Collections

Although there are several websites that provide free access to collections of cases (*e.g.*, CanLII, law library websites, and some courthouse websites), these collections generally only go back in time to the year when the courts first began providing them. In most instances this was the mid-1990s.

These free access case collections also tend not to be "value added" in that they do not provide case summaries, digests, headnotes, commentaries or hyperlinks to other considered cases. So they tend to not be as helpful when trying to research histories or judicial considerations of cases.

In addition, because these cases are not edited or compiled by publishers, they may not be as easy to search as those on commercial services. Because they often do not contain headnotes or key search terms, your subject search may be very cumbersome. As always, it is best to refine your search as much as you can before going online or you may be overwhelmed by all the information available.

HOW TO FIND CASES IN A LAW LIBRARY

Step 1: Locate the Case

If you do not have access to an online collection of cases or cannot locate a case in an online collection, you will need to look in the library. You can look for the case by case name, by case citation or by subject.

Finding a Case by Name or Citation in the Library

The main printed tool for locating cases is called the *Consolidated Table of Cases*, which is part of the larger set known as the *Canadian Abridgment*. Published by Carswell, it is a multi-volume comprehensive list of thousands of reported Canadian cases. It includes the titles of almost all published cases in Canada and of many British and some international cases. It contains case histories (*e.g.*, appeals) and citations for each case. Carswell also publishes new cumulative revisions of the *Consolidated Table of Cases* from time to time (see Illustrations 9.1 and 9.2).

Illustration 9.1
Consolidated Table of Cases (Canadian Abridgment)

THE
CANADIAN ABRIDGMENT
THIRD EDITION

CONSOLIDATED
TABLE OF CASES

TABLE GÉNÉRALE DE
LA JURISPRUDENCE

APRIL – DECEMBER
AVRIL – DÉCEMBRE
2009

VOLUME 1
A – L

Containing all cases digested in Alternative Dispute Resolution Reissue Volume 2, Bankruptcy and
Insolvency Reissue Volumes 3, 4, 4A and 4B, Contracts Reissue Volumes 27, 27A, 27B, 27C and
27D and in the [2009] Canadian Current Law — Case Digests issues 4 to 12.

Comprend toutes les décisions résumées dans Alternative Dispute Resolution réédition volume 2,
Bankruptcy and Insolvency réédition volumes 3, 4, 4A et 4B, Contracts réédition volumes 27, 27A,
27B, 27C et 27D, et dans [2009] Canadian Current Law — Sommaires de la jurisprudence
numéros 4 à 12.

CARSWELL®

Reprinted by permission of Carswell, a division of Thomson Reuters Canada Limited.

Illustration 9.2
Consolidated Table of Cases — Entry

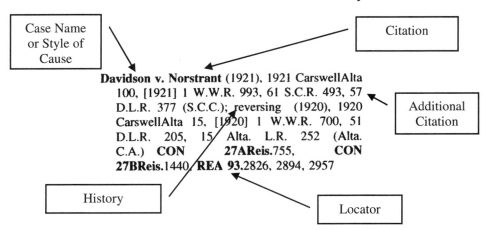

The Canadian Abridgment Third Edition "Consolidated Table of Cases — Supplement April – December 2009 Reprinted by permission of Carswell, a division of Thomson Reuters Canada Limited.

The *Consolidated Table of Cases* is just one of several aids within the *Abridgment*. Use of the *Abridgment* is described in more detail below, but the main rule when searching any of the parts of the *Abridgment* is to search in the hardbound volumes first, then the softbound volumes, then the loose-leaf volumes (*i.e.*, search from oldest to most recent). Once you have located a case citation in the *Abridgment*, it is always advisable to go to the actual case report to make sure the citation is correct.

Finding a Case by Subject in the Library

A case is more difficult to locate by subject than by title. This is because, as mentioned above, cases are published in a variety of ways in a variety of case reports and in a variety of databases.

Typically, researchers use secondary materials to gain a general understanding and, at the same time, to gather citations of cases and statutes. These cases often provide a springboard for further case research. Use of these and other secondary materials is discussed in detail in Chapter 6 (How to Find Secondary Materials). The top three are: the *Canadian Encyclopedic Digest* (CED); *Halsbury's Laws of Canada*; and law textbooks. A more specific tool for locating cases, once you have narrowed down your topic, is the *Canadian Abridgment* and its Key Classification system.

The ***Canadian Encyclopedic Digest* (CED)**, a legal encyclopedia, is often the first place researchers will go when looking for cases because it provides references to leading cases as part of each entry. It is available in paper (multi-volume) and online through Westlaw Canada, and can be searched fairly easily.

The paper version (multiple loose-leaf volumes) is fairly easy to access because of its highly developed subject classification scheme. To locate a case in the print version of the CED, you need to first find your subject in the classification scheme (found in the first few volumes) in the *Contents Key* and *Index* (this is described in detail in Chapter 6). Be careful when searching the online version as a poorly thought out search might uncover too much information. Start by reviewing the online list of topics (Index) before delving into the full text.

Halsbury's Laws of Canada is similar to the CED in that it is a comprehensive encyclopedia of Canadian law. It is available in both print and online through LN/QL. It is divided into logical categories, topics and detailed subheadings so it is fairly easy to use. At the end of each volume is a detailed subject index, a recommended list of additional secondary sources for further research and a glossary of relevant terms. There is also a consolidated master index to help with research.

Law **textbooks** and **legal journals** (often called commentary) are very useful when looking for cases since they often provide summaries and synthesis with specific case citations. Armed with a current case directly on point, you can go directly to online services and look for other cases that considered it. More and more textbooks and journals are becoming available through aggregated collections sold by commercial online providers such as HeinOnline. Refer to Chapter 6 to learn more about these sources and how to use them.

The ***Canadian Abridgment*** is several research tools in one. The two sets that are most useful for locating cases are *Case Digests* and *Canadian Case Citations*. But to use these effectively you need to understand the Key Classification System.

Long ago, Carswell, the publisher of the *Canadian Abridgment* set, went to great trouble to develop a subject classification scheme for use in its whole set of research aids. It is called the Key Classification System and sorts every case and case digests by a coded sequence of numbers and letters. This classification system is very similar to that used in the CED because Carswell is the publisher of both tools.

Therefore, researchers need only find the way in which the subject they are researching is categorized in order to find cases, summaries and case digests in that category. This may sound easy, but in order to locate a case by subject you must first know the particular subject area and how it is categorized. As you can imagine, this is not an easy task for a person unfamiliar with a particular area of law. Many legal subjects fall into a host of areas of the law; different publishers often categorize the subjects differently and those categorizations may not be consistent with your thinking. To avoid searching under the wrong subject, most researchers first read about the law generally in secondary sources in order to achieve a clearer sense of the way the law is categorized before delving into subject classification schemes and case reports.

In order to locate a case by subject in these digests (or any part of the *Canadian Abridgment*) it helps to first find your subject in the classification scheme, which is contained in the *Key & Research Guide*. The *Key* is a thick, single loose-leaf volume that contains the Key Classification System (see Illustrations 9.3 and 9.4) and a Subject Titles Table (see Illustration 9.5). Both list legal topics and are good starting points for research.

Illustration 9.3
Key Classification System (Canadian Abridgment)

CANADIAN ABRIDGMENT
KEY CLASSIFICATION SYSTEM

EDITOR'S NOTE: *All case digests in the Abridgment are classified and organized according to the subject titles which form part of the Abridgment's classification system. To facilitate research, each of the subject titles has a Scope Note describing its contents and parameters. In addition, an extensive system of cross-references enables the researcher to locate specific topics and related issues.*

AB INITIO — *see Torts XX.1.d*

ABANDONMENT — *see Natural resources II.3.c.v; Public law II.12.a.v.A; Real property V.10.b.iv.D*

ABATEMENT — *see Estates and trusts I.6.i; Public law II.12.a.v.C*

ABDUCTION — *see Criminal law VI.2–VI.6, VI.52, VI.72, VI.93*

ABETTING — *see Criminal law I.6.b*

The Canadian Abridgment Key and Research Guide, Third Edition. Reprinted by permission of Carswell, a division of Thomson Reuters Canada Limited.

Illustration 9.4
Key Classification System (Canadian Abridgment) — Excerpt from Torts — Negligence section

---

6. Strict liability (rule in Rylands v. Fletcher)
— *liability for environmental damage, see ENVIRONMENTAL LAW II; strict liability in nuisance, see XVII.3; vicarious liability, see XVI.7*
  a. General principles
     i. Non-natural user of land
     ii. Escape
  b. Particular dangers
     — *liability of owners of animal, see XVI.10; tortious liability of public utilities generally, see PUBLIC LAW IV.3.b*
     i. Chemicals
     ii. Electricity
        A. Installation
        B. Maintenance
        C. Miscellaneous
     iii. Explosives
     iv. Fire
        — *statutory liability for fires in tort, see XVI.11.a.i*
     v. Firearms
        — *liability of police officer, see LAW ENFORCEMENT AGENCIES I.2*
     vi. Poisons and drugs
     vii. Gas and fumes
     viii. Gasoline and oil

From Canadian Abridgment Key and Research Guide. Adapted by permission of Carswell, a division of Thomson Reuters Canada Limited.

Illustration 9.5
Subject Titles Table (Canadian Abridgment)

SUBJECT TITLES TABLE

EDITOR'S NOTE: The list of subject titles below is supplemented in the Key by an extensive system of cross-references. The cross-references appear in bold-face and may be of assistance in locating specific topics or related issues. In addition, each subject title includes a Scope Note describing its contents and the location of related issues in other subject titles.

i   Key & Research Guide 2009–2

Using Case Digests (Canadian Abridgment)

A great but often underused case-locating tool is called *Case Digests*. This is a set of many volumes and forms the bulk of the *Canadian Abridgment* set. *Case Digests* is a 160-plus-volume collection of summaries/digests of cases, and includes almost every reported Canadian case and many more recent unreported cases. From these summaries a researcher can quickly find a case, decide if the decision is relevant and find other related cases. To find a case, you first need to find your classification number.

Illustration 9.6
Case Digest (Canadian Abridgment)

Excerpt from Volume 114

Digest Number

293.   **(XVI.6.b.i)**
Negligence — Strict liability (rule in Rylands v. Fletcher) — Particular dangers — Chemicals —— Car battery exploding.

Classification Number

Narrative: Background Facts of the Case

Defendant attached jumper cables from his car to plaintiff's car battery. Defendant also removed the air filter on the carburetor and used gas line anti-freeze. The anti-freeze ignited and in turn ignited the hydrogen gas produced by the charging battery and exploded the battery injuring plaintiff. Plaintiff sued. **Held:** The action should succeed. Defendant was wholly at fault in using a highly flammable anti-freeze in the carburetor for a purpose for which it was not intended. Where a person chose to employ an inherently dangerous method to procure a desired result and injury followed, he must be held liable.

The first phrases in the caption repeat the classification key phrases.

Deposition: Reasons for Disposition

Boudreau v. Paquin (1979), 25 N.B.R. (2d) 271, 51 A.P.R. 271, 1979 CarswellNB 111 (Q.B.).

Case Name and Citation

As you can see from the excerpt in **Illustration 9.6** these digests are in order by "classification number" (see top right hand of digest: XVI.6.b.i) and the case of *Boudreau v. Pacquin* was classified under XVI.6.b.i. If you look in the classification scheme in **Illustration 9.4**, you will see that XVI.6.b.i represents the following subjects:

Torts
XVI: Negligence
6:     Strict liability (Rule in *Rylands v. Fletcher*)
b: Particular dangers
i: Chemicals

In addition, the first loose-leaf volume consists of the General Index, which is an alphabetical subject index of legal concepts arising out of the case law digests.

Tips When Using the Abridgment

When using the library set of the *Abridgment* you must look in *all* of the following parts:

- *Key & Research Guide*: Look in the Subject Titles Table and Key Classification Scheme.
- *Main Set*: Look under your title (*i.e.*, subject), note the classification number, and refer to the pages and specific digest numbers.
- *Supplements* (softcover): Refer to your subject and classification number.
- *Canadian Current Law – Case Digests* and *Canadian Case Citations*:[1] Look at these for further updates.

Many Canadian researchers have become frustrated with the *Canadian Abridgment*, arguing that it is too difficult to use because of the number of supplements. This requires explanation. Because the *Canadian Abridgment* is a vital aid to case law research, it is important that researchers understand the underpinnings of the system.

As soon as the paper volumes of the *Canadian Abridgment* are published they are out of date. Therefore, the publisher, Carswell, must continually update these hardbound volumes with supplements. As soon as the supplements accumulate to a certain point, these supplements are bound. This process is continuous so that each source typically has one original volume or volumes (called the *Main Set*), as well as both hardbound and softbound supplements. Periodically, the entire set is consolidated. As a result of this ongoing process, the researcher is required to look in a number of volumes to find the information needed. As a rule of thumb, the three general steps in using the *Canadian Abridgment* are as follows:

- Check Hardbound
- Check Softbound
- Check Loose-leaf

If you search in each of these volumes, you can ensure that your information is correct and up to date. If you are confused, ask a law librarian for assistance. Once you know the basic steps, the *Abridgment* becomes an invaluable aid.

---

[1]   These are other parts of the *Canadian Abridgment*.

Steps 2 and 3: Update and Note Up the Cases in a Library

After you have located the cases that are relevant to your situation, you will need to update them and note them up. This means ensuring that the cases are still "good law". This requires:

- Updating: Find the history of the cases. Have they been appealed or overturned?
- Noting-up: Find the judicial treatment of the cases. Have they been considered in other cases, and have these cases overruled them or followed them, *etc.*?

There are two paper-based research aids specifically designed to answer these two queries: tables of cases, which list all decided cases and their history; and case citators, which list all cases, their history and their treatment (how they were considered in other, later cases). The two main Canadian sources are published by Carswell and are also available on WC:

- To update, use the *Consolidated Table of Cases (Canadian Abridgment)*.
- To note up, use the *Canadian Case Citations (Canadian Abridgment)*.

Consolidated Table of Cases

The *Consolidated Table of Cases (Canadian Abridgment)* lists alphabetically almost every Canadian case, the history of the case and citations. It is typically used to locate the citation of a case or to find out if a case has been appealed. It is available in print and on Westlaw Canada.

Some individual case reports, both topical and jurisdictional, also have indexes that provide information about the history and judicial treatment of cases. A researcher could consult case tables in those case reports where a case would likely be reported to locate this information. For example, if looking for a British Columbia tort case, a researcher might look in *British Columbia Law Reports* (B.C.L.R.) or *Canadian Cases on the Law of Torts* (C.C.L.T.).

Canadian Case Citations

The main tools used to update or note up cases are called case citators. These citators are lists of cases that are compiled by editors. Under each case there is information about whether the case has been appealed (history) and how the case has been considered in other cases (treatment). These tools greatly assist the ability of our courts to apply the rule of precedent.

The only cross-Canada print citator is called *Canadian Case Citations (Canadian Abridgment)*. It consists of a set of 22 hardbound volumes and their supplements. It contains two types of information: prior and subsequent history (*e.g.*, the prior or subsequent treatment of that case in a lower or higher court), and treatment of the case by other cases.

Illustration 9.7
Canadian Case Citations (Canadian Abridgment)

Cuddy Chicks Ltd. v. Ontario (Labour ——— The decision of the Ontario
Relations Board) Labour Relations Board can be
(May 6, 1988), Doc. 0310-87-R found in all of these reports

[1988] O.L.R.B. Rep. 468, 88 C.L.L.C.
16,049, 19 C.L.R.B.R. (N.S.) 286 (Ont.
L.R.B.)

affirmed / confirmé (November 2, 1988),——— The decision of the Ontario
Doc.469/88 (1988), 66 O.R. (2d) 284, 32 Labour Relations Board was
O.A.C. 7, 88 C.L.L.C. 14,053, 33 Admin. affirmed by the Ontario
L.R. 304 (Ont. Div. Ct.) Divisional Court

The decision of the Ontario ——— **which was affirmed / qui a été confirmé**
Divisional Court was affirmed (September 8, 1989), Doc. CA 67/89 (1989),
by the Court of Appeal for 39 Admin. L.R. 48, 62 D.L.R. (4th) 125, 35
Ontario. O.A.C. 94, 89 C.L.L.C. 14,051, 44 C.R.R.
75, 70 O.R. (2d) 179, [1989] O.L.R.B. Rep.
989 (Ont. C.A.)

which was affirmed / qui a été confirmé ——— The decision of the Court of
(June 6, 1991), Doc. 21675 (1991), 91 Appeal for Ontario was affirmed
C.L.L.C. 14,024, 3 O.R. (3d) 128 (note), 50 on appeal to the Supreme Court
Admin. L.R. 44, 122 N.R. 361, 81 D.L.R. of Canada
(4th) 121, [1991] O.L.R.B. Rep 790, 47
O.A.C. 271, 4 C.R.R. (2d) 1, [1991] 2 S.C.R.
5 (S.C.C.)

...

The Ontario Divisional Court ——— **Cases citing Ont. Div. Ct.**
decision was followed in this
case Ⓕ B.G. (L.G.A.), Re (1989), 101 A.R. 92
(Alta. Prov. Ct.)

...

The Ontario Court of Appeal ——— **Cases citing Ont. C.A.**
decision was considered in these
cases Ⓒ R. v. Lepage (1994), 23 C.R.R. (2d) 81
(Ont. Gen. Div.)

Ⓒ Health Sciences Assn. of Alberta v.
Calgary General Hospital (1991), 91
C.L.L.C. 16,044 (Alta. L.R.B.)

...

Cases citing S.C.C.

Ⓓ P&S Investments Ltd. v. Newfoundland ——— The decision of the Supreme
(Human Rights Commission) (1994), 2 Court of Canada was
C.C.E.L. (2d) 287 (Nfld. T.D.) distinguished in this case

Ⓕ K Mart Canada Ltd. v. U.F.C.W., Local
1518 (1994), 24 C.L.R.B.R. (2d) 1
(B.C.L.R.B.)

Ⓕ Canada (Minster of Employment & The decision of the Supreme
Immigration) v. Agbasi (1993), 10 Admin. Court of Canada was followed in
L.R. (2d) 94 (Fed. T.D.) these cases

Ⓕ Tétreault-Gadoury v. Canada
(Employment & Immigration
Commission) (1991), 91 C.L.L.C. 14,023
(S.C.C.)

The decision of the Supreme ——— Ⓒ G. (M.) c. Gazette (The) (November 28,
Court of Canada was considered 1996), no C.A. Montréal 500-09-002434-
in these cases 967, 500-09-002305-969 (Que. C.A.)

Ⓒ Falkner v. Ontario (Ministry of
Community & Social Services) (1996),
140 D.L.R. (4th) 115 (Ont. Div. Ct.)

...

From Canadian Abridgment: Canadian Case Citations: User's Guide. *Adapted by permission of Carswell, a division of Thomson Reuters Canada Limited.*

Illustration 9.8
Terms and Symbols Used in Canadian Case Citations
(Canadian Abridgment)

Affirmed Decision affirmed on appeal or on reconsideration; or application for judicial review refused

Amended Correction of wording of decision by decision maker to conform to intended meaning

Additional reasons Additional reasons for decision

Allowed leave to appeal Leave to appeal to an appellate court allowed

Refused leave to appeal Leave to appeal to an appellate court refused

Referred for further consideration

back by an appellate court to lower level for further consideration or clarification

Granted reconsideration or rehearing Application for reconsideration or rehearing of decision by same court granted

Refused reconsideration or rehearing Application for reconsideration or rehearing of decision by same court refused

Reversed Decision reversed on appeal or on reconsideration

Varied Decision varied or modified by either the decision maker or an appel-

---

TREATMENT OF DECISIONS

(N) **Not Followed/Overruled** *Cited case expressly overruled, not applied or judged bad law*

(F) **Followed** *Principle of law in cited case adopted*

(D) **Distinguished** *Cited case inapplicable because of difference in facts or law*

(C) **Considered** *Some consideration given to cited case*

From Canadian Abridgment: Canadian Case Citations: User's Guide. *Adapted by permission of Carswell, a division of Thomson Reuters Canada Limited.*

HOW TO FIND CASES USING NO-FEE SERVICES

There are more and more no-fee websites that provide access to Canadian cases. The main ones today are CanLII; the federal, provincial and territorial court websites; and Rawlaw. These services are described in more detail in Chapter 5 (How to Find the Law and Legal Information).

Using CanLII to Find Cases

CanLII (<http://www.canlii.org>) provides access to court cases from both the trial and appellate level courts for all Canadian jurisdictions. It has a few drawbacks:

Coverage: Its coverage goes back to only about 1990 with each database of cases having a different inception date. You need to check the Scope of

Databases link to see what each of the databases includes and may have to go to printed reporters for older cases. It does, however, include cases from administrative tribunals.

Not value added. CanLII is not a "value-added site" like the commercial databases. This means it does not always provide summaries, headnotes and hyperlinks to other cases. However, "key terms" are automatically generated for each of the decisions retrieved. It also provides some hypertext linking between its case law and legislation content.

CanLII is most useful if you know the name of your case or the citation. In fact, it will direct you to your specific court website. CanLII has direct links to the court websites from its case law pages.

Illustration 9.9
CanLII Search Page for Cases in a Particular Court

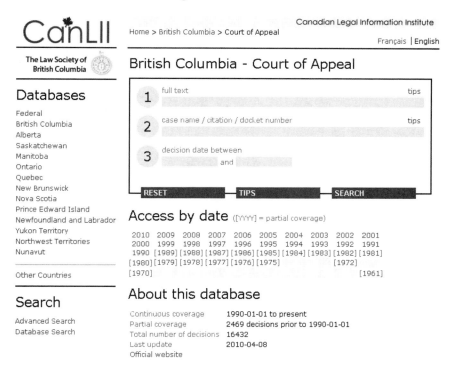

Reproduced by permission of CanLII.

Step 1: Locate a Case on CanLII

In CanLII you can search by name, citation or word search. As you can see from Illustration 9.9, you have a choice of doing a global search (all databases) or a specific search (by jurisdiction database).

By case name or citation: If you know the **citation** for the case, the fastest way to retrieve it is to enter the citation into Search Field 2 on the site's main search template. If you know the name of the case but not the citation, it is more efficient to select the jurisdiction first and then search for the case name in Search Field 2. This way you will not need to discard irrelevant cases from other jurisdictions.

By subject: To locate a case by **subject**, you can search the full-text box (Search Field 1) for your topic. Once again it is best to select the jurisdiction first in order to filter out irrelevant cases. Remember it is always best to use secondary sources to identify keywords or topics before delving into vast case law databases.

It is also possible to browse for cases, but in order to do so you must know the jurisdiction, court and date of the decision. If you have all that information, you have what you need to do a more precise search.

Steps 2 and 3: Update and note up a Case on CanLII

Once you have located your case you can note up the case by clicking on the CanLII "Noteup" link. If there are any cases in CanLII's databases that have referred to your case, you will see a list of those cases with links to the full text of those decisions. CanLII does not provide any indication of the judicial treatment or history of a case. You will have to read the case through to see if it has been overruled, followed, distinguished, considered or merely referred to.

Using Courthouse Websites to Find Cases

Most courts in Canada provide access to their more recent cases via their websites. The courts do not provide any value-added information or the ability to note up or update a case. If searching for a case from a particular court website, it is better to use CanLII in order to take advantage of the searching and noting-up features available. CanLII does provide links to all the court websites if the researcher thinks it is necessary to visit them. (See also Appendix 9B: Courthouse Electronic Cases for a list of courthouse websites.)

Using RawLaw to Find Cases

RawLaw (<http://www.mlb.nb.ca/>) is another free case law database, provided by Maritime Law Book. This database provides access to cases reported in the Maritime Law Book print reporters with the headnotes and subject key numbers stripped out (hence the name RawLaw). Individual cases with the headnotes and editorial content can be purchased. These cases cannot be updated or noted up.

Illustration 9.10
RawLaw from Maritime Law Book Main Search Page

Reproduced by permission of Maritime Law Book.

HOW TO FIND CASES USING COMMERCIAL PROVIDERS

The three main commercial service providers are LN/QL, Westlaw Canada and BestCase. These services are described in detail in Chapter 5.

Each of the commercial providers has many databases of cases: reported, unreported and in digest form. Many of the databases are combined into global databases to make the searching of multiple case collections easier. For example, lawyers have the ability in LN/QL to make up their own customized combinations of databases and save these combinations for repeated use.

Searching by Case Name or Citation

All three providers have a quick way to search for a case by case name or citation. Usually from the landing page, you can simply enter the information you have and a search will be conducted of all the available databases.

In practical terms this means that you can do a very quick search without having to search through several different databases. The search engine will use the citation to search only relevant databases.

This tool is primarily for busy lawyers who know the case they want and may be looking for more current cases like this one, which they can find through hyperlinks.

If you know what database your case is likely to be in, you can do a similar word search in that specific database.

All three providers have powerful citators. These electronic citators can be used to both update and note up cases. For example:

1. If you are in the case you need, you can select the citator or note-up function and you will be hyperlinked to all the history and judicial treatment of this case. Each database has its own particular method of identifying the judicial treatment of a case. LexisNexis/Quicklaw and Westlaw Canada use symbols, while BestCase describes the treatment textually. Each database provides an information link or button that explains the meaning of these symbols. Always be on the lookout for negative treatment of the case you are researching.

2. You can go directly into the particular citator database and you can do a word search for your case. Just as in the paper version, it will list all those cases that mentioned your case.

Using Westlaw Canada to Find Cases

Illustration 9.11
Westlaw Canada Main Search Page

Reprinted by permission of Carswell, a division of Thomson Reuters Canada Litmited.

If you know the case's name or citation, as with legislation, you can use the "Find" search on Westlaw Canada's default search page. If your search is less specific, use the more detailed search templates in the "Cases" database.

Illustration 9.12
Westlaw Canada Cases Search Page

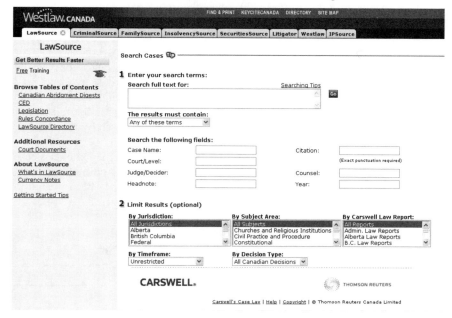

Reprinted by permission of Carswell, a division of Thomson Reuters Canada Limited.

This template enables the researcher to search by case name, citation, keywords or even by judge or counsel.

If you are searching by subject, you can also search the full text using "Terms and Connectors" or "Natural Language" searching. Natural language searching is where you formulate your search in terms of a question. "Does a Treaty Indian have the right to hunt and fish without a licence?", for example. Prior to conducting a subject search, you should consult secondary sources in order to have a good idea of the terms and concepts for which you should be searching. *Case Digests*, the CED and *Words and Phrases* are all good sources to use to start your research.

Once you have located a case, you can note it up using KeyCite Canada. Keycite provides the history of the case along with citing references and links to secondary sources that refer to the case if available.

Using LexisNexis/Quicklaw to Find Cases

Like other commercial providers, LN/QL essentially gives you two choices: conduct a global search by entering a case name or citation, or do a database search by selecting a specific database.

In LN/QL you typically start on the "search default page" (Illustration 9.13). You will see "Find a document", which allows you to find a case quickly by entering a case by name, citation, *etc.* You can insert words into the "Find a case by name" or "Find by citation" search boxes. Or, you can go into a separate database by clicking on the top tabs that list the various databases, such as Court Cases, Tribunal Cases, Legislation, Commentary, Journals, *etc.*, and use the templates provided to search. LN/QL has the most extensive collection of tribunal cases of all the case law databases.

The best place to start a subject search is in secondary sources. If you go to the Commentary database (tab on top) you will find several secondary sources such as "Words and Phrases", *Halsbury's Laws of Canada* and "the Canada Digest". You can look through the indexes or enter a word search and read generally. Some secondary sources are hyperlinked to specific cases to make research easy. If you are searching by subject you can also search the full text of the case database by keyword. You can also narrow your search by jurisdiction, court, judge or counsel (see Illustration 9.14).

Once you have located your case you can note it up using the Quickcite case citatory, which provides the history of the case along with its citing references. Quickcite uses a series of icons that illustrate how the case has been treated in the courts.

Illustration 9.13
LexisNexis/Quicklaw Default Search Page

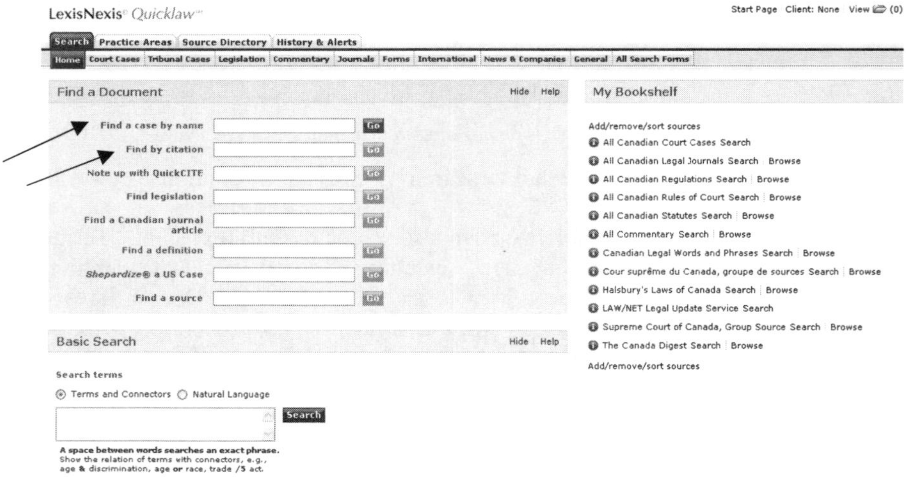

Illustration 9.14
LexisNexis/Quicklaw Court Cases Search Page

| Search | Practice Areas | Source Directory | History & Alerts |

| Home | **Court Cases** | Tribunal Cases | Legislation | Commentary | Journals | Forms | International | News & Companies | General | All Search Forms |

Court Cases

Court Cases	**Search terms**	[ ] **Search**
QuickCITE™ Case Citator		**A space between words searches an exact phrase.** Show the relation of terms with connectors, e.g., age **&** discrimination, age **or** race, trade /5 act. View connectors...
The Canada Digest		
Breach of Contract Quantums		Refine search by area(s) of law
Child Support Quantums		**Search Term Equivalents** [✓] Singular and plural [✓] Masculine and feminine
Defamation Quantums	**Sources**	*All Canadian Court Cases [▼] ⓘ
Dependants' Relief Quantums		Find more sources...
Matrimonial Property Quantums		**+ Show document segments**
Medical Negligence Quantums	**Case name**	[ ]
		To find Smith v. Jones, enter: Smith **and** Jones
Property-Related Torts Quantums	**Citation**	[ ] Citation help
Sentencing Quantums	**Specify date**	All available dates [▼]
Spousal Support Quantums	**Summary**	[ ]
		Search for words that appear only within the summary of the case
Wrongful Dismissal Quantums	**Jurisdiction**	[ ] All Jurisdictions
Carlson Personal Injury		[ ] Federal
		[ ] Alberta
Wrongful Dismissal Notice Searcher		[ ] British Columbia Reset list
Related Searches	**Court**	Select a jurisdiction from the list above.
Tribunal Cases		
International Cases (Common Law)		Reset list
Shepard's® Citations		
International Cases (Civil Law)	**Judge, Panel or Arbitrator**	[ ]
How do I...?	**Counsel**	[ ]

Using BestCase to Find Cases

BestCase from Canada Law Book provides electronic access to the contents of the Canada Law Book print reporters including *Dominion Law Reports*, *Canadian Criminal Cases* and a number of other regional and subject reporters. The database also includes unreported decisions, the *All-Canada Weekly Summaries* and the *Weekly Criminal Bulletin*. Because Canada Law Book has a long history of legal publishing in Canada, BestCase may contain older cases not available from some of the newer commercial providers. To locate cases, go to the main search page (see Illustration 9.15) and you will see four choices.

Illustration 9.15
BestCase Main Search Page

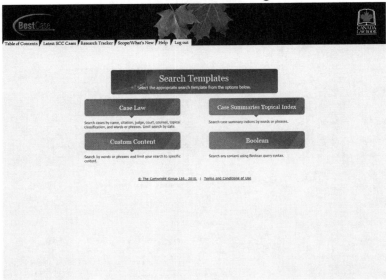

Reproduced from BestCase with the permission of Canada Law Book, A Division of The Cartwright Group Ltd. (1-800-263-3269, <www.canadalawbook.ca>).

Illustration 9:16
BestCase Case Law Search

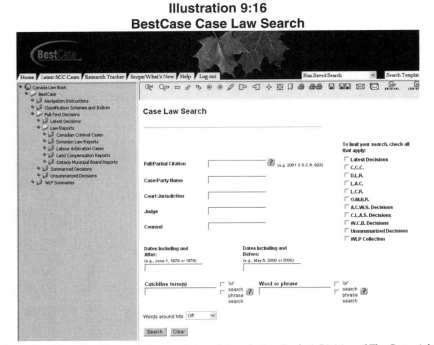

Reproduced from BestCase with the permission of Canada Law Book, A Division of The Cartwright Group Ltd. (1-800-263-3269, <www.canadalawbook.ca>).

Researchers can search BestCase by case name, citation, court, judge, counsel or subject. The best place to start is either in the "Case Law Search" template to conduct a global search, or in the specific database or law report by selecting from the list of law reports.

If searching by subject, users can search the full text by keyword. In addition, users can browse the classification schemes for each of the print reporters as well as their tables of contents. Classification schemes are subject keys devised by the editors of Canada Law Book. Once a search is completed, "Select Decisions", that is, cases that have established any important legal principles, are identified with a diamond symbol.

Cases can be noted up by clicking the Note-Up tab. The results list will provide the history of the case and all citing references. The database also provides links to the full-text cases that are available on the database.

Using Google Scholar

Google Scholar (<http://scholar.google.ca/>) has a law-specific search engine which can be accessed by selecting the "Legal Opinions and Journals" button on the Google Scholar webpage. This collection provides links to Canadian as well as U.S. federal and state cases. Although Google has not specifically indicated the extent of case law covered, they do, at a minimum, cover all the U.S. Reports. In addition, the search engine has indexed a number of legal journals including those provided by HeinOnline. As always, when searching the Internet you should make sure that cases come from an authoritative source.

HOW TO WRITE A CASE CITATION

The citation of cases is fairly rigid. This is primarily because each component of the citation is necessary to enable a person to locate a case.

An example of a case citation is as follows:

Style of Cause	Date	Volume	Case Report	Series	Page	Court
↓	↓	↓	↓	↓	↓	↓
Jones v. Gas Co.	(1980),	2	D.L.R.	(2d)	555	(B.C.C.A.)

The following are some basic rules of case citation. For detailed rules of citation it is best to refer to a specific book on the topic.

Style of Cause

The style of cause is the title of the case or the names of the parties involved in the action. Some of the rules of citation of the style of cause are as follows:

- Always underline or italicize style of cause, including the *v.*, which stands for *versus*.
- Do not use full names of parties.

- Refer to the Crown as *R*.
- *Re* means "Reference" or "in the matter of a party named". These cases are usually applications to a court for an opinion or interpretation of someone's rights.
- Omit "the" before most styles of cause.
- *Ex Parte* means "on application of a party who is not present".
- In some family or sexual assault matters only initials are given (*e.g.*, *M. v. L.*).

Date/Year

The year in the citation means either the date the case was published or the date of judgment.

If there are round brackets around the year, it means the date of judgment. If only round brackets are in the citation, you also need the volume number to locate the case. Square brackets are used to enclose the year of publication. In some cases it may be necessary to include both square and round brackets.

Volume

The volume is the number of the volume in which the case is published. Some reports resume numbering at volume 1 at the beginning of each year. Citations to these reports will have a year in square brackets followed by a volume number.

Case Report

The title of the case report is abbreviated. There are specific books in the library that provide the abbreviation of case reports.[2] Do not try to guess what the abbreviation is.

One really useful and comprehensive free website for interpreting abbreviations is the *Cardiff Index to Legal Abbreviations* at <http://www.legal abbrevs.cardiff.ac.uk/>.

Series

The series number is an essential piece of information. Many case reports have several series spanning many years (*e.g.*, 1st, 2d, and 3d series). When citing a case report, you must cite the series in brackets after the title (*e.g.*, D.L.R. (2d)).

---

[2]   *E.g.*, Iosipescu & Whitehead, *Legal Writing and Research Manual*, 6th ed. (Markham, Ont.: LexisNexis Butterworths, 2004); *Canadian Guide to Uniform Legal Citation*, 6th ed. (the "McGill Guide") (Scarborough, Ont.: Carswell, 2006); and Carswell's *Canadian Abridgment, Consolidated Table of Cases*, at the beginning of Volume 1.

Page or Paragraph Number

The citation includes the page at which the report begins. If you are referring to a specific page within a case, include that page number at the end of the citation, preceded by "at" (*e.g.*, 434 at 437).

Most modern judicial decisions now have numbered paragraphs. Numbering begins with the first paragraph of the judge's actual words and ensures very accurate reference to the exact text you wish to point out. Everything above that is editorial matter and is not numbered. If you wish to refer to a specific paragraph within a case, include that paragraph number at the end of the citation, preceded by "at para." (*e.g.*, 345 at para. 21). Alternatively, this information can be indicated by use of the paragraph symbol (*e.g.*, 345 ¶ 21); do not put "at" before the symbol.

Court

The court is also part of the citation, and each court has its own particular citation (*e.g.*, B.C.C.A. stands for the British Columbia Court of Appeal). If the court is obvious from the title of the report, then the court does not need to be included in the citation (*e.g.*, S.C.R. includes only decisions of the Supreme Court of Canada).

Parallel or Alternate Citations

A parallel or alternate cite is another citation of the same case in a different case report or online. This is to assist those who may only have access to certain case reports or online services.

The date does not need to be repeated in an alternate cite, but square-bracketed years must be included when they are necessary to locate the case by volume. Alternate citations are separated by a comma.

See below for discussion of the recent "neutral citation" innovation for identifying cases.

Punctuation

General Rules about Punctuation in Citation	
Comma	Precedes date in square brackets Follows date in round brackets Between parallel citations
Period	After all abbreviations At end of citation
Brackets	Around date (round if date of judgment; square if date of volume) Around court Around series
Underline or italicize	Style of cause only, including the "v."
Semicolon	Between citations of different cases

History of a Case

The history of a case is the course of a case through all levels of appeal. Prior history means all that happened before. Subsequent history means all that happened after.

Use of *Sub Nom.*

The term *sub nom.* is the abbreviation for the Latin *sub nomen*, meaning "under the name of". It implies that the case also has an alternate title. In the citation, this other name appears in round brackets before the name of the case report in which it appears.

For example, *W. v. R.* (1984), [1985] 1 W.W.R. 122, (*sub nom. Re Walton and A.G. of Canada*) 13 D.L.R. (4th) 379 (Ont. C.A.).

ELECTRONIC CITATIONS

Generally, if the case is published in a printed reporter it is sufficient to cite to the printed reporter only. Otherwise, if a case is taken from an electronic source it is necessary to add that information to the citation. After the citation, add a comma and then the word "online" followed by a colon. If a commercial online system was used, add the abbreviation for the provider (*e.g.*, LN/QL). If a free public website was used, add the name of the website followed by the name of the specific part of the site, then the URL (Uniform Resource Locator) in angled brackets.

NEUTRAL CITATION

Starting around 2000, Canadian courts began assigning a "neutral" citation to each decision they released. This number provides the year, court and unique decision number of each case, so that such a decision can be identified regardless of which printed reporter and/or online database published it.

Here is a fictitious example of a typical "neutral" citation:

Smythe v. Myers Upholstery Ltd., 2003 ABQB 312 at para. 16.

This fictitious case is the 312th decision released in 2003 by the Alberta Court of Queen's Bench. The information following the names of the parties is assigned by the court and cannot be changed. Note that the jurisdiction (AB) and level of court (QB) are shown in the neutral citation and do not have to be repeated elsewhere in the citation, nor does the year (2003). There are no periods in the identifiers for the court and jurisdiction. In the example, the reader's attention is drawn to paragraph 16 of the case by adding "at para. 16." at the end. (Alternatively, this can be signified by "¶ 16".)

Current guidance suggests that a reference to a printed reporter should follow as a parallel citation to the neutral citation. In this fictitious example, this decision was reported in the *Alberta Law Reports* (abbreviated A.R.), second series, on page 109 of volume 97. Thus, the recommended form would be:

Smythe v. Myers Upholstery Ltd., 2003 ABQB 312, 97 A.R. (2d) 109 at para. 16.

(Note that "para. 16" can be cited alternatively, by "¶ 16".)

At the present time, there is no universal agreement about how to use the "neutral citation" in conjunction with "unreported" decisions that appear *only* in databases of commercial online providers. If a researcher locates an "unreported" (or perhaps a "not yet reported") decision on one or more of the commercial online services, common sense dictates that a parallel citation to that service be provided, as a help to his or her readers. Thus, in the fictitious example above, if the case had never appeared anywhere in a printed reporter BUT had been captured online by, for example, LN/QL, one might use the following form:

Smythe v. Myers Upholstery Ltd., 2003 ABQB 312, [2003] A.J. No. 808 at para. 16.

Upon seeing the above parallel citation, a reader would quickly discern that he or she could find the case in LN/QL because of the designation [2003] A.J. No. 808.

Similarly, if the decision has been captured by WC, one might use the following form:

Smythe v. Myers Upholstery Ltd., 2003 ABQB 312, 2003 CarswellAB 3560 at para. 16.

Upon seeing the above parallel citation, a reader would quickly discern that the case appears in WC because of the designation 2003 CarswellAB 3560.

Neutral citation is a dynamic subject at present. The best guidance for new legal researchers is to inquire about neutral citation from a law librarian, work supervisor or legal editor, or follow the lead of local practitioners.

For a more detailed discussion of neutral citation, see <http://www.lexum. umontreal.ca/ccc-ccr/index_en.html>.

SELF TEST

The following is a self test based on the information provided in this chapter. The answers to these questions are found at the back of the book in the "Answers to Self Tests" section.

1.   Describe what a case report is.
2.   Name a few case reports.
3.   Name a research aid that assists in locating a case by name.
4.   Name a research aid that assists in locating a case by subject.
5.   What does "updating" a case mean?
6.   Name a research aid that assists in updating a case.

SAMPLE EXERCISES —
FINDING AND UPDATING CASES

Objectives

At the end of this exercise you should be able to:

*   Locate cases by title
*   Locate cases by subject using *Case Digests (Canadian Abridgment)*
*   Locate case reports
*   Update and note up cases
*   Cite cases properly

Instructions

*   Do background reading on how to locate, update and cite cases.
*   Keep a record of all the steps and the time taken to complete the exercise.

1. Find Cases by Title

Go to the *Consolidated Table of Cases* (in the *Canadian Abridgment)* and give the proper citation for the following case. Provide an alternate citation as well.

Berwick v. Canada Trust Co. (S.C.C.)

Citation:

Alternate citation:

2. Find Cases by Subject Using *Case Digests* *(Canadian Abridgment)*

Read the following research situation and answer the following questions.

Research Situation

Ms. Keener

Your client, Ms. Keener, a recent graduate from law school, has been going through the articling interview process over the last few weeks. She has received no offers and, although she admits that there is a recession, she has recently become suspicious of the interviewing process. In particular, at her last two interviews, she was asked whether she had ever been to a psychiatrist or suffered from any mental disorder. Being an honest person, Ms. Keener told both interviewers that she had indeed been to a psychiatrist and has a family history of mental disorders. She has asked you to find some case law that defines discrimination in order to determine whether her human rights have been violated.

a. Before entering the library, brainstorm for possible legal subject areas. List five or more words relating to the above research situation that you might search for in the library.

Words:

b. Go to the *Key & Research Guide* (in the *Canadian Abridgment, 3d ed.*) and look at the section entitled Key Classification System. Find subjects relevant to the research situation. List one or two relevant subject titles, and also their subtitles and reference numbers (*e.g.*, Torts; XVI Negligence; 2. Duty and Standard of Care; e. After accidents).

Titles; Subtitles; Reference Numbers:

c. Using these Key Classification numbers, go to the multi-volume set of *Case Digests (Canadian Abridgment, 3d ed.*), and find the volume that contains your subject. Within that volume, find a case that appears to discuss your research situation. Give the citation for that case. Recall that you must look in the hardbound and softbound volumes.

Citation:

3. Find Case Reports Using *Canadian Case Citations* (*Canadian Abridgment*)

Go to the relevant case report and then the *Canadian Abridgment, Canadian Case Citations* and provide the style of cause and citations for the following cases.

a.   [1973] 4 W.W.R. 417.

Citation:

b.   (1976), 12 O.R. (2d) 253.

Citation:

Alternate Citation:

c.   (1982), 139 D.L.R. (3d) 407.

Citation:

Alternate Citation:

4. Find the History of a Case

Go to *Canadian Case Citations* (in the *Canadian Abridgment*) and list the courts that heard the following case. Provide one citation for each level of court that heard the case, starting with the highest level of court.

Industrial Acceptance Corp v. Canada Permanent Trust Co.
(Supreme Court of Canada)

Courts:

Citation one (S.C.C.):
Citation two (S.C.C.):
Citation three (S.C.C.):
Citation four (N.B.C.A.):
Citation five (N.B.K.B.):

5. Find Cases Judicially Considered

Go to *Canadian Case Citations* (in the *Canadian Abridgment*) and give the citation for the case by the Alberta Court of Queen's Bench that followed *Slavutych v. Baker*, [1976] 1 S.C.R. 254.

Citation:

6. Find Cases in Electronic Sources

a. Using CanLII, locate a case from the Nova Scotia Small Claims Court in which a tattoo artist was sued for misspelling the word beautiful as "beatiful".

Citation:

b. Using LexisNexis/Quicklaw or Westlaw Canada, locate a 2010 case from Alberta in which the judge indicates that disbursements for costs for electronic research might in the future be allowable as electronic research is now "expected of counsel" and that a lawyer who "forgoes electronic research is negligent in doing so", and provide its neutral citation.

Citation:

ANSWERS TO SAMPLE EXERCISES

1. Find Cases by Title

Berwick v. Canada Trust Co., [1948] S.C.R. 151.

Alternate citation: [1948] 3 D.L.R. 81 (S.C.C.).

2. Find Cases by Subject Using *Case Digests* (*Canadian Abridgment*)

a. Human Rights; Discrimination; Employment; Labour; Articling.
b. Human Rights; III. What Constitutes Discrimination; 7. Handicap; b. Mental Handicap; ii. What constitutes: III.7.b.ii.
c. In volume 50, Human Rights, under section III.7.b.ii there are many cases. One is *Walmer Developments v. Wolch* (2003), 67 O.R. (3d) 246, 230 D.L.R. (4th) 372 (Ont. Div. Ct.).

3. Find Case Reports Using *Canadian Case Citations* (*Canadian Abridgment*)

a. *Bank of Montreal v. Sperling Hotel Co.*, [1973] 4 W.W.R. 417 (Man. Q.B.).

Alternate Citation: (1973), 36 D.L.R. (3d) 130 (Man. Q.B.).

b. *Mahood v. Hamilton-Wentworth (Region) Commissioners of Police* (1976), 12 O.R. (2d) 253 (Ont. H.C.).

Alternate Citation: (1976), 68 D.L.R. (3d) 437 (Ont. H.C.).

c. *Sherwood v. Sherwood* (1982), 139 D.L.R. (3d) 407 (N.S.T.D.).

Alternate Citation: (1982), 29 R.F.L. (2d) 374; *or* (1982), 52 N.S.R. (2d) 631; *or* (1982), 106 A.P.R. 631.

4. Find the History of a Case

Courts: Supreme Court of Canada (three times), New Brunswick Court of Appeal, and New Brunswick King's Bench.

Citation one: [1932] S.C.R. 661 (reversed)

Citation two: [1931] S.C.R. 652 (set aside)

Citation three: [1931] S.C.R. 503 (refused leave)

Citation four: [1931] 4 D.L.R. 348 (N.B.C.A.) (affirmed)

Citation five: [1931] 2 D.L.R. 663 (N.B.K.B.)

This is a good exercise because it is such a complicated example. These are five decisions by five courts about the same situation. The case was first heard in the N.B.K.B. and then the N.B.C.A. It was considered by three different sittings because leave was sought, refused, then overturned, and eventually heard.

5. Find Cases Judicially Considered

Dudley v. Jane Doe (1997), 53 Alta. L.R. (3d) 272 (Q.B.) (followed)

6. Find cases in Electronic Sources

a. *Ullock v. Slaunwhite*, 2010 NSSM 22 (CanLII)

b. *Aram Systems Ltd. v. NovAtel Inc.*, 2010 ABQB 152

Appendix 9A: Format of a Printed Decision

1. The *style of cause* names the parties in the case. The name of the plaintiff (or on an appeal the name of the appellant) appears first.	**BUDAI v. ONTARIO LOTTERY CORP.**
	Ontario High Court of Justice, Divisional Court. O'Leary J. January 20, 1983.
2. The *name of the court* that decided the case.	**Torts — Negligent misstatement — Plaintiff wrongly informed that he had won lottery prize — Plaintiff spending money to celebrate — Whether defendant liable for prize or for money spent.**
3. The *name of the judge or judges*.	The plaintiff was, because of a computer error, wrongly informed by the defendant that he had won $835.40 in a lottery. He spent $480 U.S. in an evening's celebration, but was informed the next day of the error. An action for the $835.40 succeeded at trial. On appeal to the Divisional Court, held, allowing the appeal in part, the plaintiff had not, by the rules of the lottery, won the prize. However, the defendant was liable for negligently misinforming him, the extent of the liability being the money lost by the plaintiff in reliance on the misstatement, in this case $480 U.S.
4. The *date of the judgment* is the date that the judgment was handed down, not the date it was heard or published.	
5. The *keywords* classify the issues in the case. They are selected by publishers to fit a subject classification scheme.	**Statutes referred to** *Ontario Lottery Corporation Act*, R.S.O. 1980, c. 344
6. The *headnote* is a brief summary of the case. It is written by the editors of the case report.	**Rules and regulations referred to** O. Reg. 251/75, s. 9 (now R.R.O. 1980, Reg. 719, s. 8)
	APPEAL from a judgment in favour of the plaintiff in an action for a lottery prize.
7. The list of *authorities* is those sources referred to by the court (e.g., cases, statutes, and literature).	*K. C. Cancellera*, for appellant, defendant, Ontario Lottery Corporation *Robert Roth*, for *amicus curiae*. No one appearing for respondent, plaintiff, Jim Budai.
8. The *history of the case* advises where the case originated.	O'Leary J.:—This appeal involves the question of the right of the purchaser of a lottery ticket, who has been incorrectly and negligently told by the lottery operator that he is a winner, to collect from that operator some or all of the amount he was incorrectly told he had won where, prior to learning of the error, he has squandered part of his expected winnings.
9. The *names of counsel are the lawyers* representing the parties in the case.	The appeal is brought by the defendant, Ontario Lottery Corporation, from the judgment dated February 29, 1980, of His Honour Deputy Judge D. Ceri Hugill, wherein he awarded the plaintiff the sum of $835.40. The plaintiff, at a cost to him of $7, in effect purchased seven tickets on a lottery operated by the defendant...
10. The *name of the judge* who delivered or wrote the decision.	

Appendix 9B: Courthouse Electronic Cases

CanLII attempts to bring together on one free, easily searchable website, many newer cases from most Canadian jurisdictions. However, a number of the free public websites listed below contain some cases that are older than those now available through CanLII.

Jurisdiction	URL
Supreme Court of Canada	<http://www.scc-csc.gc.ca> (official site for history, *etc.*) OR <www.lexum.umontreal.ca/csc-scc/en/index.html> (for judicial decisions)
Federal Court of Appeal	<http://decisions.fca-caf.gc.ca/en/index.html>
Federal Court	<http://www.fct-cf.gc.ca/>
Tax Court of Canada	<http://decision.tcc-cci.gc.ca/en/index.html>
British Columbia	<http://www.courts.gov.bc.ca>
Alberta	<http://www.albertacourts.ab.ca>
Saskatchewan	<http://www.sasklawcourts.ca>
Manitoba	<http://www.manitobacourts.mb.ca>
Ontario	Court of Appeal <http://www.ontariocourts.on.ca/coa/en/> Superior Court of Justice <http://www.ontariocourts.on.ca/scj/en/> Ontario Court of Justice <http://www.ontariocourts.on.ca/ocj/en/>
Quebec	<http://www.jugements.qc.ca>
Newfoundland and Labrador	<http://www.court.nl.ca/>
Prince Edward Island	<http://www.gov.pe.ca/courts/>
Nova Scotia	<http://www.courts.ns.ca/>
New Brunswick	<http://www.gnb.ca/cour/index-e.asp>
Yukon	<http://www.justice.gov.yk.ca/prog/cs/courts.html>
Northwest Territories	<http://www.justice.gov.nt.ca/dbtw-wpd/nwtjqbe.htm>
Nunavut	<http://www.canlii.org/en/nu/> Available on CanLII

Appendix 9C: Checklist: How to Find and Update Cases

All case law research involves three steps: finding the case (by name, citation or subject), finding out if it has been appealed or overturned (updating it) and finding out whether it has been considered in other cases (noting it up).

HOW TO FIND A CASE BY NAME OR CITATION

You can find a case by name or citation by using any of the following sources. Your accuracy in electronic searching will improve if you know how to conduct effective searches, recognize the limitations of electronic searching and understand the workings of the various search engines. Spend time reading the online information on how to search and use advanced search templates where available.

☐ **In a library:** Use the *Consolidated Table of Cases* (in the *Canadian Abridgment* set). This multi-volume set lists all cases alphabetically. Each volume has a supplement containing more recent cases. Locate your case in the Table and note its citation and where it is located in the *Case Digests* (in the *Canadian Abridgment* set) in print or online.

☐ **Commercial providers**: LN/QL, WC and BestCase. These commercial providers allow you to search by name or citation from their main screens. Alternatively, you may select a specific jurisdiction (database) and conduct a word search using the template.

☐ **Public (no-fee) websites**: CanLII (<http://www.canlii.org>), court websites and RawLaw (<http://www.mlb.nb.ca/>) are all non-fee websites that provide many current full-text cases, but few older historical cases. Search by case name or citation in the templates provided — by jurisdiction if possible.

HOW TO FIND A CASE BY SUBJECT

When you know your topic but do not have any case names, the most direct way to identify relevant cases is by reading secondary materials and finding the cases cited therein. See Chapter 6 (How to Find Secondary Materials). Unless you are an expert, conducting an online word search will either pull up too many cases or, worse, not locate the relevant cases. The following describes how to use the most useful secondary materials.

☐ Read about your topic in a textbook, the *Canadian Encyclopedic Digest* (CED), *Halsbury's Laws of Canada* and periodical articles. All of these secondary materials are in print, and some are online. The CED's are on Westlaw Canada. *Halsbury's* is on LN/QL. Record citations of relevant cases.

☐ Use the *Canadian Abridgment Key & Research Guide* volume to discover how your subject is categorized in its Key Classification Scheme. Write down the key classification number (*e.g.*, Torts, X.3.a.).

☐ Using this Key Classification, find the relevant *Case Digests* (in the *Canadian Abridgment* set) volumes containing your topic and classification number. Read the digests and any supplements, and record the citations of all relevant cases. Locate these cases in print (in the volumes of Case Reports) or in electronic sources. Read each case and do not depend on summaries.

☐ Once you have a better sense of your subject, to find more cases, do a keyword or phrase search in a commercial service (*e.g.*, LN/QL, WC or BestCase). First, search any case digest databases and read summaries, then search full-text databases and read only the most relevant cases.

☐ Alternatively, use a public (no-fee) website (*e.g.*, CanLII or court websites) and do a word search in the various jurisdiction-based databases. Remember that these usually do not have digest databases.

HOW TO UPDATE AND NOTE UP A CASE

Ensuring that cases are still "good law" requires both **updating** cases and **noting up** cases. *Updating* means finding the history of the cases and ensuring your cases have not been appealed or overturned by a higher court. *Noting up* cases means looking at the judicial treatment of a case to ensure the cases have not subsequently received adverse judicial consideration in later decisions.

In a Library

* To **update** a case, use the *Consolidated Table of Cases* (part of the *Canadian Abridgment*). It lists all decided cases alphabetically and sets out their history. Check supplements as well.

* To **note up** a case, locate a case citator. These loose-leaf books list cases, their history and their treatment by other cases. The main all-Canada citator is called *Canadian Case Citations* (part of the *Canadian Abridgment*), available in print and online through WC.

Online

The most comprehensive electronic case citators are LN/QL's *Quickcite* and WC's *KeyCiteCanada* (the latter is the online version of the printed *Canadian Case Citations*). You can locate these citators in two ways:

- by going to the actual citator database directly for your case; or
- by hyperlinking from inside a case you are viewing on the screen.

Introduction to Legal Analysis 10

The skill of legal analysis is one that evolves over years of practice. It is sometimes called "thinking like a lawyer" and involves determining what law is relevant, understanding it and applying it to the situation at hand. In simple terms, you must take all the law that you have found, read it, interpret it and apply it to your facts.

The skills of reading, interpreting and applying the law are continually learned throughout law school, professional legal training and in practice. However, to complete the full five steps in the FILAC model of legal problem solving, you need to know how to do legal analysis. This chapter, therefore, serves as a basic introduction to the skill of legal analysis.

Legal analysis requires researchers to construct a picture of the law and apply this picture to a set of facts. This chapter explains how to analyze cases and statutes and how cases build upon each other and combine with statutes to form the law. It teaches legal analysis in a direct and simple manner and is not intended to replace the long-term development of legal analysis skills.

LEARNING OBJECTIVES

At the end of this chapter you will be able to:

- Describe the doctrines of precedent and *stare decisis*
- Name the three basic levels of court in Canada
- Name the three steps in case analysis
- Define what is meant by synthesizing the law
- Explain what "distinguishing between cases" is
- Name a rule of statutory interpretation

CASE ANALYSIS

The ultimate goal of research is to find cases and statutes that are relevant to a particular situation, analyze them and apply them to that situation.

Analysis of cases involves determining the relevance of cases, reading these cases and synthesizing them into a statement of law. It involves asking the following questions about the cases you find:

- Does the case apply to the situation? (determining relevance of cases)

- What does the case say? (reading cases)
- What does the case mean? (synthesizing cases)

Only after completing these three steps and doing a similar type of analysis for relevant statutes can you synthesize the law and then apply it to your legal problem. Each step is discussed here.

Determining Relevance of Cases

The first step in case analysis is determining whether the cases you have found apply to your situation or will be considered relevant by a court.

Relevant cases are those that have similar facts and issues and are persuasive or binding on the court that is likely to hear the case if it goes to trial.

Therefore, determining the relevance of cases involves determining which cases are similar, binding or persuasive. An understanding of the system of common law and the Canadian court system is necessary to be able to determine relevance.

The Common Law

The system of common law developed through the use of precedents or decided cases. Precedents were, and continue to be, used as examples or authorities to assist judges in deciding cases.

From the system of precedent evolved the doctrine of *stare decisis*, which literally means "to stand by the decision". *Stare decisis* requires courts to follow prior decisions of courts from the same jurisdiction to the extent that those cases have similar facts and issues.

The doctrines of precedent and *stare decisis* promote consistency in law, ensure certainty and provide tools to predict the likely outcome of a case. A coherent body of law results if these doctrines are applied consistently.

The Court System

The court system in Canada is structured in tiers of increasing authority. The courts form a hierarchy, whereby appeals from lower courts are heard by the higher courts and lower courts are bound by the decisions of higher courts. In Canada, there are three levels of courts: trial level, appellate level and court of last resort. Each province has a trial and an appeal court. The court of last resort is the Supreme Court of Canada.

Trial courts are courts of original jurisdiction. This means they are the first courts to hear cases and make determinations about both fact and law. Often trial courts are divided by type of claim, amount of claim or territorial jurisdiction. For example, the provincial court in British Columbia consists of the following divisions: Family Court, Criminal Court and Small Claims Court.

Appellate courts hear appeals from trial courts. They do not, as a rule, review factual determinations of trial courts, but review errors of law. There is no trial *per se* in the appellate court since no evidence is heard. The court instead reviews written briefs on the law (*i.e.*, factums) and hears arguments only.

The court of last resort in Canada is the Supreme Court of Canada. Prior to 1949 the court of last resort was the British Privy Council. Today, the Supreme Court of Canada hears cases that are appealed from the various appeal courts. It also hears cases that are specifically referred to it for a determination about the meaning or application of a law. These are called "references".

There is also a federal court system that deals exclusively with federal matters, such as immigration and tax law. The system includes a trial and an appeal level: the Federal Court and the Federal Court of Appeal. Appeals from this court go to the Supreme Court of Canada. There are also a federal Tax Court of Canada and a Court Martial Appeal Court of Canada, which hear cases limited to tax issues and appeals from military court martials, respectively.

Illustration 10.1
Canadian Court Structure

Supreme Court of Canada
⬈   ⬉
Provincial Courts of Appeal   Federal Court of Appeal
⬆   ⬆
Provincial Trial Level Courts   Federal Court

In Canada, all courts are bound by decisions of the Supreme Court of Canada and all courts are bound by higher courts in their own jurisdiction. For example, trial courts are bound by appeal court decisions. Appeal courts from one jurisdiction are not bound by appeal courts from another jurisdiction. For example, the British Columbia Court of Appeal does not bind the Alberta Court of Appeal.

Similar, Binding or Persuasive

Those cases most similar to your legal problem are the best indicators of the likely outcome of your case. In other words, a case's predictive value is greatest when its facts and issues are most similar to yours. The converse is also true.

If a court is compelled to follow a case, that case is considered to be *binding*. There are a number of factors that will determine whether a case is binding on a court: the level of court, the jurisdiction of the court, the history of the case, the judicial consideration of the case and the currency of the case. In other words, when determining whether a case is binding, the following questions should be asked about each case:

Court Level: What is the court level? Is the decision from a higher level court?

Jurisdiction: What is the jurisdiction? Is the decision from the same jurisdiction?

History: What is the history of the decision? Has the decision been appealed or overturned by another court?

Judicial Consideration: Has the decision been considered by another court (*e.g.*, distinguished, applied, or followed)?

Currency: Has the decision been superseded by legislation?

The answers to these questions will not only determine whether a case is binding but will also contribute to the amount of weight the decision will be given by a court. Precedents that are binding are referred to as "mandatory", whereas those that are not binding are referred to as "persuasive". Although not binding, persuasive cases often assist judges in deciding cases. For example, a case from the United States will not be binding on a Canadian court but may be persuasive if the facts and issues are similar.

After selecting relevant cases, the researcher must read them and synthesize them into a coherent whole.

Reading Cases

Reading cases involves some skill. Most cases follow a particular format and, after reading several cases, the researcher should be able to find relevant information quickly without getting bogged down in irrelevant facts.

At the most basic level, researchers should be familiar with the format of published cases. A description of this format is provided in Appendix 9A. This format is also important for computer research, since computer searches are often conducted by selecting a specific location in the text of reported cases (*e.g.*, by title or date).

Each case is the result of a judge's attempt to move through the legal problem-solving process. Therefore, as you read cases you will learn how to elicit from each case the products of the legal research process: FILAC — facts, issues, law, analysis and conclusion. By reading and dissecting cases, researchers enhance their problem-solving skills.

Synthesizing Cases

After all the relevant cases have been gathered and read, they must be synthesized into a coherent description of the law. Synthesis requires comparing cases, recognizing their similarities and differences, and attempting to weave them together into a single picture of the law. It involves the exploration of the relationships between cases.

Judges do exactly this in their decisions as they apply the rule of precedent. Since similar cases must be decided in a similar manner, a crucial step for judges is to recognize the differences and similarities between the facts and issues of decided cases and the facts and issues of the case before the court.

Synthesis involves briefing cases, comparing them and then constructing a description of the law.

Briefing Cases

A skill that can greatly assist researchers in synthesizing cases is briefing cases. Most law students become fairly proficient at the skill of summarizing cases into briefs, since much of law school learning is through cases.

Briefing cases involves summarizing cases into short, organized and easily understandable formats. The basic format of a case brief is as follows:

1.	**Style of Cause:**	Name and citation of the case
2.	**Procedural History:**	Previous judicial treatment of case
3.	**Facts:**	Summary of relevant facts in the case
4.	**Issues:**	Specific legal questions that the court must answer
5.	**Decision:**	Disposition by the court of the case
6.	**Reasons:**	Reasons provided by the court for the answers to the legal issues
7.	***Ratio Decidendi*:**	Rule of law for which the case stands
8.	**Commentary:**	Dissenting opinions, personal views on the case and connections to other cases

Attached as Appendix 10A to this chapter is a sample case brief.

The obvious benefit of a briefed case is that it is in a form that can be reviewed quickly. Case briefs provide snapshots of the law as applied to a particular situation. These snapshots can then be pulled together to form a complete picture of the law.

Comparing Cases

The goal of legal research is to find cases that are so similar that they will predict the results of the current situation.

In order to find similar cases, the facts and issues of each case must be compared and reconciled with other cases and your situation. This is called analogizing and distinguishing. Analogizing is extracting the similarities between the cases. Distinguishing is noting the differences. Analogizing and distinguishing are very important intellectual skills in case analysis.

Whether a case is viewed as similar or different often depends on the level of generality and creativity applied. For example, a case that held that a landlord must supply a tenant with a heater could be considered similar to a situation in which a tenant complained that she had no running water. On the other hand, the case could be seen as fundamentally different because heating is a necessity of life but running water is not.

Often it is useful to gather together all of the case briefs into a one-page schedule like the following:

Illustration 10.2
Case Comparison Schedule

	Case 1	Case 2	Your Facts
Binding or Persuasive			
Facts			
Issues			
Decision			
Reasons and *Ratio*			
Commentary			

When comparing cases, sometimes it is best to compare the decision of the court first and work back through the reasoning of the judge. For example, if the facts and the issues are very similar but the decisions are not, working back through the analysis might enable you to locate the distinguishing features or perhaps the different approaches taken by different judges. Do not assume, however, that because the decisions are the same, the same analysis was applied.

Constructing a Description of the Law

After a comparison of the relevant cases, the law should be synthesized into one general statement.

Synthesis involves pulling all the individual relevant cases together to form a complete picture of the law. Synthesis involves finding a collective meaning from the relevant cases. Synthesis does not simply involve describing case after case, but, rather, describing the law as a unified whole. Synthesis weaves the law together like a spider web. The result of synthesis is the development of a new "rule" from all of the cases that have been decided as they apply to your particular fact situation. Synthesis takes practice and is a skill that develops over time.

The difficulty of synthesis is finding common ground among the cases when there are wide-ranging similarities and differences. The following is a simple example of a synthesis.

Example of Synthesis

Slip and Fall

Facts: A woman slipped and fell on a banana peel on the sidewalk in front of her neighbour's house. The banana had been on the sidewalk for days and had rotted in the sun, making it particularly slippery. She has sued the neighbour for negligence.

Case 1: A man fell on an icy sidewalk of a big department store. The sidewalk had been cleared of ice daily but there had recently been a massive snowfall. The department store was not liable because, although it was foreseeable that such an accident could occur, the store did all it could do to prevent the accident.

Case 2: A boy slipped and fell on an icy sidewalk. The ice was caused by faulty eavestroughs, which dripped water onto the sidewalk. The owner was liable because he could have foreseen the accident and did nothing to prevent it from occurring.

Case 3: An owner posted a sign on her property stating "enter at own risk" because she had flooded her property for irrigation purposes. A man slipped in the mud. The owner was not held liable because she had posted a warning.

Possible Synthesis: An owner or occupier of property will be held liable for injuries that occur on his or her property if the injury was reasonably foreseeable and the owner did nothing to prevent the injury from occurring.

Application to the Facts: The neighbour will likely be liable to the woman who slipped on the banana peel. Because the banana peel had been there for days, it was likely reasonably foreseeable that such an accident might occur. In addition, the owner did nothing to prevent the accident from occurring.

STATUTE ANALYSIS

The system of common law has been altered significantly by the introduction of statutes. Indeed, some academics have argued that the law in Canada is no longer a true system of common law because of the weighty effect of statutes on almost every area of the law.

Statutes are codifications of the law. They are legal rules set out in legislative form to alter or clarify case law, or to create new areas of law. They cannot be separated from case law.

The law develops through both the creation of statutes and the interpretation of statutes by the courts in deciding cases. The rule of precedent suggests that the courts must apply statutes similarly to each set of facts.

As within case analysis, statute analysis involves finding relevant statutes, reading these statutes and interpreting them. It involves asking the following questions about the statutes you find:

- Does the statute apply to the situation? (relevance)
- What does the statute say? (reading statutes)
- What does the statute mean? (interpreting statutes)

Relevance

The first step in statute analysis is to determine whether the statute applies to a particular situation. This entails reading a statute and determining if the legislation was designed to cover the current situation.

Like case analysis, statute analysis involves distinguishing and analogizing the facts. The "facts" in a statute, however, are the words used in the statute. These words describe whether and how the statute applies. These "facts" must exist in order for a statute to apply to a situation. For example, all criminal law offences require that there be an act (*actus reus*) and intent (*mens rea*). Thus, a legal problem must involve both an act and intent to be considered a criminal offence.

Statutes are rules that apply to specific people or activities. If the current situation involves those specific people or activities referred to in the statute, then the statute probably applies. Often statutes have definitions at the beginning of the statute that describe the persons and activities covered in the statute. For example, s. 2 of the British Columbia *Insurance Act*[1] states as follows:

> This Act, except as provided, applies to every insurer that carries on any business of insurance in British Columbia and to every contract of insurance made or deemed made in British Columbia.

If it is not readily apparent whether the statute applies, you may need to resort to the rules of statutory interpretation described below.

Reading Statutes

If a statute is applicable, you must read those parts of the statute that are relevant.

Most statutes follow a particular format. Recognizing this format will help you better read and interpret statutes. The six components of a statute are essentially as follows:

1. Long title
2. Chapter number
3. Date of Royal Assent
4. Short title
5. Definitions
6. Parts, sections and subsections

---

[1]   R.S.B.C. 1996, c. 226, s. 2.

Statutes are discussed in detail in Chapter 7 (How to Find and Update Statutes).

Interpreting Statutes

Statutory interpretation involves some skill. There are three different, and often competing, approaches taken by the courts in interpreting statutes. They are as follows:

Literal or Grammatical Method

The literal or grammatical method of statute interpretation stresses the literal or plain meaning of a statute. This method assumes that complete understanding of the statute can be found within the ordinary meaning of the words of the statute. Therefore, interpretation is restricted to the actual text of the statute.

Aids used to interpret the statute, outside of the text, such as the intent of the legislators and previous versions of the statute, are not considered relevant. Taken to the extreme, this method requires interpretation of the ordinary meaning of the words within the statute even if it leads to an absurdity or inconsistency within the statute. Although the literal method is not appropriate where the wording of a statute is ambiguous, it is still the primary and preferred approach to interpreting statutes.

Contextual Method

The contextual method of statutory interpretation employs the "Golden Rule". This rule allows the court to depart from the literal meaning of a statute if it would lead to absurdity. Contextual interpretation is based on the assumption that statute law is meant to be rational and coherent. All legislation should be internally coherent and each must be coherent with any higher enactments; *e.g.*, a regulation must be coherent with its authorizing statute. Thus, the plain wording of a statute should be interpreted in a manner that will avoid any absurdity or inconsistency.

Purposive Method

Purposive interpretation of a statute gives primary importance to the intent of the legislators, rather than the words used, in enacting the legislation. This approach is called the "Mischief Rule". The original aim of this rule was to determine what mischief the legislators sought to overcome in enacting the legislation and to see that their goal was met. Today purposive interpretation of a statute is not limited to remedying mischief but rather to determining the purpose behind the legislation. With this method, in contrast to a literal interpretation, external aids such as legislative committee reports may be crucial to determining the purpose of the legislation.

Synthesis of the Three Approaches

According to E.A. Driedger in the *Construction of Statutes*, there is only one approach to statutory interpretation:

the words of an Act are to be read in their entire context, in their grammatical and ordinary sense harmoniously with the scheme of the Act, the object of the Act, and the intention of Parliament.[2]

Just as important to statutory interpretation are court decisions that have construed statutes. These cases provide the opinions of both lawyers and judges on how the statute applies and what the statute means. The cases can be from other jurisdictions if those jurisdictions have similar statutes.

Thus, when looking at a statute, you should look at the specific words, the entire statute (*i.e.*, context), the history or creation process, the rules of construction of statutes and cases that have considered the statute.

Because there will always be several interpretations of a statute, the skill required in statutory analysis, like case analysis, is to use analogy to extend or limit the application of the statute. For example, a statute that restricts vehicles from parks may or may not extend to skateboards or roller skates, depending on the interpretation.

This discussion is by no means exhaustive and other tools of interpretation can be found in treatises dealing specifically with statutory interpretation.

Recall the situation of Paul and Melody first mentioned in Chapter 2 (Factual Analysis). They were separating and Melody wanted to keep the $20,000 gift that her grandmother had given to her. We saw that the *Family Property Act* (fictitious) applied to all residents of British Columbia and all marriages entered into in British Columbia. We also saw that ss. 8 and 9 of that statute related to the division of family property upon marriage breakdown. One case had considered this statute. A synthesis of the statute and case law might look like this:

Example of Synthesis of Law

Paul and Melody

Statutory law in British Columbia provides that upon marriage breakdown, "family assets" must be shared equally between the marriage partners. Family assets include gifts and inheritances obtained while in the marriage. However, a court may alter this division if the division would be unfair, having regard to a number of factors including "the extent to which property was acquired by one spouse through inheritance or gift". Cases that have interpreted this statute primarily look at whether the gift was intended to become part of the family assets. For example, in those circumstances where a gift of money was kept in a separate bank account and was received fairly close to the time of the marriage breakdown, the gift was not considered to be part of the family assets.

---

[2]	E.A. Driedger, *The Construction of Statutes* (Toronto: Butterworths, 1974), at p. 67.

APPLYING THE LAW TO THE FACTS

Once the cases and statutes have been read, analyzed and synthesized, and the researcher has a good understanding of the law, the law may be applied to the current facts. This involves looking at the current facts and attempting to predict what would happen if the situation were brought to trial.

At this point, researchers should place themselves in the position of a judge. This entails looking at the law and stating how and why the law applies to the current facts. However, since researchers are not judges, they should not reach a final decision, but should only provide a best assessment of the outcome. In describing the outcome, words such as "probably" or "likely" should be used to show that the conclusion is only a prediction and not an absolute.

An example of application of the law to the Paul and Melody situation might look something like this:

Example of Application of Law

Paul and Melody

It is likely that Melody will be able to keep the $20,000 gift from her grandmother and not share it with Paul when they separate.

Although the gift would likely initially be included in the "family assets" which must be shared equally between the marriage partners on marriage breakdown, it is likely that a court would alter this division on the basis that the division of the $20,000 would be unfair. Case law indicates that it would be considered unfair because the money was not intended to become part of the family assets. This is evidenced by the fact that the money was kept in a separate bank account and was received fairly close to the time of the marriage breakdown.[3]

A WORD ON POLICY

When analyzing the law, policy should also be considered. Policy refers to the purpose or intent of the law or the reason behind the law. Policy usually relates to the underlying rights, interests and obligations the law attempts to protect. Examples of policy are often found in the reports and other publications of law reform commissions at the federal, provincial and territorial levels. Occasionally these secondary sources are presented to courts as persuasive authority to be considered in judicial decisions, but they are not binding because they are only an interpretation of where the law stands or what it might become.

Policy can be used in two ways. It can be used to support the *status quo* or to introduce a change in the law. Often, if a case appears to be unfair, there is an

---

[3] This is an example only and should not be taken as an accurate description of the law.

underlying policy reason for the decision. This policy reason may be referred to when comparing cases and reconciling the differences.

As mentioned, courts are concerned with consistency in law and, therefore, will refer to policy in ensuring that the results reflect the intention of the law. But policy is not the law and should be used sparingly in legal analysis.

SELF TEST

The answers to these questions are found at the end of the book in the "Answers to Self Tests" section.

1. What is the doctrine of precedent?
2. What is meant by *stare decisis*?
3. What are the three basic levels of court in Canada?
4. What are the three steps in case analysis?
5. Define what is meant by "synthesizing the law".
6. What is the "Golden Rule" of statutory interpretation?

SAMPLE EXERCISE AND ANSWERS

The following exercise and answers demonstrate how the steps of legal analysis come together.

Try to do a legal analysis for the following fictional problem by reading the law (statutes and cases), determining its relevance, synthesizing it and applying it to the following facts.

Problem

Janet Smith

Janet Smith is a single woman who lives alone in Edmonton in a second-floor apartment with a balcony. She was recently the victim of an attempted sexual assault. A series of similar sexual assaults on single women living alone in second- and third-floor apartments with balconies had occurred recently, all within a few blocks of Smith's home. Although the police were aware of the assaults, the investigating constables chose not to warn women at risk, partly for fear of causing hysteria.

It was discovered that the chief of police had reassigned several officers from Ms. Smith's neighbourhood to the downtown area to protect personal property in response to rumours of rioting. As well, the board of police commissioners had decided to allocate funds to public relations rather than to a seminar for police officers entitled "The Female Victim and the Myth of Hysteria".

Question

You have been asked to answer the following question: Did the police constables breach a private law duty of care by failing to take steps to warn Smith about her particular risk from this attacker?

The Law

The following is a brief fictional description of the law relating to the duty of care of police officers. It consists of the *Police Act* (fictitious) and the following four cases.

The *Police Act* applies to all police officers in Alberta. It sets out the duties of a municipal police force and liability for police action. The relevant section of the Act is as follows:

> 21(1) No action for damages lies against a police officer ... for anything said or done or omitted to be said or done in the performance or intended performance of duty or in the exercise of power or for any alleged neglect or default in the performance or intended performance of duty or exercise of power. (fictional)

Four cases that discuss the duty of care of public officials are as follows:

Anders v. Calgary Council (Alta. C.A., 1915) (fictional)

A local building authority was sued when structural damage occurred in a residential building block. Although the building's plans had been approved by the authority, it was discovered that the block had not been constructed in conformity with the plans. Anders, the lessee, alleged that the building authority had a duty to ensure that the building was constructed in accordance with the plans, and that it had been negligent in not inspecting it. The Court of Appeal found that the authority owed a *prima facie* duty of care to the lessees of the building based on the relationship between them, that is, that there was "a sufficient *relationship of proximity* or neighbourhood such that, in the reasonable contemplation of the former, carelessness may have been likely to cause damage to the latter".

R. v. Dorse Boat Co. (H.L., 1930) (fictional)

Several prisoners escaped from custody and stole a yacht, and while escaping collided with the yacht of the plaintiffs. It was alleged that the officers in charge of the prisoners' custody had been negligent in their supervision. The majority of the court found that the fact that the damage had been caused by third parties did not exempt the officers from a duty of care towards the plaintiffs because of the *foreseeability* of the damage caused as a result of their negligence in supervising the prisoners. A concurring majority decision found that the duty of care arose from the *special relationship* between the officers and the prisoners due to the former's *control* over the latter.

Hall v. Chief Constable of West Sheffield (H.L., 1969) (fictional)

An action was brought against the police by the estate of the last victim of the "Yorkshire Ripper", on the grounds that it was foreseeable that this criminal would commit further offences against young women in Britain in the future. The court found that the police did not owe a general duty of care to individual members of the public absent a special *relationship of proximity* between the victim and the police, and that the identification of the victim as a young woman was not sufficient to locate her in a special class of persons to whom a private duty was owed. The court further held that the police should not be liable in such a situation.

Air Alaska Disaster Claimants v. Air Alaska (Ont. Dist. Ct., 1988) (fictional)

An action was brought against the police for not preventing, through proper security measures, an aircraft disaster caused by a bomb. The court held that, although a private law duty to the public generally could not be imposed on the police (as decided in *Hall*), this did not exclude the possibility of a duty of care to a more *limited* class of individuals such as the passengers of the aircraft. The court went on to suggest an expansion of the special relationship criteria to include such factors as the *control* that the defendants had over the situation (*i.e.*, the passengers and baggage allowed on board the aircraft), and the fact that they *knew or ought to have known* of the danger to Air Alaska flights.

Step 1: Determining Relevance of Statutes and Cases

The *Police Act* is relevant because it applies to all police officers in Alberta. The particular section of the statute has not been amended or repealed.

The relative relevance of the cases can be determined from the jurisdiction, dates and court level of each of the cases. The only binding case is the Alberta Court of Appeal Decision, *Anders*. However, it is factually different (and fairly old), so may be fairly easily distinguished. Although two cases are from England, they are persuasive because they discuss duty of care. Therefore, although they are not binding, the court will likely apply them to Janet Smith's situation. *Air Alaska* is the most recent Canadian case and carries some weight in terms of precedent because it is a Canadian case — although an Alberta court is not bound by decisions from Ontario. The case that is most similar in fact to Smith's situation is *Hall*.

Step 2: Synthesizing the Law

Statute law and case law can be restated in a simplified form as follows:

The *Police Act* imposes on police a public duty to protect the public. In this role, the police are immune from liability. However, the common law has established that public officials can be found to have a private law duty of care to members of the public. This occurs in situations in which: there is a prior knowledge of the danger; harm is foreseeable; a special relationship of proximity exists between the police and that particular group or segment of the public; and the police have control over the situation.

In establishing the existence of a private law duty of care for police officers, the law appears to require four main elements: the foreseeability of harm; prior knowledge of the danger; the existence of a special relationship between the police and the member of the public; and control of the situation.

Step 3: Applying the Law to the Facts

An application of the law to Janet Smith's situation looks like this:

It is likely that the police constables owed a duty of care to Janet Smith. The police constables should have foreseen the possibility of another assault on a single woman in Smith's neighbourhood because they knew of the conditions surrounding the previous assaults and of the danger to women in the neighbourhood. The foreseeability of harm caused to a segment of the public is likely enough to establish a "special relationship" between the constables and the women in that neighbourhood, including Smith.

In addition, it is likely that there was a special relationship between the police and Ms. Smith based on Smith's membership in a small and identifiable group of potential victims. Smith and other women like her would likely be recognized by a court as being a sufficiently narrow class of potential victims and, as such, they may fit into the rule outlined in *Air Alaska*. Janet Smith's case can, therefore, be distinguished from *Hall*, for, unlike the "Yorkshire Ripper", for whom all young or fairly young women in Britain were targets, the assailant in this case targeted only single, white women living alone in second- or third-floor apartments with balconies, in Smith's neighbourhood.

There is no "control" factor in Janet Smith's case. No public authority exercised direct control over Smith's attacker. However, it seems unlikely that the lack of control over the assailant will affect the duty owed by the constables, given the extent to which the other elements apply.

Appendix 10A: Sample Case Brief

Style of Cause

Christie v. Davey, [1893] 1 Chancery Division 316.[1]

Procedural History

No previous judicial action.

Facts

Christie worked as a music teacher and had pupils in her home 17 hours per week. Her daughter, son, and a boarder frequently sang and practised their instruments. Davey had lived in the adjoining semi-detached house for the past three years. He worked out of his home as an engraver and had a musical evening once a week. Davey came to object to the noise from Christie's home and wrote a letter of complaint to Christie. Christie did not respond and the next day Davey began to make shrieking, banging, whistling and pounding noises whenever Christie commenced musical activity.

Christie filed an action for an injunction to prevent Davey from making noises to annoy or injure Christie. Davey filed a counterclaim to prevent Christie from constant music to injure Davey.

Issue

May the occupier of property engage in an ordinarily legitimate activity on the property if the sole purpose for engaging in the activity is to deliberately annoy the neighbour?

Decision

The court allowed the claim by Christie and an injunction was issued restraining Davey from making noises in his house to annoy Christie, except for noise which resulted from his engraving trade or his weekly musical evenings, which existed before the dispute.

The court disallowed the counterclaim by Davey, finding that Christie's music lessons were not unusual or malicious.

---

[1]   [1893] 1 Ch. 316, 62 L.J. Ch. 439, 3 R. 210.

Reasons

The court held that Christie was making reasonable use of her home, evidenced by no complaints by Davey in the past three years. Davey was making unusual noises to annoy and disrupt in a deliberate and malicious manner. Davey was not permitted to complain about a legitimate use of Christie's home.

Ratio Decidendi

An occupier of property may not engage in an activity on the property in a manner ordinarily legitimate if the sole purpose of the activity is to deliberately annoy the neighbour.

Comments

No dissenting opinions. The history of the situation and reasons for the noise (*i.e.*, pleasure or intentional annoyance) are important factors. No cases with which to compare.

Legal Writing

11

The final stage in the research process involves writing the results. Writing is a skill that develops over time. With practice, all writers can become more accurate, brief and clear.

This chapter discusses the basics of good legal writing and introduces a three-stage process of legal writing. It then describes the format of legal writing and discusses two devices by which the law is communicated: the legal memorandum and the opinion letter.

LEARNING OBJECTIVES

At the end of this chapter you will be able to:

- Name a few rules of good writing
- List the three stages in the legal writing process
- Describe the five parts of a memorandum of law
- Explain the order in which to revise writing
- Describe the form of a typical opinion letter

GOOD LEGAL WRITING

Good legal writing is accurate, brief and clear. Good writers use plain English and target their writing to their readers. Although a lot has been written about the use of plain language in the law, the essential ideas are well articulated by Richard Wydick in his book *Plain English for Lawyers*.[1] Wydick's six basic rules are as follows:

1. Omit surplus words.
2. Use familiar, concrete words.
3. Use short sentences.
4. Use base verbs and the active voice.
5. Arrange words with care.
6. Avoid language quirks.

---

[1] (Durham, N.C.: Carolina Academic Press, 1985).

Legal writing involves not only good basic writing skills, but, more specifically, the ability to write about the law. This may sound self-evident, but many lawyers who are good writers and knowledgeable about the law are still often unable to convey the law in a clear and concise manner.

Because legal writing is the articulation or written expression of legal thought, it requires all of the skills of good writing plus an ability to put the law in a form that is understandable. As researchers learn more about the law, their ability to communicate it improves: clearer thinking leads to clearer writing. However, before researchers can put pen to paper, they should have a general understanding of the process of legal writing and the way in which the law is usually articulated (*i.e.*, the form of legal writing).

THE PROCESS OF LEGAL WRITING

The process of legal writing, like other writing, has three basic stages:

1. Planning
2. Writing
3. Revising

Stage 1: Planning

Planning involves the following four steps:

Step 1: Identify the reader.
Step 2: Determine the purpose of the writing.
Step 3: Gather, analyze, and organize the information.
Step 4: Prepare an outline.

The following situation provides an example of the four-step planning process:

Scenario

A biology professor is deciding which first-year biology textbook to purchase and use in her first-year university biology class. You are a Ph.D. candidate in biology and the professor has asked you to review the available books and recommend one. She wants a book that is easy to read, inexpensive and includes all of the topics that should be taught in a first-year biology course.

Step 1: Identify the Reader. The reader of your response is a biology professor who is very busy. It is likely that she expects thoroughness as well as conciseness. She will be familiar with the language of biologists and may even be familiar with some of the more popular biology textbooks.

Step 2: Determine the Purpose. The purpose of the project is to select a textbook to be used in a first-year biology class. The textbook should be easy to read, inexpensive and cover all first-year biology topics. You must provide enough information to enable the professor to make an informed decision.

Step 3: Gather, Analyze and Organize the Information. It is likely that you will go to a bookstore and contact publishers to gather information about first-year biology books available. Once you have gathered this information, you will be able to formulate a list of all of the books and organize and summarize the information. This information could then be organized into a schedule indicating the differences between the various options.

Step 4: Prepare an Outline. Once you have summarized all the information, you must decide how you will present it. Drafting an outline will enable you to put your ideas in order.

The following are samples of two potential outlines for the above example:

Sample Outline A:

1. Introduction
2. Body
    a. Book 1: Ease of reading, cost and topics covered
    b. Book 2: Ease of reading, cost and topics covered
    c. Book 3: Ease of reading, cost and topics covered
3. Conclusion

Sample Outline B

1. Introduction
2. Body
    a. Ease of reading: Books 1, 2 and 3
    b. Cost: Books 1, 2,and 3
    c. Topics Covered: Books 1, 2 and 3
3. Conclusion

Beginning researchers often do not spend enough time on planning. New researchers should avoid the temptation to begin writing before the planning process is complete. Each of the four steps of planning are described here in more detail as they relate to legal writing.

Step 1: Identify the Reader

Writers should always keep in mind who their readers are. Identifying the audience enables a writer to focus on an audience's particular wants and needs and adjust the content, organization and style accordingly. It also gives specific purpose and direction to writing. Some questions that might be asked in order to identify readers are:

- Who are the potential readers?
- How much do the readers already know about the subject?
- What do the readers want or expect in the writing?
- How busy are the readers?
- What are the readers' ages, gender, language, education, *etc.*?

Step 2: Determine the Purpose

Determining how writing will ultimately be used and why a topic is being researched enables writers to convey the information in ways that are practical and useful. For example, if the writing is to be used in preparation for a trial, it will be written persuasively, whereas if the writing is to be used to advise a client, it will be written objectively and informatively. The following examples of audiences and purposes of writing indicate how the audience and purpose affect writing:

Types of Writing, Audiences and Purposes				
	Poetry	**Exams**	**Legal Memo**	**Opinion Letter**
Audience	Public	Professor	Lawyer	Client
Purpose	Inspire	Assess	Inform	Advise

Each purpose requires a different type of writing in terms of content, form and organization.

Although readers of legal writing will often be other lawyers, it is advisable not to assume that these lawyers are knowledgeable about the research topic. As you delve into the law, you become somewhat of an expert. Therefore, it is good practice to always introduce the subject at a basic level and work towards the more complicated, as if you were giving instruction about the law. There is some skill involved in deciding in how much detail the basics should be discussed.

Step 3: Gather, Analyze and Organize the Information

After identifying the purpose of the writing and the readers, researchers should gather together the law, read it and attempt to make sense of it.

At this stage, relevant statutes and cases should be briefed and important concepts and quotations should be noted. The cases should be organized in terms of importance and relevance. This step is described in detail in Chapter 9 (How to Find and Update Cases).

Step 4: Prepare an Outline

The use of an outline cannot be overemphasized.

Researchers who develop comprehensive outlines spend significantly less time later at the writing stage. Although it is often difficult to hold back from writing, the benefits of doing so are numerous. Without an outline, your thoughts are less organized and it is difficult to be objective about them. Using an outline will encourage you to be more critical of your words and ideas. Outlines have other advantages. Drafting an outline:

- highlights gaps and overlaps in information and discussion;
- indicates where each case and statute will be discussed and the connections between each;
- shows logical inconsistencies; and
- forces you to stay on track and to be systematic and logical.

An outline should include all issues, ideas and law in tabulated form. It should, ideally, fit onto one page and refer to cases and statutes in support of each proposition.

Stage 2: Writing

Writing involves describing the law and its application to the facts in a comprehensive and concise way. If you prepare a solid outline, you will know prior to writing what you generally want to say and how it will be organized. Therefore, the focus at the writing stage is on putting thoughts into words and connecting the thoughts together into a whole.

The first attempt at writing should be a fast, rough draft and should not take as much time as either planning or revising. Lawyers often dictate a first draft. This enables them to quickly get thoughts down and recite quotes from the actual text of cases without rewriting entire quotations. It is recommended that the entire first draft be written in one sitting — even if in point form — so that there is some flow to thoughts.

It is not necessary to wait until your analysis of the law is perfect before beginning your writing. Often thoughts become clearer as they are put into writing. It is important not to get caught up in words at this particular stage. Instead, focus on content and organization. Put everything you want to say in writing and edit it later.

Content

What you decide to include in your writing will obviously depend on a number of factors, such as time, complexity of the law and the nature of the problem. For example, if a researcher has only one hour to find an answer to a legal problem, the written response may be only one page. However, if a researcher has a week and the law is particularly complex, it is likely that a comprehensive analysis will be more than just a few pages.

How Many Cases to Include

One of the most common questions of the novice researcher is: How many cases should I include and how much should I say about each case?

You should include as many cases as are necessary to describe the law in a clear and concise manner. Although this may sound elusive, once you begin your research you will begin to recognize cases that are critical and those that are subsidiary.

Try not to include cases that say almost the same thing. At a point in your research, certain cases begin to be repeatedly referred to in other cases. This is one of the first clues that your research is beginning to gain focus. Another key turning point in research is when you find a case that refers to a number of other key cases related to your topic. These cases are particularly helpful because they often summarize the law from the other cases. To ensure brevity, legal researchers should refer to the most recent cases and only mention cases separately if they are foundation cases, are critical to the analysis or have particularly relevant facts.

Deciding on the number of cases to include is always a balancing act. Often novice researchers, in a desire to include all of the research, include cases that are not necessary. One of the most difficult tasks of legal writing is paring down the law so that just enough, but not too much, information is included. It is said that a famous writer once wrote, "I would have written you a shorter letter but I didn't have time."

You can be sure that judges are bombarded with cases in trials, yet their decisions include only those that are important to the outcome of the case.

How Much Information to Include about Each Case

There should be enough said about each case to indicate to the reader why the case is important to your situation. In other words, what does the case add to the analysis?

When including cases, researchers must make decisions about whether to include the following components of each case:

- Name of case and citation;
- How the case fits into the analysis;
- Brief outline of facts;
- Issues; and
- Holding or reasoning.

There is no "right" amount of information to include. The amount and type will be different in each situation, but there are some general patterns. For example, typically a discussion of the law begins with a general overview of the law and moves towards a more detailed description of particularly relevant cases. In other words, the discussion usually moves from the general to the specific, like a funnel:

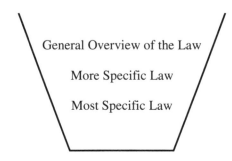

General Overview of the Law

More Specific Law

Most Specific Law

The general overview is a broad statement of the law. It often includes the principles of a few foundation cases and includes only a few facts from each of those cases. In some areas of the law, in which the law is relatively settled, there may be no need to include the facts of a well-known case. Providing the rule of law or the principle resulting from this case may be sufficient.

As researchers begin to go into more detail about particularly relevant cases, the discussion of the cases expands. At this stage, the facts and issues of each case are important for purposes of distinguishing cases and, therefore, should be included in the discussion. At the same time, the writer should try to link each case to both the prior case and the following case, so that the reader is able to see how the law developed.

Organization

Organization is critical to legal writing and the successful communication of thoughts. Lack of organization is the most frequent cause of miscommunication in legal writing. Organization means putting thoughts in an order that permits ideas to flow smoothly from the beginning of the writing through to the conclusion. The reader should be led from one idea to the next and never stumble over ideas. Keep the following rule in mind: "State where you are going; go there; and then state where you have been."

Always provide introductions to new thoughts and conclusions at the end of these thoughts. It is the writer's responsibility to lead the reader through the discussion.

The order of your discussion will depend on the area of law discussed, the particular set of facts, the audience and your personal style. There is no single, right way to organize, but here are a few tips.

Discuss Each Legal Issue Separately

The most important organizational tip in legal writing is: discuss each legal issue separately. For each issue there should be a discussion of:

- the law pertaining to that issue;
- how that law applies to the particular facts; and
- a conclusion.

This method of organization is not always as simple as it looks. Most cases include several issues, so one of the more difficult tasks in legal writing is deciding how to divide the issues and where and how often to mention a case. This is discussed further below under The Legal Memorandum heading.

Organize Issues Logically

Dividing the law into separate issues requires deciding how to divide the issues clearly and logically.

Many legal problems have natural divisions. For example, in criminal law, two necessary components to a criminal offence are the *actus rea* and the *mens rea*. Therefore, the first issue may be: Was there a criminal act? And the second issue may be: Was there intent? Researchers should avoid falling into the trap of categorizing legal matters in the same way that legal textbooks do. Textbook writers often divide legal issues into those categories that are easiest to teach. These divisions are not always applicable to real-life situations. Some sense of how to organize legal issues can be elicited from the cases being researched.

Theoretically, there may be a different way to organize the legal issues in every new legal problem. Your task is to search for the one that explains the law to the reader in the clearest fashion.

Select a Specific Order for Statutes and Cases

You must make a decision not only about what cases and statutes to include, but also about how you will include them and where. Regardless of how you decide to order the cases and statutes, there must be some logic to the order. It should never be random.

For example, it may be desirable to discuss the statute first and the cases second. It may also be preferable to mention the oldest cases first and work forward, or to mention the most recent case first and work backwards. Each decision about organization must be rational. Some logical legal patterns are chronological, historical, or general to specific.

When drafting an outline, some of the questions you might ask yourself are:

- Why did I put the cases in that order?
- Do the cases flow logically from one to the next?
- Why did I put the statute where I did?

Your decisions should be driven not only by the subject matter, but also by the expectations of your readers and the rules of good communication.

Stage 3: Revising

Revising involves ensuring that the content, organization, paragraphs, sentences, words and style are effective at conveying thoughts and information.

Revision is a long and sometimes tedious process. A significant amount of time should be spent on revision. It is recommended that the original draft be revised up to five times — each time for a different purpose. Revising requires the writer to amend what has already been written and then walk away and come back later for further revisions. The writer must be particularly rigorous at this particular stage and be prepared to edit seriously. The recommended way to revise legal work is in the following order:

1. Content
2. Organization
3. Paragraphs
4. Sentences
5. Words
6. Style
7. Form

A writing checklist is included in Appendix 11C, which summarizes the things to look for when editing and revising.

Content

Revising content primarily involves scaling the work down to that which is relevant. This first edit should focus on the bigger concepts and not on the words. Some questions you might ask yourself are:

- Have I covered all the main legal issues?
- Have I included the key statutes and cases for each issue?
- Did I include any cases that basically say the same thing?
- Is there a reason why each case is included?
- What does each case add?

Organization

Revising organization involves ensuring that the facts, brief answers, issues, analysis and conclusion are in an order that best conveys and expresses your ideas. You should ask yourself the following questions after you have completed your memorandum to ensure that your organization is appropriate:

- Have I explained my organization to my reader?
- Have I told my reader where I am going?
- Is the organization I have selected easy to follow? Does it flow?
- Is there a reason why I have put these issues in this particular order?

Paragraphs

Revising paragraphs involves ensuring that your thoughts flow logically from paragraph to paragraph. Recall that the main rule of organization is to state where you are going; go there; and state where you have been. In order to do this, the writer must provide the reader with "sign posts". Often, new legal writers do not articulate each of the steps in their analysis because they are so immersed in the subject that they forget that the reader needs to know each step that led to the analysis. To assist the reader, it is a good idea to make use of transitions between paragraphs and to tell the reader in the first sentence of each paragraph what that paragraph will include. Transitions provide the reader with directions. They state where the writer has come from and where the writer is going.

The following are examples of transitions. Select the one you like the best.

Examples of Transitions Between Paragraphs

1. In *Brooks v. Goet* a purchaser of a doll sued a toy manufacturer after her child swallowed one of the doll's eyes.
2. Another case involving liability of a manufacturer was *Brooks v. Goet*. In that case, the purchaser of a doll sued ...
3. Several other cases held toy manufacturers liable for faulty construction of dolls. One of theses cases was *Brooks v. Goet*. In that case ...

4.   The issue of liability for faulty toys was considered most recently in the case of *Brooks v. Goet*. That case involved ...

You should ask yourself the following questions to ensure your paragraphs are appropriate:

- Have I provided "sign posts" for the reader?
- Would a layperson who knows nothing about the law be able to pick up my writing and understand it?
- Does the first sentence in each paragraph tell what the paragraph will be about?
- Does the last sentence in each paragraph tell what the next paragraph will likely include?

Sentences

Revising sentences involves eliminating excess words, ensuring sentences are short and using an active rather than passive voice. Although variation in sentence structure keeps the writing interesting, too much variation can be unsettling to a reader.

Words

Revising words involves selecting words that are clear and understandable to the reader. This means using plain English, avoiding Latin, using gender-neutral language and avoiding jargon. Correct spelling and punctuation are also very important.

Style and Form

The last edit involves revising the style and form of writing. Revising style involves detecting tones that may emerge in your writing. The most important rule with regard to style is to remain objective. The purpose of a legal memorandum is to provide a summary of the law in an impartial manner. While the tone of a memorandum should be objective, there is another style of legal writing besides the informative — the persuasive style.

To achieve objectivity, it is important to avoid identifying too closely with a particular client's concerns. It is better to try to anticipate the other party's position. Even if required to answer to one party in a dispute, researchers should avoid the compulsion to argue in their favour, or the temptation to make their case sound better than it is. Phrasing a letter or memorandum in terms of an argument can split the law into pros and cons unnecessarily and often does not describe the law as a whole. Students who use an argumentative style tend to find it difficult to come to a final decision because the argument necessarily fragments the law and the discussion.

Generally, it is improper in informative writing to include personal opinions about the law. For example, words such as "promising" or "unfortunately" should be saved for persuasive writing. Your writing, even if friendly, should always have a professional tone. For example, you should not use slang and you should never be flippant.

Form and presentation are also very important. The look of the print and the use of divisions and subheadings should invite the reader to read on.

FORMAT

Most legal writing, including judgments, case briefs, letters to clients and legal memoranda, tends to follow a particular format. This is not the only way law can be communicated, but this particular format has become an acceptable and commonly used means of discourse in the law.

Many readers of law, such as lawyers and judges, expect legal writing to follow a particular format. The format allows them to read the law much more effectively because they know ahead of time where the information they are looking for will be located in the text. It is therefore important to recognize the format when reading and writing about the law.

Other types of writing follow their own particular formats as well. For example, newspaper articles tend to follow a pyramid format: providing the most important information in the first paragraph and expanding on this information in sequential paragraphs. The pyramid format allows readers to move quickly through newspapers selecting the information needed. Newspaper readers have come to expect this type of format and can become frustrated if the format is not followed.

The format used most frequently in legal writing is called FILAC (Facts, Issues, Law, Application and Conclusion). You will note that the FILAC format of writing is similar to the five-step process recommended for researching the law. In legal writing, however, it looks like this:

Facts — State the legally relevant facts
Issues — State the legal issues
Law — Describe the law (cases and statutes)
Application — Describe how the law applies to the facts
Conclusion — Conclude and state the likely outcome

There are several benefits to dividing the discussion into these five components. First, the reader can quickly select what to read. Second, the reader can see the separation between the law and the application of the law. This is important because the description of the law is totally objective. The application of the law, on the other hand, necessarily includes the opinions of the writer, since it is an estimation of how a judge will apply the law to a particular circumstance. If the reader does not agree with the application, he or she can still benefit from the objective description of the law and attempt an alternative application.

FILAC is not the only format of legal discourse. Legal writers should understand why it is an effective format and strive to improve it by adding their own particular style and creative touches.

The Legal Memorandum

A legal memorandum is a written document that expresses the results of legal research. It is a summary of the law and the application of the law as it applies to a particular situation. It is used as a basis for advice to a client. Although clients rarely see legal memoranda, the memoranda are used to assist lawyers throughout the entire life of the file. Decisions such as whether to proceed with, settle or abandon a claim will be made on the basis of the information and analysis provided in the memorandum. Based on a memorandum, lawyers will often write letters to clients providing opinions about the merits of a case and the likelihood of success.

Before describing how best to put a legal memorandum together, imagine the following situation:

Situation

You are a judge. The two lawyers in the case before you have provided you with about 60 cases and one statute, which they suggest is the law pertaining to the case before you. You have heard the witnesses in the case and have a good idea of the facts involved. Your task is now to write a decision. This means you must restate the facts as you see them, summarize the law as you read it, and tell the parties how the law applies in this particular case. You must then come up with a decision that makes some sense and is clear and concise. How will you do this?

A judge's job is very similar to a legal researcher's, except that, instead of coming to a decision, researchers predict the likely outcome of the case. A legal memorandum, if properly written, will look very similar to a well-written judgment. Although each judge has a particular style, readers can quickly detect which judgments are easiest to follow and get to the point quickly. The same qualities you appreciate as a reader of cases should be incorporated into your own legal writing.

Format of a Legal Memorandum

There is no required format for a legal memorandum. Since memoranda are usually law office documents, the format will usually be dictated by the particular law firm or legal department. The format recommended here is one used in a number of law firms. It is designed to communicate the law in the most useful way for a busy lawyer. Researchers, however, should remain flexible with the format and be as creative as a particular situation may require. The recommended format is as follows:

1. Facts
2. Issues
3. Brief answers
4. Analysis (law and application)
5. Conclusion

You will note that this format follows both the research process and the common discourse in law, which was described earlier. Each component is discussed below.

Facts

The facts in a legal memorandum are the legally relevant facts of the problem presented. A recital of the facts in a legal memorandum should look much like those facts found in judgments. Although the way in which facts can be articulated is unlimited, the goal is to include only relevant facts. This is discussed in more detail in Chapter 2 (Factual Analysis).

Often a first attempt at summarizing the facts is incomplete. As researchers become more familiar with the law pertaining to their case, they begin to recognize the importance of the facts that have been taken into consideration in other cases. Therefore, the facts should be reviewed periodically as research progresses. Any necessary assumptions should also be stated.

Issues

The issues are the legal questions to be answered. Proper drafting of issues enables a reader to know exactly where the writer is headed. Drafting of issues is discussed in more detail in Chapter 3 (Issue Determination).

Drafting issues is not a one-time task. Ideally, the issues should be redrafted as the research and writing progress. It is always good practice to review the legal issues at the very end of writing to ensure that these are the specific questions that have been answered in the legal memorandum.

Some tips when drafting issues are as follows. Legal issues should:

- be drafted as a single question;
- include both facts and law;
- use the actual names or roles of the parties in the issue (*e.g.*, not "plaintiff" or "defendant"); and
- be divided into sub-issues where possible.

Brief Answers

The brief answers in the memorandum are the likely outcome of the case supported by reasoning. A sample brief answer is as follows:

It is likely there is no contract between Mr. Job and Type Company because there was no consideration flowing from Mr. Job when Type Company forwarded merchandise that was not included under the original contract.

It is advisable to use words such as "likely" or "probably" in the brief answers since there is rarely a situation where the outcome of a case is guaranteed. It is also good practice not to include references to specific statutes or cases in the brief answer unless they are critical to the outcome of a case.

Analysis

The analysis part of the memorandum is the bulk of the memorandum. It includes an analysis of the law and a determination of how the law applies to the facts.

Organization is critical to the analysis. As indicated above, it is important to keep each legal issue separate. It is also important to keep the description of the law separate from a description of how the law applies to the facts. For each issue, state the relevant law first (*i.e.*, cases and statutes), synthesize this law into a paragraph or two, and then apply this law to your particular facts. This is discussed in more detail in Chapter 10 (Introduction to Legal Analysis).

Any discussion of policy should appear at the end of the analysis.

Conclusion

The conclusion in a legal memorandum summarizes the information contained in the memorandum. It essentially gathers all of the conclusions reached under each of the issues into one or two concise paragraphs. It is important not to include any new information in the conclusion. Nothing in the conclusion should surprise the reader, since it is simply a brief restatement of what has already been said. Often a reader will only read the issues, the brief answer and the conclusion of a memorandum. Therefore, the conclusion should include the likely outcome of the case and the reasoning.

It is rare to include case names in the conclusion unless they are very important to the analysis. Mention of policy for the first time in the conclusion should be avoided.

The Opinion Letter

An opinion letter is a letter to a client advising about the state of the law and how it applies to a situation.

Opinion letters are usually written on the basis of legal memoranda and include the same components as the legal memorandum: the facts, the law, the application of the law to the facts and a conclusion. However, the format is much more flexible. The ultimate aim is to answer the client's question.

Both the format and the language used should enhance understanding. If the law does not support the client's position, this should be made clear and alternatives should be briefly considered. To test the clarity and conciseness of a letter it is a good idea to ask a layperson to provide feedback. A layperson should be able to understand what you have written.

The suggested format of an opinion letter is as follows:

Part 1:   Introduce yourself (if necessary) and define your task. State where you are going and what you are going to say. Sometimes it is good to state the conclusion right up front.

Part 2:   Introduce the subject at hand generally and give a simple overview of the relevant area of law. Then describe the law in more detail by focusing on the specific wording of statutes or the factors that the courts have taken into consideration in determining past cases. You may want to refer to a specific case if it is very similar to your client's situation.

Part 3: Apply the law to the client's situation and describe the likely outcome of the case if it were to go to trial.

Part 4: Conclude and describe the next steps to be taken.

SELF TEST

The answers to these questions are found at the end of the book in the "Answers to Self Tests" section.

1. Name a few basic rules of good writing.
2. List the three stages in the legal writing process.
3. Name the four steps involved in planning.
4. What are five parts of a legal memorandum?
5. In what order should you revise your writing?
6. What is the form of a typical opinion letter?

Appendix 11A: Sample Memorandum of Law

The following memorandum of law was prepared by a first-year law student. It is only an example and should be critiqued by students.

To: M.F. Fitzgerald
From: Michael Lee
Re: Ravi and May — Liability of Partners
Date: November 24, 2009

STATEMENT OF FACTS

Ravi, May and Jan formed the law partnership of "JMR Legal Services" to provide traditional legal and mediation services. Their partnership agreement stated that all profits from the law practice were to be shared and the firm's name and facilities were only to be used for activities related to the law practice.

In building their practice, Ravi and May regularly referred clients requiring mediation work to Jan. However, Jan eventually decided that since her mediation work was separate from the traditional law practice, she would keep the profits generated from this work. Consequently, she started "Jan's Mediation Services" (JMS), set up her own bookkeeping, banking and advertising, and met her mediation clients at home. Although Jan tried to keep the two areas of her practice separate, she occasionally asked the secretary at JMR to type correspondence relating to her mediation work. It is assumed that the secretary did not use JMR letterhead.

Viewing the mediation services as integral to the firm's practice, Ravi and May wrote a protest letter to Jan stating that the mediation profits should be shared. However, before this dispute was resolved, Jan was charged with theft for misappropriating $30,000 from the Regal Bank, which had retained Jan to provide mediation services. During the mediation process, Jan had held the money in a trust account under the JMS name. Since Jan had no assets, the bank sued Ravi and May as partners in JMR. It is assumed that there was no previous relationship between Regal Bank and JMR and that the bank did not know that Jan was a lawyer.

ISSUES

The main issue of whether Ravi and May are liable for Jan's misappropriation of funds may be divided into two issues: (1) Was Jan's provision of mediation services to Regal Bank and subsequent misappropriation of funds within the ordinary course of the business of the firm? (2) Was Jan acting within the scope of her apparent authority when she provided mediation services to Regal Bank and misappropriated the funds?

BRIEF ANSWER

Under the *Partnership Act* of B.C., a partner is liable for the wrongful act of another partner if he or she was acting in the ordinary course of the firm's business, or within the scope of his or her apparent authority. Case law identifies the following factors as acting in the ordinary course of business where: (1) there is no agreement excluding the activity from the firm's business; (2) the firm's staff and facilities are used; and (3) the profits from the activity are shared. Acting in the scope of apparent authority can be defined as when: (1) a partner uses the firm's name and its facilities to hold himself or herself out as acting with the approval of the other partners; and (2) a client is under the impression that the individual is acting within his or her authority as a partner in the firm. Most of these factors were not present in this case, so it is unlikely that Jan could be viewed as having acted either in the ordinary course of the firm's business, or within the scope of her apparent authority. Consequently, Ravi and May likely will not be found liable.

ANALYSIS

Issue 1: Ordinary Course of the Firm's Business

The Law

The applicable statute law is s. 12 of the *Partnership Act*[1] of B.C., which states:

> Where by any wrongful act or omission of any partner acting in the ordinary course of the business of the firm, or with the authority of his co-partners, loss or injury is caused to any person not being a partner in the firm, or any penalty is incurred, the firm is liable for that loss, injury or penalty to the same extent as the partner so acting or omitting to act.

In *Patchett v. Oliver*,[2] the Supreme Court of B.C. applied the *Partnership Act* to find Oliver's law partner liable for Oliver's wrongful acts, because he was acting within the ordinary course of the business of the firm and within the scope of his apparent authority. From the case it may be inferred that the important factors in making this determination were Oliver's acting as a solicitor and using the firm's bookkeeper and accounts to carry out his wrongful acts.

In *Public Trustee v. Mortimer* ("*Mortimer*"),[3] the Ontario High Court of Justice applied the *Partnership Act* of Ontario, which is similar in language to

---

[1] *Partnership Act*, R.S.B.C. 1979, c. 312.
[2] [1977] 5 W.W.R. 299 (B.C.S.C.).
[3] (1985), 16 D.L.R. (4th) 404 (Ont. H.C.).

the B.C. Act. The defendant, Mortimer, a solicitor in a law firm, acted as an executor and trustee of an estate. Using the staff and facilities of his law firm to administer the estate, Mortimer stole money from the estate. The court found the defendant partners liable for Mortimer's wrongful acts because he was acting within the ordinary course of the firm's business. To reach this decision, the court outlined several *indicia* as possible ways to separate a partner's activities as an executor of an estate from the ordinary course of the firm's business [p. 413]:

> There would probably be an agreement between the partners to that effect, and one might expect to find that the partner would not charge the estate on an account issued in the firm's name, would personally keep any fees and compensation paid, rather than treat them as revenues of the firm, would keep the funds of the estate in an account separate from his firm's trust account, and would keep a set of accounting records from the estate separate from those of his firm. If he wanted to be careful to make it clear that his work as an executor was not part of the firm's business, he would not use the firm letterhead when writing as an executor.[4]

None of these *indicia* were met by Mortimer and his firm. In addition, Mortimer used a junior solicitor and the firm's management company for the typing and bookkeeping work on the estate. The executor's fees were also directed into the firm's revenues. Consequently, the court concluded that Mortimer's activities as an executor were within the ordinary course of the business of the firm.

In *Tomiyama v. Riley* (*"Tomiyama"*),[5] the defendant, Riley, asked his client, Mrs. Tomiyama, for a personal loan in exchange for a mortgage on three residential lots owned by Riley. He asked her to make separate discharges of the mortgage, then sold the lots, but failed to repay her. The Supreme Court of B.C., in applying the *Partnership Act* of B.C., found that Riley's firm was liable for Riley's wrongful act, because he was acting within the ordinary course of the business of the firm. This finding was based on Riley's use of his secretary, the firm's facilities and his position as a partner in the firm to carry out these transactions. For example, the court cites that Riley applied for the releases of the mortgage as a member of the firm and used his firm's business address. As Riley had not separated his activities from the firm, the court inferred that these releases were secured in the ordinary course of the business of the firm.

In *Korz v. St. Pierre* (*"Korz"*),[6] Korz, a solicitor in a law firm, entered into a business agreement with two clients to form a company and serve as its directors. He did not contribute his share of the financing, nor did he help his two clients settle the debts when the company went bankrupt. The Ontario Court of Appeal, applying the *Partnership Act* of Ontario, found Korz's partner liable for Korz's wrongful acts because he was acting in the ordinary course of the business of the firm. This finding was based on Korz acting as the solicitor to the company and, by extension, the directors, and on his long record of solicitor work for both clients prior to the company's formation. In addition, all meetings of the company's directors were held in Korz's law offices.

---

[4]   *Ibid.*, at 43.
[5]   [1987] B.C.J. No. 1942 (B.C.S.C.).
[6]   (1988), 43 D.L.R. (4th) 528 (Ont. C.A.); leave to appeal refused (1988), 62 O.R. (2d) ix (S.C.C.).

Synthesis

From these cases, the factors defining when a partner is acting in the ordinary course of business of a law firm are where: (1) there is no agreement excluding the activity from the firm's business; (2) the firm's staff (including lawyers, secretaries and bookkeepers), facilities (including accounts and offices) and name (including letterhead) are used; and (3) the profits from the activity are shared.

Application of Law to Our Situation

These factors must now be applied to determine whether Jan's activities were in the ordinary course of the business of the firm. As in *Mortimer*, there was no agreement excluding mediation work from the firm's business. Rather, the partners had an understanding, reaffirmed in Ravi and May's protest letter, that the practice was to include mediation work.

However, Jan separated her mediation activities from the business of the firm. Meeting several of the key *indicia* laid out in *Mortimer*, Jan kept separate accounting records and bank accounts and did not share the profits from her mediation work. Although Jan occasionally used the firm's secretary for correspondence related to her mediation activities, this use of the firm's staff was minor compared to Mortimer's use. Jan did not use a junior solicitor of the firm or employees of the firm's management company for bookkeeping. In addition, unlike the *Korz* case, Jan did not use the offices of the firm to conduct meetings with clients regarding mediation services. Jan also did not conduct her mediation activities under the firm's name, as opposed to the *Tomiyama* case. As a result, it is unlikely that her activities would be found as having taken place within the ordinary course of the business of the firm.

Issue 2: Apparent Authority

The Law

The applicable statute law is s. 13(*a*) of the *Partnership Act* of B.C., which states:

> where one partner acting within the scope of his apparent authority receives money or property of a third person and misapplies it ... the firm is to make good the loss.

In *Mortimer*, the Ontario High Court of Justice, in considering the claim of the managing partner that Mortimer's activities were not in the course of the firm's business, also reviewed the use of apparent authority. Despite the managing partner's claim, Mortimer was allowed to use the facilities of the firm to carry out his activities as an executor. The court held that the firm: "by permitting Mortimer to use the stationery, accounts, staff and other facilities of the firm in connection with his activities as executor and trustee, had vested Mortimer with apparent authority to receive the money or property of the estate which he subsequently misapplied".[7] In this way, through his use of the firm's accounts, letterhead and staff, Mortimer's activities appeared to be authorized by the partners in his firm.

In *Tomiyama*, the Supreme Court of B.C. applied the decision from the *Mortimer* case regarding apparent authority to suggest that Riley's use of the "trappings of the firm" to carry out his fraud was analogous to Mortimer's activities. The court found that Tomiyama was under the impression that Riley was acting within his authority as a senior partner in the firm. This impression was in part based on her long history of dealings with Riley in a solicitor-client relationship. Tomiyama was also under this impression because Riley carried out these activities using the firm's facilities and staff, such as his secretary. The court summed up Riley's use of his apparent authority: "[w]ithout the aid of his secretary and the trappings of the firm Riley could not have accomplished fraud upon her in the manner that he did. Theoretically perhaps he could have perfected the fraud personally and outside the scope of his firm, but he did not."[8] In this way, Riley, by using the firm's name and facilities, took advantage of his apparent authority.

Synthesis

From case law, the factors defining acting within the scope of apparent authority are: (1) when a partner uses the firm's name and its facilities to hold himself or herself out as acting with the authority of the other partners; and (2) when the client is under the impression that the individual is acting within his or her authority as a partner in the firm.

Application of Law to Our Situation

These factors must now be applied to determine whether Jan was acting within the scope of her apparent authority. Jan had the authority of her partners to carry out her mediation work, because of the partners' understanding that their practice was to include mediation work. She also did not sever her partnership with JMR. In addition, like the *Mortimer* case, her partners permitted her to use the firm's facilities to carry out her mediation work.

However, in forming JMS, Jan separated her activities from the firm and did not use her authority as a partner in JMR. Unlike both *Mortimer* and *Tomiyama*, Jan did not use the facilities of the firm to give the appearance that her activities were authorized by her partners. In using her own promotional materials and facilities, Jan carried out her mediation activities under a separate business name — unlike Riley, who acted as a partner of his firm. Consequently, it is unlikely that Jan will be found to have been acting within the scope of her apparent authority.

---

[7] *Supra*, note 3, at 414.
[8] *Supra*, note 5, at 5.

CONCLUSION

It is likely that Ravi and May will not be held liable for Jan's misappropriation of funds from the Regal Bank because Jan was not "acting in the ordinary course of the business" of the firm and not likely acting within the scope of her apparent authority. She had effectively separated her mediation work from the firm's practice. She did not use the firm's facilities or her position as a partner in the firm to give the impression to the bank that she was acting with the authority of her partners. In short, the action against Ravi and May is likely to fail. A recurrent policy theme in case law is holding partners responsible for their partners' wrongful acts where there is a sharing of profits. Should this policy consideration be given more weight, the argument in Ravi and May's favour would not be weakened because Jan kept her mediation work profits separate from those of JMR.

Appendix 11B: Sample Opinion Letter

The following is a sample opinion letter written by a first-year law student. It is only an example and should be critiqued by students.

November 14, 2009

Ravi and May
JMR Legal Services
Victoria, B.C.

Dear Ravi and May:

Re: <u>Liability in Jan's Misappropriation of Funds</u>

I have been assigned your case by Ms. Fitzgerald, and am responding regarding your potential liability in Jan's misappropriation of funds from the Regal Bank. Ms. Fitzgerald gave me the facts of your case and, based on this information, the following letter outlines the issues, case law and application of the law to your situation.

Under the *Partnership Act* of B.C., you would be liable for Jan's wrongful acts if she was either acting in the ordinary course of the business of the firm, or within the scope of her apparent authority.

The factors used by the courts to define acting in the ordinary course of the firm's business are: (1) there is no agreement excluding the activity from the firm's business; (2) the firm's staff and facilities are used; and (3) the profits from the activity are shared. The factors defining acting in the scope of apparent authority are: (1) a partner uses the firm's name and its facilities to hold himself or herself out as acting with the authority of the other partners; and (2) a client is under the impression that the partner is acting within his or her authority as a partner of the firm.

In applying these factors to your case, it is likely that, although there was an understanding that the firm's practice included mediation work, Jan effectively separated her mediation activities from the law practice. She informed JMR, made arrangements for separate bookkeeping, banking and advertising, and kept the profits separate from JMR. Although Jan may have had your authority to do mediation work as part of the firm's practice, she did not use the firm's staff, facilities or name to make it appear as though her activities were authorized by you, her two partners. Rather, Jan used her own facilities and conducted her mediation activities under her own company name.

Therefore, it is likely that the court will find that Jan was neither acting in the ordinary course of the firm's business, nor acting within the scope of her apparent authority. In our opinion, it is unlikely that a court would find you liable for Jan's wrongful act.

Should you wish to discuss this opinion further, please contact me.

Yours sincerely,

Student

Appendix 11C: Legal Writing Checklist

The following checklist summarizes many of the tips provided in Chapter 11. It can be used as a guide for legal writing or as a checklist on completion of your writing to ensure that you have written in an accurate and concise manner.

Content

❑   The purpose is clearly stated.

❑   All relevant facts are identified and necessary assumptions are stated.

❑   The main issues and sub-issues are identified and worded as questions.

❑   The probable outcome is briefly summarized.

❑   The law is synthesized and applied to the facts.

❑   The analysis reconciles or distinguishes conflicting case law.

❑   The conclusion briefly summarizes the law and states the probable outcome.

❑   The text is consistent with the stated purpose.

Organization

❑   The information is presented in logical order.

❑   Topics are discussed in a logical sequence.

❑   There are smooth transitions.

❑   The conclusion summarizes the discussion.

❑   Issues are discussed separately.

Paragraphs

❑   Each paragraph explains no more than one main idea.

❑   The main idea is stated at the beginning of the paragraph.

❏ Each paragraph flows logically from one to the next.

Sentences

❏ Sentences are short, accurate and clear.

❏ Each sentence is connected to the surrounding sentences.

❏ Complex sentence structure is avoided.

❏ Active rather than passive voice is used.

❏ Sentence structure varies.

Words

❏ Language is concise (*e.g.*, no repetition or wordiness).

❏ Language is precise, and concrete words are used (*e.g.*, no ambiguity or vagueness).

❏ Language is consistent and objective.

❏ Language and tone are suitable for the purpose of writing and the reader.

❏ Legal jargon is avoided.

❏ Legal terms are explained where necessary.

❏ Gender-neutral language is used.

❏ Correct punctuation and spelling are used.

Style and Form

❏ Headings and definitions are used effectively.

❏ A suitable format is adopted.

This Legal Writing Checklist is adapted from: Modern Writing for Lawyers (Continuing Legal Education Society of British Columbia, 1992) Writing Guide, p. 3. Used and adapted with permission.

A Research Plan

12

Legal research should be done as quickly and inexpensively as possible. This means that researchers should devise ways to conduct research effectively and efficiently. Time is money — the time cost of research has to be taken into account just as costs to do online research must be.

There are many ways to conduct legal research. There is no single, best way. The research method used will depend on a number of factors, such as the nature of the problem and the researcher's abilities. Because legal research is as much an art as a science, the ability to research the law will develop with practice. As lawyers become more familiar with legal sources and more proficient with the research process, they learn short cuts. Solving legal problems effectively and efficiently, however, should be done in a systematic way. Irrespective of ability and knowledge, researchers are continually confronted with new problems and issues. In these situations, it is advisable to go "back to the basics" of research.

Regardless of the approach taken, each researcher must have a plan prior to beginning the research process. Before heading to the library or logging onto an online resource, researchers should plan where they intend to look and what they hope to find. This gives some direction to the research and keeps researchers from sinking in the myriad of books and databases. Developing a plan eliminates wasted effort in looking at irrelevant sources and provides a checklist indicating steps taken.

This chapter explains what a research plan is, describes some practical considerations, lists some research tips and describes how to develop a research plan. Appended to this chapter is a sample research plan.

LEARNING OBJECTIVES

At the end of this chapter you will be able to:

- Explain what a research plan is
- Explain why a research plan is necessary
- Name a few practical considerations in preparing a research plan
- Describe the basic parts of a research plan
- Describe some advantages to note-taking

WHAT IS A RESEARCH PLAN?

A research plan is a written plan describing how research will be conducted. As soon as a problem is presented, a researcher will begin to think about possible ways to solve the problem. Some problems will be easy to solve and require little research, whereas others will require extensive research. Each legal problem requires a unique research plan.

At a minimum, a research plan should consist of the five broad steps of the legal research process: Factual analysis, Issue determination, finding the Law, Analyzing the law, and Communicating the law (FILAC). However, the details of how each step is accomplished will vary from problem to problem.

Although there is no magic plan, all research plans should indicate, in as specific terms as possible, where the researcher intends to go and what she or he hopes to find. A research plan evolves as the research progresses and, thus, should remain fairly flexible.

PRACTICAL CONSIDERATIONS

When devising a research plan, some practical factors must be taken into consideration.

Before diving into the research process, researchers must know something about the persons requesting the research (audience), why the research is necessary (purpose), and limitations on the research, such as time and cost. All legal research depends on these factors.

The audience and the purpose of the research are very important considerations when defining the scope of the research. The most typical purpose of research is to advise a client, in preparation for trial or in preparation for negotiation. Although the research process will be similar in either case, the purpose of the research will define exactly how deeply a researcher may delve into a particular area. For example, if the research is being done for a knowledgeable client or a lawyer, the researcher may decide not to include some very basic information on a particular area. However, if the research is being prepared directly for a less sophisticated client, then the researcher may want to include more general or basic information about the particular legal subject.

There will almost always be constraints placed on researchers. Typically, there are time or financial constraints. If, for example, a client is disputing a contract with a value of $100, it would not be practical or proper to spend days researching the issue, especially if the extensive use of online resources is contemplated.

Researchers are also often limited by availability of information. Many libraries do not carry information that could be useful, but the rapidly expanding array of commercial online providers and products opens up new ways to conduct research, even if you work or live quite far from a law library. A researcher must be aware of what information is available and at what cost. One of the first things a new researcher should always do is to familiarize himself or herself not only with the online services available in the workplace, but also with whatever physical law collections are handy, such as academic or courthouse law libraries. Within those libraries, the researcher should ask about the kinds of locally prepared tools that are likely to be on hand, such as an index to a local law society newsletter, a collection of local municipal bylaws or a listing of cases that have interpreted provincial statutes. Often, these kinds of aids can save hours of time.

RESEARCH TIPS

The following are some tips for legal researchers. The first group of tips deals with the legal research process. The second group deals with note-taking, and the third deals with knowing when to stop.

The Legal Research Process

These tips will assist legal researchers during the legal research process.

- *Think through the whole research process.* It is very important to think through the entire research process thoroughly before beginning research. Although this may seem like an obvious task, time spent here will save you time and effort in the long run.

- *Move from broad to specific.* Researchers should almost always move from the broad to the specific when conducting research. This means that research should begin at the general level and move towards research of more specific legal issues. It is important not to get trapped into a narrow category of law early in the research. Think of this process as an inverted triangle — start at the top with a very broad legal topic, such as torts. Then work your way toward more and more specific subdivisions of that topic, until you arrive at the bottom, at a narrow and manageable specific level. For example, when perusing indexes for a legal topic, do not consider your search complete if you find one relevant topic. Often legal subjects span a number of legal areas.

- *Try not to jump back and forth between sources.* It is usually not efficient to interrupt your review of one source and immediately go to another source. It is best to use one source completely so that you do not have to go back to it and wonder how far you have read in that particular source. If you feel compelled to jump ahead, make detailed notes about where you are so that you can return to the source without retracing steps. When using physical materials in a library, it is a good idea to make a note of exactly where in the building the materials are, to avoid having to relocate things later.

- *Look for "meaty" quotes.* Often court cases are well written and include excellent summaries of the law. Therefore, when reading cases, researchers should be on the lookout for "meaty quotes", which can ultimately be included in the final written product. A good habit is to photocopy important quotations. Handwritten quotations leave room for error when transcribed. Photocopies can also be used to proof the final product.

- *Stay flexible.* Perhaps the most important tip is to stay flexible. If you find yourself off on a tangent, be prepared to abandon what you have done and start again. Try not to be narrow in focus, and continually ask yourself whether the route you are taking is the most effective and efficient. Remain open to new ideas as they present themselves.

Note-Taking

Since legal research can often take weeks or months and can uncover vast quantities of information, researchers must be organized and devise systems to record research steps taken. Some of the suggestions made below should assist researchers in doing this.

- *Summarize the facts and issues on one page.* It is a good idea to summarize the facts and legal issues on a separate page. This page can be carried into the library and referred to as necessary and revised as the research progresses. You might also jot down the relationships among the parties in a fact situation, such as physician–patient, or parent–child.

- *List the keywords that you search.* Listing the words or phrases that are searched is particularly important because these words are often forgotten later. It is helpful to dedicate a specific page for a list of descriptive words that could be searched. This way the list can be lengthened or shortened. This list is particularly helpful when narrowing down the legal issues and later in the research process when computer searches are conducted.

- *Devote a separate page to each legal issue.* It is recommended that a separate page be devoted to each legal issue. This ensures that the legal issues are dealt with separately and thoroughly. If the information on legal issues is combined, it is very difficult to separate the legal issues later.

- *Record citations as you conduct your research.* It is always a good idea to record the full citations of cases, statutes and secondary sources as you are conducting your research. This cannot be over-emphasized. Many researchers know how frustrating it is to have to search for a citation of a source later, when only a scrawl has been recorded. Another suggestion is to also record references to material that you considered to be irrelevant at the time and why you thought so. Your opposition may present these to the court and you will have to defend yourself regarding your decision **not** to use them as authorities.

- *Photocopy statutes.* When referring to statutes it is critical that the exact numbering, wording and format of the statute be maintained. Therefore it is best to photocopy the relevant sections of the statute or bookmark them within your web browser.

- *Record particular insights.* Often as research progresses, researchers are struck by particular insights. It is a good idea to jot down the ideas you may have, although they need not be researched at that particular moment. These insights often provide the basis for policy discussions later in the analysis.

- *Photocopy key cases.* It is recommended that very important cases that are referred to repeatedly be photocopied or printed out from databases. This is to enable researchers to re-read cases a number of times and highlight the important parts. These cases often include citations and summaries of other relevant cases.

- *Devote a separate page to a list of sources referred to.* It is a good idea to keep a separate page listing authorities referred to. This will be your bibliography. Sometimes researchers will be asked to produce this list to ensure that the research is complete and that all relevant sources have been canvassed. It is recommended that a specific coloured page be devoted to the bibliography because of the importance of keeping a record of the sources referred to. Again, you may wish to keep a separate list of authorities you decided not to use, in case you are questioned about them.

- *Date every page.* Often, dating pages of notes serves as a reminder of the series of steps taken. It can also trigger a researcher's memory so that tracks can be retraced if necessary.

Knowing When to Stop

There is no simple way to know when to stop. If you are consistent and thorough, you will begin to see your research coming into focus. The most obvious clue is discovering that the sources you are referring to refer you back to the same ones you have already examined. If you are getting no new leads or no new references to new legal sources, the research is nearing completion. When you get the sense that you are repeating steps or that the sources are becoming exhausted, you can stop your research.

DEVELOPING A RESEARCH PLAN

Although a research plan will constantly evolve, the framework of each plan should ideally remain constant. In other words, the five-step process (FILAC) should remain the same, although the steps taken within each of those steps might vary.

In earlier chapters, a number of other steps are recommended within this five-step process. These steps are summarized in a sample research plan and are appended to this chapter.

The step that requires significant advance planning is finding the law in the law library. There are two fundamental steps in finding the law: refer to secondary materials, and then refer to primary sources. The way in which secondary materials and primary sources are found and used will vary. However, each researcher should have an idea about which secondary materials will be reviewed and which primary sources he or she hopes to find in the library.

SELF TEST

The answers to these questions are found in the back of the book in the "Answers to Self Tests" section.

1. What is a research plan?
2. Why is a research plan necessary?
3. Name a few practical factors to consider when preparing a research plan.
4. Describe the basic parts of a research plan.
5. Describe some advantages to note-taking.

Appendix 12A: Sample Research Plan

The exact steps taken to research a legal problem depend on a number of factors. The following plan is a guideline consisting of the basic steps in the process of legal research. It should be adjusted to the particular needs of the research and researcher.

Name of Researcher:_____ Date Assigned:_____

Research For: _____ Date Due: _____

File number (if applicable):_____

PRELIMINARY STEP: IDENTIFY AUDIENCE, PURPOSE, LIMITATIONS AND QUESTIONS

❑ Determine the purpose of the research, who the research is for and any limitations on the research, such as time and cost. At this stage, you should estimate how much time should be spent on the total research. A record should be kept of all steps taken.

STEP 1: ANALYZE THE FACTS

❑ Gather and organize the facts (*e.g.*, identify the parties, events and possible claims).
❑ Identify the legally relevant facts by reading generally about the law in secondary materials such as textbooks, the *Canadian Encyclopedic Digest*, or *Halsbury's Laws of Canada*.
❑ Summarize and formulate the relevant facts.
❑ Reformulate the facts later in the research process as the legally relevant facts become clearer.

STEP 2: DETERMINE THE LEGAL ISSUES

❑ Determine applicable areas of law by brainstorming, word association and/or using the subjects of law courses.
❑ Identify the general legal issues by consulting secondary materials such as journal articles, *Halsbury's Laws of Canada*, the *Canadian Encyclopedic Digest* or textbooks and reading about the law generally. When reading about the law, move from general to specific.

☐   Formulate the specific legal issues by reading about the law in more detail. Articulate the issues as questions of law and fact.

☐   Reformulate the legal issues later in the research process as they become clearer.

STEP 3: FIND THE LAW

Some Preliminary Questions

Some preliminary questions you will want to keep in mind as you begin your search for the law are:

- What information are you looking for?
- Where is that information likely located?
- Which resources are available for your use? At what cost?
- What resource likely contains your content?
- How easy is it to use the resource?

A. Refer to Secondary Materials

☐   Locate and read secondary materials to gain an overview of the law. While reading, record references to specific cases, statutes and other secondary materials. Here are a few secondary materials:

- *Halsbury's Laws of Canada* or the *Canadian Encyclopedic Digest* (*Western* or *Ontario*): Look in subject indices in the first few volumes to locate your topic. It will lead you to a few titles and volumes that cover your topic. Go there and read generally at first. After you have focused your research, record cases and statutes that are referenced. If you have access to an electronic version of these encyclopedias, scan the table of contents first, then read the text.

- *Textbooks*: Look in a computer catalogue to locate textbooks or go to library shelves and browse. Scan the textbook's table of contents or index first. Read the relevant sections and record the relevant cases and statutes that are referenced. Some researchers photocopy relevant pages from textbooks for future reference. If you have access to electronic textbooks, scan the table of contents or index before conducting a word search.

- *Legal Periodicals*: Periodical indexes, in print or online, can be used to locate the titles of articles by subject. Libraries often purchase collections of electronic journals and journal indexes which can be located through the library catalogue. In addition to commentary, journal articles include references to statutes and cases. Locate electronic journals or articles on your topic by looking in any of the following indexes. Then find and read the text of the articles.

- *Index to Canadian Legal Literature* (available in print and on LN/QL and WC).
- *LegalTrac* (available through the library catalogue) provides not only references to journal articles but links to some of the full text.
- *Index to Legal Periodicals and Books* (available through the library catalogue) provides references to journal articles.
- HeinOnline *Law Journal Library Search* (available through the library catalogue) provides links to the full-text articles available in the HeinOnline *Law Journal Library*.
- Or, other electronic collections of journals.

Online service providers such as LN/QL or WC provide searchable databases of full-text journal articles.

B. Statutes: Find and Update Relevant Statutes

❑   If you know the **title** of the statute, consult:

- government websites, CanLII (<http://www.CanLII.org>) or law library websites that provide links to statute databases.
- commercial online providers such as WC, LN/QL or BestCase.
- print versions of the federal, provincial or territorial tables of public statutes. Statutes are listed alphabetically and direct you to the printed source.

❑   If you are researching by **subject**, you can locate statutes in the following sources:

- secondary materials, such as *Halsbury's Laws of Canada*, the *Canadian Encyclopedic Digest*, textbooks and periodicals. These sources refer to relevant statutes.
- federal or provincial subject indexes of statutes. Search these indexes for descriptive words that will lead you to relevant statutes.

❑   Ensure the statute is **effective** (CIF) by determining whether it has a delayed effective date. If there is a commencement clause (*i.e.*, it is brought into effect at a later time), you must determine the effective date of the statute (see Chapter 7). Most electronic versions (with Westlaw Canada being the exception) state the effective date in the statute.

❑   Determine whether a statute has been **amended** by looking in the federal, provincial or territorial *tables of statutes* or tables of legislative changes. Statutes can also be updated unofficially by looking in commercially published statute *citators*, which include not only amendments to the statutes but also cases that have considered statutes. Not all researchers will have these commercial citators readily available.

❑   You can also go to **electronic versions** of statutes on CanLII, WC, LN/QL and government websites. These sets are usually consolidated so any changes to the statutes have been incorporated. Thus, you need only search for more very recent amendments to these versions.

☐ To further update a statute and its amendments, look in the most recent gazettes or publications from the various legislatures (see Chapter 7).

☐ Look for cases that have considered statutes (**note up**) by looking in statute citators — in electronic or print form. For example, the *Canadian Abridgment Canadian Statute Citations* lists all cases alphabetically, the history of each case and judicial considerations. Alternatively, use this citator feature online in WC.

☐ If necessary, search for regulations pertaining to the relevant statutes (see Chapter 8).

C. Cases: Find and Update Relevant Cases

☐ If you know the **title** of a case, look in electronic collections of cases from any of the following:

- provincial, territorial and federal court websites;
- commercial online providers such as LN/QL, WC or BestCase;
- *The Consolidated Table of Cases* (part of the *Canadian Abridgment* set), which lists all cases alphabetically along with their parallel citations (also available on WC).

☐ If you are researching by **subject**, the most direct way to locate cases is through secondary materials such as the following:

- *Canadian Encyclopedic Digest, Halsbury's Laws of Canada*, textbooks and periodicals (above). Locate and read those cases cited and note other cases that are referred to in those cases.
- *Case Law Digests* (part of the *Canadian Abridgment* set). Look at the first few volumes of the set and figure out how your subject is categorized in the "key classification scheme". Find the volumes of case digests on that subject. Read the digests and record the citations of relevant cases.

☐ Check if the relevant cases have been appealed (*i.e.*, **update** the cases) or considered in other cases (*i.e.*, **note up** the cases) through the following sources:

- electronic citators through commercial online providers such as LN/QL, WC or BestCase;
- *Consolidated Table of Cases* (part of the *Canadian Abridgment* set) which lists all cases alphabetically along with the history of each case (in print and on WC);
- *Canadian Case Citations* (part of the *Canadian Abridgment* set), which lists all cases alphabetically, the history of each case and judicial consideration of each case (in print and on WC).

STEP 4: ANALYZE THE LAW

❑ Read the secondary materials and primary sources.
❑ Analyze and brief cases and identify which cases are similar and whether they are mandatory ("binding") or merely persuasive.
❑ Analyze the relevant statutes.
❑ Synthesize the law (distinguish and analogize cases and merge with statute law).
❑ Apply the law to the legal problem.

STEP 5: COMMUNICATE THE LAW

❑ Consider options or ways to communicate the results of the research (*e.g.*, legal memorandum or opinion letter).
❑ Plan your writing:

1. Identify the reader.
2. Determine the purpose.
3. Gather, analyze and organize the information, selecting the best authorities from among all you have found.
4. Prepare an outline.

❑ Write a first draft focusing on content and organization.
❑ Revise your writing in the following order:

1. Content;
2. Organization;
3. Paragraphs;
4. Sentences;
5. Words; and
6. Style and form.

Answers to Self Tests

CHAPTER 1

1. The five steps of legal research are:

    - Facts — Analyze the facts
    - Issues — Determine the legal issues
    - Law — Find the relevant law
    - Analysis — Analyze the law and apply it to the facts
    - Communication — Communicate the results of the research

2. Factual analysis involves gathering the facts and determining which facts are legally relevant.

3. Issue determination involves determining what the legal issues or questions are.

4. Legal analysis involves three tasks: reading the law, synthesizing the law and applying the law to the facts.

CHAPTER 2

1. The three steps of factual analysis are:

    - Gather and organize the facts
    - Identify the legally relevant facts
    - Formulate the facts

2. PEC stands for Parties, Events and Claims.

CHAPTER 3

1. The three steps in determining legal issues are:

    Step 1: Determine applicable area of law
    Step 2: Identify the general legal issues
    Step 3: Formulate the specific legal issues

2. Some methods that might assist you in thinking about applicable areas of law are: first-year law courses; brainstorming or word association; or using library sources such as the *Canadian Encyclopedic Digest*, *Halsbury's* and textbooks.

3. Library sources that might assist in determining legal issues are the *Canadian Encyclopedic Digest*, *Halsbury's*, textbooks and legal periodical indexes.

4. Correctly formulated legal issues include both facts and law.

5. Yes, legal issues should be drafted as questions.

CHAPTER 4

1. The two types of law are legislation or government-made law, and case law or judge-made law.

2. The term "common law" originates from the travelling courts in England.

3. Legislation is law made by federal and provincial legislatures and municipalities. It includes statutes, regulations and municipal bylaws.

4. The law-making process consists of governments making laws (legislative powers), governments enforcing laws (executive powers), and courts interpreting the laws through specific cases (judicial powers).

5. Primary sources are the law. Secondary materials are aids in understanding and locating the law.

CHAPTER 5

1. The six steps of efficient legal research require that you ask the following six questions:

- What information are you looking for?
- Where is that information likely located?
- Which sources are available for your use? At what cost?
- What resource likely contains your content?
- How easy is it to use the service?
- How will you formulate your search?

2. Some questions to ask when formulating an online search are:

- What words or phrases do you want the computer to locate?
- How should the words be grouped?
- Do you want to limit the search by dates?
- Do you want to limit the search by other factors such as judge's name, jurisdiction, or level of court?

3. The four doors to the law library are: (1) general materials such as textbooks; (2) journals and periodical indexes; (3) legislation; and (4) cases.

4. Canadian commercial online providers include LN/QL, WC, BestCase, Canada Law Book Online, CCH Online, Maritime Law Book Online, SOQUIJ, and Canadian Human Rights Reporter Online.

5. Sources of free legal information include: government websites, CanLII, law library websites, Social Science Research Network, law firm newsletters, law blogs, legal wikis and listservs.

CHAPTER 6

1. A textbook can be located by using a library computer catalogue and searching by author, title, keyword(s) or subject. Or you could conduct an online search in Google or through a commercial provider.
2. To locate journal articles by subject, you could do three things: 1. Go to the library and look in a print-based periodical index. 2. Do an electronic search of a periodical index online. 3. Do a search of full-text electronic database such as HeinOnline.
3. The *Canadian Encyclopedic Digest* is an encyclopedia of all of the law in Canada, arranged by subject.
4. A book of words and phrases includes alphabetical lists of words and phrases that have been considered by the courts.
5. A case digest is a brief summary of a case. These digests are compiled in periodic publications and sorted by subject area.
6. A citator is an annotation of the law. There are case and statute annotators. They include information about whether the law is still current and accurate, and they list cases that have interpreted statutes and prior cases. Most citators *do not contain the text* of cases or statutes but are helping tools that list these.

CHAPTER 7

1. Statutes can be located on public websites (no-fee) on the Internet; on provincial government websites; in law libraries and on CanLII.
2. Statutes are located in a designated area in a law library, sorted by jurisdiction.
3. A table of statutes is an alphabetical listing of statutes. There is usually one for each set of statutes published by each jurisdiction and they are usually consolidated.
4. Two commercial service providers who provide access to electronic statutes are WC and LN/QL.
5. A statute citator is a book that lists statutes, their revisions and any cases that have considered these statutes.

CHAPTER 8

1. A regulation is law that is created through delegated authority. It is also called subordinate legislation and is made pursuant to a statute.
2. Regulations become law by order-in-council.
3. A consolidation of regulations contains all of the regulations in place up to a particular point in time. It consolidates prior regulations so you need not look "behind" a consolidation.

4. A regulation can be found through use of consolidated indexes of regulations, either by title of the statute that empowered it or by the title of the regulation.

CHAPTER 9

1. A case report is a series of books that contain decided cases.
2. A few case reports are: *Supreme Court of Canada Reports* (S.C.R.), *Dominion Law Reports* (D.L.R.) and *British Columbia Law Reports* (B.C.L.R.).
3. To locate a case by name, go to the *Consolidated Table of Cases* (in the *Canadian Abridgment* set) or the tables of cases in individual case reports.
4. To locate a case by subject, use the *Canadian Encyclopedic Digest*, a textbook, or the *Case Digests* (in the *Canadian Abridgment* set).
5. Updating a case means ensuring that the case is "good law". This involves finding its history and any judicial considerations of it at any levels of appeal.
6. To update a case you can use the *Canadian Case Citations* (in the *Canadian Abridgment* set) or individual case report research aids.

CHAPTER 10

1. The doctrine of precedent means that courts use precedents or prior decisions as examples or authorities to assist in deciding cases. The doctrine of precedent is designed to promote consistency in law and provide a tool to predict the likely outcome of a case.
2. The doctrine of *stare decisis* means "to stand by the decision". This doctrine means that courts must follow prior decisions of certain other courts.
3. The three basic levels of court in Canada are trial, appeal and court of last resort.
4. The three steps in case analysis are: determining relevance of cases, reading cases and synthesizing cases.
5. "Synthesizing the law" means merging all the law from the relevant cases and statutes into one general statement of law.
6. The "Golden Rule" of statutory interpretation means that the plain meaning of the words in a statute is to be applied unless it leads to some absurdity or inconsistency. If so, the statute should be interpreted to avoid this.

CHAPTER 11

1. A few rules of good writing are: omit surplus words, use short sentences, use the active voice, arrange words with care and avoid language quirks.
2. The three stages of the legal writing process are: planning, writing and revising.

3. The four steps of the planning process are: identify the reader; determine the purpose; gather, analyze and organize the information; and prepare an outline.

4. The parts of a legal memorandum are: facts, issues, brief answer, analysis and conclusion.

5. Revisions should take place in the following order: (1) content; (2) organization; (3) paragraphs; (4) sentences; (5) words and style; and (6) form.

6. A typical opinion letter has four parts: introduction, description of the law, application of the law to the facts, and conclusion.

CHAPTER 12

1. A research plan is a written plan of how research will be conducted. Each legal problem requires a unique research plan.

2. A research plan is necessary to give some direction to the research and keep researchers from sinking in the myriad of books. Developing a plan eliminates wasted effort and provides a checklist indicating steps taken.

3. A few practical factors to take into consideration are audience, purpose, cost and time.

4. The basic parts of a research plan are FILAC: factual analysis, issue determination, finding the law, legal analysis and communicating the results.

5. The main advantage of note-taking is that it provides a record of steps taken. This enables researchers to interrupt research without losing position and provides a reminder of what has been done to avoid gaps and repetition.

Index

Note: Page references followed by "*i*" indicate material in illustrations; page references followed by "*n*" indicate material in footnotes.